The Preschool Scientist

by

Robert A. Williams, Elizabeth A. Sherwood, Robert E. Rockwell, and David A. Winnett

Resource provided by:

SEEDS **Supporting Early Engagement and Development in STEM**

SCIENCE * TECHNOLOGY * ENGINEERING * MATH

A program of the
Foundation for Family Science & Engineering
www.familyscienceandengineering.org

Dedication

To all my new teacher and children friends in Texas.
You have made me feel welcome. Thanks
and let's teach those kids science!

R. A. W.

To Will and Jeneé, Jennifer and Lee, and
grandchildren, Phillip and Anna,
our youngest scientists.

E. A. S.

To Donna, who has been a friend, wife, mother, grandmother,
and great-grandmother extraordinaire. To Susan and Janet,
my daughters, who are living the joys of grandparenthood.
To my grandchildren, Teri, Robert, Amanda, Kathryn,
and Michael, and my great-grandchildren
Tyler, Megan, Ethan, Delilah, Mya, and
Stella, who give me endless joy.
I love you all.

R. E. R.

To my beautiful wife Sharon, who
has put up with my dreams and
schemes for over 40 years.

D. A. W.

The Preschool SCIENTIST

Using Learning Centers to Discover and Explore Science

Robert A. Williams | Elizabeth A. Sherwood
Robert E. Rockwell | David A. Winnett

©2010 Robert A. Williams, Elizabeth A. Sherwood, Robert E. Rockwell, and David A. Winnett
Published by Gryphon House, Inc.

PO Box 10, Lewisville, NC 27023

800.638.0928 (toll-free); 877.638.7576 (fax)

Reprinted October 2011

Visit us on the web at www.gryphonhouse.com

Library of Congress Cataloging-in-Publication Data

Williams, Robert A.
  The preschool scientist / by Robert A. Williams . . . [et al.].
    p. cm.
  Includes index.
  ISBN 978-0-87659-130-7
  1. Science—Study and teaching (Preschool) I. Title.
  LB1140.5.S35W57 2010
  372.3'5049—dc22
                           2010008480

Bulk purchase

Gryphon House books are available for special premiums and sales promotions as well as for fund-raising use. Special editions or book excerpts also can be created to specification. For details, contact the Director of Marketing at Gryphon House.

Disclaimer

Gryphon House, Inc. and the authors cannot be held responsible for damage, mishap, or injury incurred during the use of or because of activities in this book. Appropriate and reasonable caution and adult supervision of children involved in activities and corresponding to the age and capability of each child involved is recommended at all times. Do not leave children unattended at any time. Observe safety and caution at all times.

Contents

Introduction

Using Science to Discover and Explore the World

Young children are eager and ready to learn. To sustain their eagerness and interest, it is important to introduce children to scientific exploration through engaging and meaningful experiences. With careful and intentional planning, we can help our preschool scientists learn the concepts and skills that will deepen their understanding of the world around them.

Consider for a moment an educational scenario. Suppose two adults, Fred and Maria, enroll in a craft class. In the first session, their teacher introduces them to working with stained glass, and they practice cutting glass and learn to connect the pieces. Fred and Maria come to the second session ready to learn more. Instead, the teacher introduces ceramics. Fred and Maria learn a little about ceramics and are excited about creating something new. Fred and Maria come to the third session ready to continue with ceramics. The clay is gone; the teacher has replaced it with equipment for wood carving. Instead of learning skills, Fred and Maria are learning frustration.

Too often, this is what we do to children. Instead of giving them the self-confidence that comes with mastering new ideas or skills, we move them quickly from one topic to the next. We are subtly teaching them to be satisfied with learning a little about many things. By limiting the number of topics presented in *The Preschool Scientist*, we are giving children more opportunities to experience feelings of competence and mastery.

Our philosophy is that it is better to help children acquire a real understanding of a few concepts than to give them fragments of many topics. Materials should be accessible, and the curriculum should be developed in such a way that children can return to or repeat experiences that they may have completed some time ago. Repetition reinforces children's awareness of their own competence, which ultimately results in confidence.

The Preschool Scientist exposes children to much more than science skills and concepts. It gives them the opportunity to explore, experiment, create, and problem solve. The approach in *The Preschool Scientist* also encourages children to refine their use of language as they talk about what they do or explain what they discover. And children can apply their emerging mathematical skills in the meaningful context of discovery. *The Preschool Scientist* provides teachers with a curricular framework that engages the spirit of excitement for discovery that dwells in the minds of all children, wherever they live and learn.

Chapter 1

Science in the Preschool Classroom

Science in the
Preschool Classroom

We know that children learn more by doing than by listening. We also know that children come to school with widely varying backgrounds, experiences, and knowledge. *The Preschool Scientist* helps teachers by providing purposeful activities that are exciting and intellectually challenging for young children in all kinds of settings.

Goals for Early Childhood Science

The goals that follow establish a foundation for early childhood science learning:

1. Provide an environment that supports active discovery.

2. Promote the development of fundamental problem-solving skills.

3. Promote the dispositions of good scientific problem solvers.

4. Promote children's awareness of careers in science, mathematics, and technology.

5. Raise children's comfort and confidence levels with science through conscious efforts to counter bias against science.

6. Promote development of a knowledge base of basic scientific principles and laws, providing the foundation upon which a clear and accurate understanding of the world can develop. A solid foundation reduces the risk of children acquiring misconceptions that may hinder their understanding of more complex science concepts later on.

Narrowing the Range of Science Themes to Promote Successful Learning

Often activity guides for young children contain a scattered collection of science concepts and terms that children are expected to absorb. A hurried exposure to science may fail to provide the opportunity for the rich conceptual development that is possible with a more coherent, thoughtful approach. Just think of the story of Fred and Maria (from the introduction) struggling in their craft class. *The Preschool Scientist* works with only three basic science process skills. This enables children ages three and four to be totally immersed in the science processes that are within their developmental capabilities. By focusing on a small number of core concepts, children will have enough time to spend with the materials and concepts to master them.

The Preschool Scientist provides many approaches for developing children's understanding of three basic and crucial science process skills:

- Focused Observing,
- Observing to Classify, and
- Organizing and Communicating Observations.

Through explorations in centers—Art, Blocks and Building, Discovery, Dramatic Play, Literacy, Messy Materials, and Outdoors—children have many opportunities to observe, classify, and communicate. The development of these skills is supported by the questions you ask children and your observations of the children as they work.

Focused Observing, Observing to Classify, and Organizing and Communicating Observations

Focused Observing

Focused observation activities allow teacher-directed quality control over the types of observations that children are making. Children are recording these observations in their minds. Later they can remember an observation and apply it in another situation that allows them to make sense of what they are doing or learning.

Because children will use the observations they make now as a basis on which to build future understanding, you have two major instructional concerns. First, there are observations about each of the activities that children need to make. If children do not make these observations, they will not begin to understand the concepts. Second, children are continually interpreting what they have observed. Some of these interpretations will be correct, while some may not be.

Over time, children should become increasingly familiar with the process of making observations, which should enable them to notice more details and ask relevant questions. You will be able to assess their understanding of science concepts through the class Discovery Books, discussion, and your own observations.

Observing to Classify

Young children naturally want to group and organize objects, and you probably will observe children classifying prior to these activities. The simplest form of classification takes place when children start to collect similar objects and materials and group them together. Encourage this behavior by asking children to share their thinking: "Why are you putting all of these objects in the same place?" Children's responses will likely indicate that they have identified a certain property and are basing the selections on that property. If this is the case, these children are well on their way to becoming skilled classifiers and will learn additional classification skills quickly. Pay special attention to those children who are not displaying the initial desire to group and organize. Encouraging children to make use of their observation skills reinforces the importance of becoming good observers.

Organizing and Communicating Observations

Science seeks to find order and structure in our world. Free Discovery (see page 20), Focused Observing, and Observing to Classify are the initial skills that young children need to begin establishing order in their world. Your task is to encourage children to describe their observations to the best of their abilities. You will assist by asking questions, providing vocabulary, and urging children to "tell more" or to show you what they know. At this age, some children understand more than they are able to verbalize. Be open to other kinds of communication. The words will come in time. Children are also exploring writing and drawing, so encourage them to use these emerging skills to communicate their observations as well.

Supporting Emerging Language and Literacy Skills

During the preschool years, children's language becomes increasingly complex. This is the time of questions. "Why" questions are constant. It is a time when you must learn to listen carefully and answer the questions children ask (not the questions you think you should answer), as well as provide the means for children to answer the questions themselves. Helping children develop their language skills is a great way to encourage them to communicate their science-related questions.

Descriptive Language

Descriptive language is an emerging skill that needs adult support. Encourage the use of all the senses and help children find words to describe what they observe. At group time, talk about shared experiences and what children saw and heard. Model descriptive language as you hold a gerbil, look at a snail in a magnifying box, or play and pour at the water table. Wonder "what if" with the children. Verbalize your own questions: "I wonder if hamsters like bananas?" "How could we find out if fish can hear?"

Comparative Language

Children at this age are just beginning to understand relationship terms such as *big* and *bigger, heavy* and *light, long* and *longer.* Use comparative language frequently as you work with children. Science experiences provide many opportunities to use comparative language as you and the children in your class investigate, explore, and discover together. Children are also learning about opposites, such as *long* and *short* and *empty* and *full.* As they make observations, encourage children to compare and classify what they discover.

Language Development

The Preschool Scientist provides many opportunities for working with language and literacy. Language is a vital means by which to explore and develop concepts. As children share ideas and observations with each other both verbally and symbolically, they will use a variety of language skills.

As educators, our job is to allow children to share what they know in whatever way they can and to use that sharing as an opportunity to enhance communication skills. In this context *The Preschool Scientist* will:

- Improve effective use and expansion of vocabulary as children seek to describe accurately their observations and to share their discoveries;

- Allow children to devise their own ways of communicating their experiences;

- Include group experiences that will model diverse uses of language and literacy;

- Familiarize children with the process of asking a question and looking for an answer, a process often confusing to young children;

- Introduce alternative methods of communication, such as demonstrations, drawings, charts, writing, and dictated text;

- Focus on effective communication and interesting and accurate content rather than precise grammar; and

- Encourage sharing and collaboration, both of which require meaningful communication.

Tracking Literacy and Language Development in the Classroom

There are several ways to track and follow children's emergent interest in and ability to use language as a means of communicating their observations and refining their questions about science and scientific exploration. The ideas below provide further means to create records of how children use science to develop their literacy skills.

Discovery Charts

Discovery Charts offer the opportunity to reinforce children's beginning understanding of the relationship between spoken language and the written word. Children are beginning to realize that writing is talk put on paper. The use of Discovery Charts helps in this process. For this reason, their development follows the progression of this book. The first section of each activity is open exploration and expansion of ideas throughout the classroom centers. Similarly, the beginning of each Discovery Chart should be equally open-ended and simple.

For example, a Discovery Chart might be titled "What Can You Tell Us About Things That Move?" or "How Do You Move a Ball, a Block, or Your Body?" Entries on the chart may include comments such as:

LaMont: I push the button on the car and it moves really fast.

Abby: I can run faster.

Tisha: I can run faster, too.

As you work with children, reread the Discovery Charts frequently. This helps children understand the permanent nature of written language—that the same Discovery Chart says the same thing each time you read it. It also tells children that you value their language and that the work they do is important enough to write about and remember.

Discovery Books

Discovery Books are a key component of *The Preschool Scientist*. Discovery Books document the children's explorations, serve as a means of communicating with others, and support emerging literacy skills. It is a rewarding experience for children to review the books, see their own entries, and remind themselves of the activities they have done. The books are also a permanent record of what they have learned that they can share with their families.

Make separate class Discovery Books for each investigation. You may also want to use several books, each focused on a specific activity. Or, alternatively, you could make a general book covering the entire theme of the chapter. The simplest way to make a Discovery Book is to staple several sheets of blank paper between two sheets of construction paper. Have the children decorate the covers. To make the books sturdier for frequent handling, it is best to laminate the covers or cover them with clear contact paper.

Classes may want to borrow each other's books to compare findings. Consider using photographs or videos to document experiences, and ask the children to provide captions or narrative.

Discovery Journals

Discovery Journals are individual books in which each child can draw and write about his discoveries and observations. Talk with the children about the difference between creative drawings and scientific drawings. Point out that Discovery Journals are for scientific drawings, which put what the children see on paper. For example, in a creative drawing, children can make birds any color they like. When they are making a drawing of a bird, lima bean, or worm in their Discovery Journals, they need to carefully consider which crayon or marker they should use to accurately show what they are observing. Help the children refine this process. They can also write labels or captions at their own developmental level or dictate information for you to write.

Science Vocabulary

Each activity in *The Preschool Scientist* contains a vocabulary list. This list contains terms that children need to understand to appreciate more fully the science concepts they are exploring. At this age, the words seem simple; however, understanding concepts such as *heavy* and *light* or how scientists define the word *animal* can be challenging for young children. Work with your preschoolers to help them develop a broader understanding of the words you introduce in the classroom.

Connecting Mathematics to Science

Science and mathematics fit together in a natural and very functional way. Mathematics is an essential component of communication for scientists. It also provides an effective way for children to process and share their discoveries.

Preschoolers are developing a beginning understanding of one-to-one correspondence and counting with purpose. They can use their hands or a double-pan balance to compare mass. *The Preschool Scientist* provides many opportunities to work with an array of concepts such as *more/less*, *alike/different*, size relationships and seriation, matching, and classifying.

Rather than teaching these concepts and others in isolation, *The Preschool Scientist* gives children the chance to gain science and mathematical knowledge together as part of a unified approach. The practical experience of connecting mathematical concepts with science experiences enables young children to begin to internalize mathematical skills, increasing the chance that they will understand and appreciate mathematics as they grow and learn.

Exploration Through Free Discovery

Children have a need to know. This natural curiosity, a fundamental drive to inquire, is as much a part of life as is breathing and eating. Free Discovery is observation and exploration at the children's own pace. It provides a way to support their curiosity about the natural and physical environment in which they live. Allowing children the freedom to explore at their own rate, without the fear of getting the "wrong" answers, is critical if children are to remain curious and excited about learning. In a secure and comfortable environment, children are able to fulfill their natural eagerness to find possible solutions to their own inquiries of why, what, how, and when in their own way. To accomplish this, Free Discovery should:

- Allow children to become familiar with the materials;

- Allow children to make observations and discoveries on their own and to feel good about them;

- Build children's self-esteem through their being in control of their own actions;

- Provide no right or wrong answers, and therefore no failure;

- Provide a nonthreatening learning time; and

- Proceed at each child's own learning pace.

Each chapter in *The Preschool Scientist* begins with Free Discovery ideas and suggestions.

The Role of Free Discovery

To be most effective, a science program must emphasize interaction with the environment, both natural and social. Using simple equipment and materials gives children unlimited opportunities to explore and interact in their own ways. There are no set parameters within the limits of acceptable behavior. Exploratory freedom reigns. This can be difficult for adults, as we often want to step in at this phase of learning, intercepting children's natural and spontaneous curiosity with questions and challenges that are not child-initiated. Children are often not ready for such interruptions. This phase of learning is the time to play with and explore materials in their own way. Free exploration and play are a need that must be fulfilled before children can see the materials as learning resources.

Free Discovery is inherent to good science, good teaching, and effective learning for adults as well as children. As adults, we have learned how to complete this process more quickly than children because of our experience and knowledge base. But how do we as adults approach learning a new skill?

Suppose that you would like to make a table but never have done any woodworking. Do you go buy some wood and some tools and get to work? No, you begin with Free Discovery. You may ask for some help from someone who has a bit more experience. Maybe you borrow a book or two and read about woodworking. You practice with the tools on wood scraps, not on premium walnut boards. The more you work and the more you practice, the better you expect to perform. The more confident you become in your skills, the more you are able to experiment and modify your techniques. With persistence, you eventually learn enough to build the table you want. This slow flow of learning—moving from inexperience to experience to modification—is a natural process for the adult learner. It is also how children learn when they are given the opportunity.

Involving Families in Science Exploration

As children's first caregivers and educators, parents and family members have both the right and the responsibility to be involved in their children's formal education. Research conducted in a variety of educational settings over many decades suggests that parents and family members who establish a learning environment in the home, stimulate their children's interest in learning, and support their children's natural curiosity foster attitudes that help ensure their children's academic achievement. In addition, involved parents and family members develop more positive attitudes toward the school and its goals.

Ideas for Family Involvement

Introducing Preschool Science: A Family Meeting

Conducting a hands-on meeting for families is a way to invite them to be a part of their preschool children's introduction to science. At the meeting, you can talk with families about the program and how you plan to implement it. The family will interact with the activities and materials in *The Preschool Scientist* in the same way that their children will. After attending the meeting, families will be more adept at supporting, modeling, and discussing science concepts and exploration with their children. The major focus of this meeting is to inform parents and family members of the strong emphasis that *The Preschool Scientist* places upon working with parents and family members as partners in the education of their children.

Family Volunteers

The Preschool Scientist can provide opportunities and access for families to volunteer both at school and at home. Family volunteers can enrich the learning process and expand the learning environment for children as they share their skills, personal expertise, and the enthusiasm of discovery.

The Classroom Learning Centers

The activities in *The Preschool Scientist* are designed to be used in learning centers throughout the classroom. The children's play in the various centers provides a myriad of opportunities for exploring science concepts and gaining information. Science with young children can and should be done in almost any setting, just as science and its applications permeate the lives of adults.

The classroom centers, by their very nature, promote problem solving and positive risk taking because children work largely on their own. They learn to make independent decisions as they explore concepts designed to teach the how-to of science rather than words and facts.

Learning Centers

Art

The Art Center provides materials for self-expression, development of fine motor skills, eye-hand coordination, and creativity along with the opportunity to explore, experiment, plan, and discover. As children work, they discover what the various materials can do, their physical characteristics, and how they can manipulate the materials with both predictable and unpredictable results. When you introduce new materials, show the children how to care for them. This will result in a longer survival rate for the materials and will allow the children to use them effectively.

In the early stages of work with any new material, the children's focus is clearly on manipulation, sensory exploration, and the process of gaining mastery and control. When children first begin to paint, their main interest is putting paint on paper. Many children will repeatedly cover the entire paper with paint. Other children will paint some lines and shapes and then cover them with another layer of paint. They are enjoying the feel of the brush on the paper, and the process, with little if any focus on the finished product.

As they become comfortable with the materials, children are self-motivated to plan for a given outcome. Their work becomes more refined and organized. If allowed the freedom to work with various media in self-directed ways, children will begin to use increasingly complex and sophisticated processes. When you introduce new materials and techniques, children will approach them with curiosity and creativity.

As the children work with the variety of materials available in the Art Center, they are learning about:

- Focusing Observations. Children use their senses to explore, experiment, and discover a diversity of textures, visual properties, and other characteristics of materials available to them.

- Observing to Classify. Children learn about the function and the use of media and equipment.

- Organizing and Communicating Observations. Children work together and share their experiences with you and the other children and dictate labels or stories about their creations.

- Balance and Stability. Children work with three-dimensional materials to create structures.

- Spatial Relationships. Children create collages, structures, or weavings and choose where to place paint or crayons on paper.

- Physical Properties of Materials. Children discover the many possibilities various media have to offer.

Blocks and Buildings

The Blocks and Building Center, an essential part of the preschool classroom, is an exciting place to introduce children to discovery and investigation. A natural progression occurs as children develop their skills in the block area. Children begin by exploring the properties of blocks through pushing and carrying them. They move at their own rate along a continuum, from flat structures and stacking to enclosures, bridges, and decorated structures. An older preschooler who has had adequate experience with blocks will build complex, well-organized structures with plan and purpose. Other than basic safety and storage rules, few limits should constrain children as they work with blocks. They explore and challenge themselves, secure in the knowledge that they can always try it again. They work with problem-solving skills as they figure out how to support a ramp, reinforce a tower so they can build it higher, or decide which block will fit into a structure precisely.

As the children work in the block area they are learning about:

- Focusing Observations. Children compare, observe, and handle the materials.

- Observing to Classify. Children sort by size, shape, color, or other attributes.

- Organizing and Communicating Observations. Children find ways to share their discoveries.

- Balance. Children carefully add blocks to buildings so they don't fall, and they use visual balance as they make symmetrical structures.

- Stability. Children work, for example, to create the best form to enable them to build a taller building.

- Spatial Relationships. Children enclose, connect, bridge, and cover space or use blocks to fill containers.

- Simple Machines. Children manipulate levers, ramps, and pulleys.

Discovery Center

The Discovery Center is the heart of *The Preschool Scientist*. It contains all of the materials needed to continue the discovery begun in the other centers. The Discovery Center provides a place for children to begin using the tools of science. Children can become proficient at using balances, magnifiers, and measurement devices while exploring here and in the other centers. Children need to use these tools with a wide variety of natural and human-made materials. They will see that the tools and materials in the Discovery Center consist of everyday items along with special "science" tools.

The children need many opportunities to make observations, classify those observations, and communicate data in an environment rich in materials, equipment, and experiences. The well-stocked Discovery Center can serve both as a hands-on area for new discoveries and as a more traditional science center. Materials in the Discovery Center should be sturdy, simple, and easy to handle. If space does not allow for a permanent center, select materials that you can set out quickly and store easily.

The Discovery Center should contain the following basic equipment:

- Safety goggles;

- Paint aprons or smocks;

- Magnifying devices such as hand lenses, bug boxes, and two-way magnifiers;

- Double-pan balance;

- Spoons, scoops, droppers, and forceps;

- Containers such as bowls, bottles, and cups;

- Sorting and storage containers such as egg cartons and clear plastic vials with lids;

- Cardboard or plastic foam food packaging trays for sorting;

- Nonstandard units for measuring length and mass, such as large metal washers, measuring cups, and interlocking cubes;

- Writing materials; and

- Clean-up equipment, such as buckets, sponges, dust pans, and hand brooms.

As the children work in the Discovery Center, they are learning about:

- Focusing Observations. Children use their senses to explore the natural and human-made objects in the center.

- Observing to Classify. Children learn to classify collections of objects according to a variety of characteristics.

- Organizing and Communicating Observations. Children share observations and discoveries with each other and with you.

- Balance. Children work with different types of balances.

- Physical Properties of Materials. Children explore and manipulate the tools and materials.

- Quantification. Children use standard and nonstandard measuring devices to quantify objects.

Dramatic Play

The Dramatic Play Center provides children with opportunities for role-playing, trying out, pretending, and acting out familiar and imaginary experiences. They learn to interact with each other, to solve problems, and to communicate effectively. Young children often initially spend time manipulating objects and seeing how they work, just as they do in other areas of the classroom. They may play dress up, put a pot on the stove, or undress a doll. Gradually their play becomes more social as they assume various roles with each other. Dramatic play also provides the opportunity for children to explore how their bodies move and how they can vary those movements.

As the children work in this area, they are learning about:

- Focusing Observations. Children use their senses to explore, experiment, and discover a diversity of textures, visual properties, and other characteristics of materials.

- Observing to Classify. Children compare shadows and movements that have similar characteristics.

- Organizing and Communicating Observations. Children find ways to share their discoveries and act out various roles.

- Matching. Children recognize shadows and movements that are alike and different.

- Predicting. Children describe what they think the shadows look like.

- Constancy. Children realize that mirror images remain the same as the objects that are reflected.

- Change and Passage of Time. Children realize how our activities change from day to night.

Literacy Center

Before you begin each chapter, visit the library to select appropriate books. *The Preschool Scientist* encourages experiences with real things, but you cannot bring the entire world into the classroom. Children will learn to expand their knowledge through the use of resource materials. A number of books appropriate for this age level are listed in each activity. Some of the books deal directly with science concepts. Many, however, have a much broader context. For example, *Hats, Hats, Hats*, by Ann Morris, which shows hats from around the world, provides an opportunity to reinforce the concepts in Chapter 2 ("Alike and Different") of *The Preschool Scientist*. Many books with text that is too complex for this age will have illustrations the children will find interesting.

Posters and recordings will also add interest to the area. Display Discovery Books, Discovery Charts, and other examples of the children's work in the Literacy Center. The classroom environment becomes a more powerful place for children's learning when you enrich it with books, magazines, posters, bulletin boards, pictures, card sets, and games. These materials help you expose children to things you cannot bring into the classroom.

Messy Materials

Sand, water, and soil are wonderful media for exploring a variety of science skills and experiences. The materials provide rich sensory experiences and are inherently attractive to children.

When children first work with fluid materials, such as sand or water, they need many opportunities to simply experience the substances and learn to manage them. Even three-year-olds can learn to use a sponge or small broom if the equipment is available. Teaching children management skills is necessary if you want to include wet and messy substances in the classroom.

Materials with fluidity provide many opportunities for children to become familiar with the use of tools, such as double-pan balances, funnels, and sieves. In the early stages, children simply pour and scoop and fill and dump, all the while exploring the texture, smell, weight, and appearance of the material. They become absorbed in the tactile sensations. They learn the various uses of equipment—cups, sieves, and scoops—that you supply. They also learn that different materials behave in different ways with the same equipment. As they become familiar with the materials and equipment, play becomes more planned and organized. They learn that a funnel can assist in filling a small container.

As the children work in this area, they are learning about:

- Focusing Observations. Children compare, observe, and handle materials of varying textures, smells, and densities.

- Observing to Classify. Children sort by size, color, and shape.

- Balance. Children use a double-pan balance to make comparisons.

- Stability. Children learn to center an object in a floating pie pan so it doesn't tip and sink.

- Spatial Relationships. Children work with volume, discovering that some containers hold more than others.

- Physical Properties of Materials. Children working with sand and water are challenged to think about volume, measurement, and comparison in concrete and meaningful ways.

Outdoors

Children find the natural world enchanting. Because they have an insatiable curiosity about their environment, you can capitalize on this enthusiasm with developmentally appropriate experiences designed to challenge and extend their learning. The outdoor world provides a whole new avenue for exploring the themes described in *The Preschool Scientist.* Take advantage of the wealth of resources available in just about any outdoor environment.

The importance of environmental education in early childhood programs is a reflection of the concern about environmental issues and the future of our planet. At this age, environmental education provides children with the knowledge, skills, and attitudes required to take environmentally responsible actions. These actions will prevent further destruction and promote the development of a sustainable society, thus ensuring the future of life on the earth. Nurturing sustainable attitudes and actions at an early age leads to environmentally responsible adults.

Introduce Outdoors time by taking the children to a somewhat private location on the school grounds. Talk with them about safety concerns and the importance of staying close enough to hear directions you may give. This is also an appropriate time to discuss environmental issues, such as littering and having respect for living things. Often, for example, the children will want to pick flowers rather than leave them so others can enjoy their beauty.

During this time, the children may investigate the area at their own pace in their own way. They need this freedom to discover on their own so when they are later asked to focus on certain outdoor features or activities, they will be less likely to wander off to explore on their own.

While the children will likely spend most of the Outdoors time in the area around your school, visiting other places to do some of the activities is also fun. Field trips to woods, prairies, and shallow creeks can be big adventures for young children. Climbing a small hill becomes a major mountain-climbing expedition for a person 36" tall. Once again, stress safety and environmental stewardship during your visits, and use these field trips as opportunities to discuss taking care of our world.

As the children work and explore outdoors, they are learning about:

- Focusing Observations. Children use their senses to explore, investigate, and discover the wealth of materials that nature provides.

- Observing to Classify. Children classify the wide variety of things they collect outdoors.

- Organizing and Communicating Observations. Children tally their collections, share their thoughts about what they see, and dictate captions for their work.

- Balance and Stability. Children work with the concepts of balance and stability as they walk on logs.

- Spatial Relationships. Children use their sense of spatial relationships as they choose how to place objects to make prints on paper.

- Physical Properties of Materials. Children discover the incredible variety of sights, textures, and smells in nature.

- Change and Passage of Time. Children observe changes in the natural environment throughout the year.

Small Group

Activities labeled as Small Group activities are done with a small group of children at a time. While the rest of the children are working in other centers or on other activities, the teacher, aide, or resource person replicates the activity with each small group until every child has had an opportunity to participate. Each child will thus have the rich experience of interacting with the presented materials and ideas, as well as working with the teacher.

Tips on Storage and Management

Storage space must be thoughtfully designed to meet each classroom's instructional needs. Several types of storage are necessary. Some materials, such as magnifiers, paper, and a balance, should be out and available at all times, promoting their use and encouraging children to find new functions for them. Shelves, tables, and pegboard are useful for this type of storage.

Some materials must be stored out of the way until you or the children need them. Our experience with storage needs has led us to depend on plastic storage tubs, which are sold in local discount stores. They have lids, come in a variety of sizes, and stack easily, allowing you to store whole sets of materials together. The availability of clear lids and a variety of colors increases their flexibility. You can make tubs available to children or you can store them out of reach.

In addition, consider the following:

- Provide clutter-free surfaces for the work areas.

- Be sure there are places on shelves, tables, or the floor where children can leave materials for an extended time or study.

- Areas should be easy to clean. Clean-up materials should be readily available. Responsibility for accidents, along with normal messes, is part of science training.

- Children need plenty of freedom, time, equipment, and materials—properly cared for and stored in areas accessible to them—to become thoroughly engaged in science learning.

Assessment

The assessment and evaluation procedures in *The Preschool Scientist* are meant to be practical and informative for an early childhood teacher in the classroom setting. Assessment and evaluation are tied closely to instruction and are embedded in the activities, eliminating many of the ill effects of assessment being "tacked on" at the end of an activity, like a caboose at the end of the train. Several train engines are spread throughout the long line of cars. These engines will give power and purpose to the learning activities.

Authentic Assessment

As educators, our interest is in improving children's skills and expanding their knowledge of the world. To ensure that our efforts in education accomplish this intended purpose, we need to monitor children's development continually. Ongoing educational assessment should be consistent with the instructional approach being used in the classroom, not an inappropriate, high-stakes assessment measure so foreign to the way children process information that it creates frustration and stress.

You are using authentic assessment when you link your assessment measures closely to your curriculum and the instructional approach you use in the learning environment. *The Preschool Scientist* uses authentic assessment measures in such a way that both teachers and children perceive the assessment as an extension of the learning process.

Be aware of the diversity of the developmental levels of children in your classroom. Nothing in your evaluation should discourage children in the growth of their inquiry skills or, even worse, set their present attitude against scientific inquiry—an attitude they may well have for the rest of their lives. The development of a willingness to think, explore, and look for answers to questions is critically important for the development of good problem-solving skills.

Curriculum-Embedded Assessment

Each activity contains ways to observe and assess children's science learning. Each chapter also includes Quick Check and Check Point activities. These are embedded evaluations that provide useful insights about how children are developing skills and understanding concepts.

• **Quick Check Activities**—Quick Check activities provide an instant assessment of how well children are learning the main activity concepts. They are simple and quick techniques for independently measuring children's learning. They also provide a reference point for the child's knowledge upon which you can continue to build as you try additional investigative activities in the classroom.

Use the following four child-performance levels in the "Close Observation" portion of the Quick Check activities to evaluate how well children understand the concepts of the activity. The ability to perform at these four performance levels is a direct indication of children's understanding of the concepts, as well as their developmental levels.

● Level One—Show It

The child is able to demonstrate an initial level of understanding by performing a specific task related to the concept being explored.

- Level Two—Tell It

  The child is able to talk with the teacher about the concept being explored.

- Level Three—Draw It

  The child is able to draw a picture about the concept being explored.

- Level Four—Write It

  The child is able to write or dictate about the concept being explored.

Discovery Charts

When you create a Discovery Chart at the beginning of an activity, it can serve as a great pre-assessment tool. Discovery Charts tell you what the children as a whole already know and can make you aware of any misconceptions the children may have. When you take the time to refer back to an old chart, add to it, or create a new one, it will help the children see the ways that they are learning. By making the Discovery Charts an ongoing part of the classroom experience, you will have a single source that contains the main body of knowledge the children have learned in a particular activity.

Using This Book

The majority of this book is made up of activities that cover a variety of science-related topics. In each activity, you will find the following sections:

- Activity Title and Introduction
- Science Content Standards
- Science Process Skills
- Science Vocabulary
- Materials
- What to Do
- Keep It Simple

- Add a Challenge
- Observing and Assessing the Child's Science Learning
- Children's Books
- Theme Connections
- Connecting Science to the Curriculum

Each activity may also contain one or more of a variety of tips covering subjects such as:

- Children with Special Needs
- Dual Language Learners
- Family Involvement
- Incorporating Technology
- Using Museums and Other Community Assets

In addition to the main activities, each chapter has a "Quick Check" activity midway through the chapter and a "Check Point" activity at the chapter's end.

The Quick Check activities (described on page 31) are similar to the main activities, though after the "What to Do" section of each activity there is a "Close Observation" section that contains four new sections designed to give you the opportunity to observe the child exploring different kinds of skills as they relate to the concept being explored in the chapter:

- Show It
- Tell It
- Draw It
- Write It

Each chapter's final Check Point activity is designed to give you the opportunity to gauge the child's exploration of the chapter's primary subject, "Alike and Different," "Working with Water," "Light and Shadows," and so on.

Chapter 2

Alike and Different

Alike and Different

Science Concepts

This chapter explores the following science concepts:

● Many objects or forms of matter in our world have similar properties or characteristics.

● Many objects or forms of matter in our world have different properties or characteristics.

● We can use the similarities and differences of objects or forms of matter to separate them into groups.

Introduction

The activities in this chapter guide children in formulating a basic understanding of the meaning of the words *alike* and *different*. It sets the stage for the development of a child's scientific discovery and observation skills. Even more importantly, the activities encourage children to develop their focused observation skills and to discover unique properties or characteristics of various forms of matter. Once children have experience with the concepts *alike* and *different*, they can use their new skills for the sophisticated challenge of classifying objects by observing their properties or characteristics.

In the world of science, everything is made up of matter. The properties of matter allow us to group materials by those properties. For example, some matter is magnetic and some is not. Some matter floats while other matter sinks. We group objects using these similarities and differences. Adult scientists group matter in very complex ways. With preschool scientists, begin with *alike* and *different*.

Getting Ready

Place the following materials, along with any other interesting objects, in the Discovery Center or other appropriate places in the classroom for the children to explore during Free Discovery:

● magnets

● materials attracted to and not attracted to magnets

- objects to sort, such as buttons, marbles, coins, counters, rocks, and shells

- texture collection, such as various fabrics, window screen, sandpaper, pieces of wood, and tiles

- leaf collection

- pattern blocks or other blocks with multiple shapes

- nut and bolt collection

- feather collection

- pairs of objects, such as rocks, shells, and nuts

Free Discovery

Begin Free Discovery by talking with the children about how various objects have properties that make them alike and different. Show the children a collection of interesting objects, perhaps an assortment of shells, rocks, and small toys that include some matched pairs. Ask the children to select things that are alike and to tell why. Ask, "Are they the same color? What else makes them alike? Perhaps they are the same shape and size." Ask the children to do the same with objects that are different. As the children share their thoughts, write them on a "How Objects Are Alike and Different" Discovery Chart. You also may want to make a chart with one column for pictures of pairs of objects that are alike and another column for pictures of pairs of objects that are different.

Allow the children ample opportunity to investigate the new materials in the classroom. While the children may need some guidance or suggestions when they first begin to explore the materials, it is important to let them explore freely. It is important not to overdirect their discovery process.

Now is the time to begin the class Discovery Books for this investigation. You may want to use several books, each focused on a specific activity. Alternatively, you could make a general book with drawings and captions showing what the children are learning about how objects are alike and different. The children can also draw and write or dictate about what they do and observe in their own Discovery Journals.

Alike and Different

Crayon Lines

In this activity, children will do simple classifying. The children group two colors of crayons by color and then line up the two groups. Once the crayons are lined up, the children use their informal measuring skills to tell by sight which color made the longest line.

Science Process Skills

Observing to classify
Measuring—linear

Science Vocabulary

color names
graph
group
line
longest
measure
most
sort

Materials

many crayons of two different
colors, such as red and
yellow
masking tape

Science Content Standards

The children will note and use similarities and differences of objects to separate the objects into groups by color properties; the children will indicate the longest line. (Science as Inquiry; Physical Sciences—Properties of Matter)

What to Do

1. Challenge the children sort the crayons by color, making two separate piles. Tell the children that they are to put the color that is the same (alike) in one pile and those that are different in another pile. If the children are having difficulty, model this action: Begin with red. Put a red crayon to one side. Then put all the crayons that are similar in color next to it. Put the rest of the crayons in a different pile. Ask, "Which color do you think will make the longest line? Let's find out."

2. Place two long pieces of masking tape on the floor parallel to each other. Show the children how to line up the crayons of one color end to end along the side of one piece of tape.

3. After the children line up all the crayons of one color, mark the spot where the crayon line ends by making a line with that color on the tape. Leave the crayons in place.

4. Have the children repeat the process with the second color along the second piece of tape.

5. After the children set out and measure both colors, ask the children which color made the longest line. Talk about the fact that the marks on the tape show how long each line of crayons is, "The marks, or measurements, we have made tell us which color made the longest line, even when we put the crayons away."

6. Encourage the children to use the same process with other colors.

Children's Books

The Crayon Counting Book by Pam Munoz Ryan, Frank Mazzola (illustrator), and Jerry Pallotta provides another way for the children to play and learn with crayons.

Alike and Different

Keep It Simple

● Presort collections of crayons to provide the children with sets of crayons that will make lines of clearly different lengths. The children can see that one color makes a long line and the other line is much shorter.

Add a Challenge

● Once the children know how to measure the crayon lines using one piece of tape for each color, show them how they can make marks to measure several lines of crayons using the same piece of tape.

Theme Connections

Colors

What else can the children find to sort by color and measure?

Friends

Have all the children wearing jeans line up head to toe (just like the crayons) next to all the children not wearing jeans. Which group makes the longest line? How many other ways can the children think of to group and measure themselves?

Dual Language Learners

Repeat the appropriate color words as the children are sorting the crayons. Invite the children to say the names of the colors in their home languages as well.

Children with Special Needs

Taping a length of clothesline to the floor provides children who have visual disabilities with a tactile guide when laying out the crayons.

Observing and Assessing the Child's Science Learning

● Working with two different colors of crayons, can the child separate the two colors accurately?

● When the crayons are lined up, can the child tell you which color made the longest line?

Connecting Science to the Curriculum

• **Language and Literacy**—Encourage the children to use color names as they sort and line up the crayons. Use comparative language as the children talk about which line is the longest, which color has the most number of crayons, and so on.

• **Mathematics**—Talk with the children about how they can use the lengths of the crayon lines to estimate the quantity of crayons in the two colors. Have the children count the number of crayons in one group and then use that information to estimate the quantity of the second group of crayons. **Note:** Only do this if the crayons are all about the same length. If you are using a number of broken crayons, estimations based on the length of the line will be inaccurate.

• **Taking It Outside**—Ask the children to find things outside to collect and line up to compare. They can use the edge of a sidewalk or a line drawn with chalk as their guide. Perhaps they could collect leaves or sticks from two different trees. **Note:** This activity requires some close examination to be sure the leaves are sorted. Then ask the children about the objects they have gathered, "Do you have rocks and acorns? What about dandelion blossoms and clover leaves?" Have the children collect litter, sort it by type (such as paper and not paper), and determine which makes the longest line. After completing the activity, show the children how to put the litter in the appropriate place, in garbage or recycling bins.

Science Process Skills

Focused observing
Observing to classify
Organizing and
communicating observations

Science Vocabulary

alike
color words
different
same

Materials

child-safe scissors (1 per child)
magazines
masking tape
materials collected from the
schoolyard
resealable bags (several per
child)
stapler
three-ring binder (optional)

Children's Books

Color Zoo, a Caldecott Honor
Book by Lois Ehlert, shows
children how colors and shapes
can make unexpected things
happen.

Of Colors and Things by Tana
Hoban illustrates an activity
similar to the one the children
just completed. Hoban collects
all kinds of different things that
are the same color.

My Color Book

Children will use resealable bags to create books. The books will all be different, because each child will have a unique approach to selecting pictures and classifying them by color. The colors, however, will be the same within each book. The children will explore similarities and differences among the books.

Science Content Standards

The children will note and use similarities and differences among pictures and objects to separate the objects into groups by their color properties; the children will begin to use simple descriptive language about the objects. (Physical Sciences—Properties of Matter; Science as Inquiry)

What to Do

1. Let the children choose the color for the books they will make. Have them search through magazines and tear or cut pictures containing primarily that color.

2. Take the children outside to find objects from the school grounds that match the chosen color. Talk with the children about the fact that some colors are hard or impossible to find in nature.

3. Bring the collected objects into the classroom.

4. Help the children place the colored pictures and collected objects into the bags. Press everything down flat. Print the color name on a cover page for the bags. Seal and staple several bags together to form color books.

5. Repeat the activity with several other colors.

6. Have the children name some of the objects pictured in their books. Do some of the books for different colors have some of the same objects? Do books for the same colors have different objects?

Observing and Assessing the Child's Science Learning

- When given a clear plastic bag, can the child collect pictures or objects of a specific color that fit in the bag?

Alike and Different

Keep It Simple

● Have the children make rainbow books or pages with all the colors of the rainbow.

● Use a three-ring binder to make a class color book.

Add a Challenge

● Have the children make class color collages using a different piece of paper for each color. Talk about how many different shades and variations there are of each color.

Theme Connections
Colors

This activity provides a great way to introduce a Colors theme. Also consider using this method to make "All About Me and My Family" or "My Favorite Things" books, since the bags allow you to include items that are not flat.

Dual Language Learners

Encourage these learners to tell the rest of the class how to say the names of the various colors in their home language. Learn the color words yourself and encourage the rest of the children to do so as well.

Children with Special Needs

Children with limited motor skills will need assistance with scissor use, placing cutouts in resealable bags, and other aspects of this activity. Encourage the children who cannot use scissors to tear pictures or pieces of colored paper.

● Can the child tell you if the objects in other children's bags are the same color as her own objects?

Connecting Science to the Curriculum

• **Language and Literacy**—After the children name the objects pictured in their books, provide markers and crayons so they can label the books at their own developmental level of writing. Provide help as needed.

• **Taking It Outside**—Go outside and make color pages using only the natural materials the children find. Which pages are hard to fill? Which are easy? In most areas during warm weather, children will find many green materials but few red items.

• Make a litter color book with the class. Is it easier to make a litter page or a nature page?

Family Involvement

● The children can take the books home and add additional pages with help from their families.

● Give each of the children a piece of paper with a color word written on it in that color. For example, write "red" with a red marker. Have the children take these home with a note asking their families to help find and attach objects that are that color. They might bring buttons, pictures, food wrappers, fabric, yarn—anything goes. Also, consider sending home resealable bags and having the children attach the materials they bring from home to a poster at school. If you give all the children the same color to find at home, you and your students will be amazed at the color collection they assemble when everyone returns to the classroom.

Alike and Different

Paint It If You Can

Paint adheres better to some surfaces than to others. This activity gives children an opportunity to discover that fact for themselves. Let them explore freely with a great variety of materials.

Science Process Skills

Focused observing
Observing to classify
Organizing and
  communicating observations

Science Vocabulary

descriptive words, such as *runny, smear,* and *puddle*
material names
sort

Materials

paintbrushes (2 per child)
painting sheets (see "Before the Activity")
paper towels (for cleanup)
water-based paints

Children's Books

Touch the Art: Feed Matisse's Fish by Julie Appel and Amy Guglielmo is a "touch and feel" journey through the work of some of the masters of modern art. It provides an appealing way for children to continue their exploration of the properties of surfaces.

In *Mouse Paint* by Ellen Stoll Walsh, three little mice discover the wonders of color mixing as they paint the floor and each other.

I Ain't Gonna Paint No More! by Karen Beaumont and David Catrow is the story of a little boy who seems to make paint stick to everything!

Science Content Standard

The children will note and use similarities and differences among the properties of materials to separate the materials into groups; the children will begin to use simple descriptive language when discussing the properties of materials. (Physical Sciences—Properties of Matter)

Before the Activity

Create the painting sheets by cutting a variety of materials—such as waxed paper, aluminum foil, plastic wrap, cardboard, newspaper, slick magazine paper, construction paper, and finger paint paper—into roughly 9"–12" squares. The greater the variety of materials you offer, the more interesting this activity will be.

What to Do

1. Place all of the materials in the Art Center. Encourage the children to paint on the different painting sheets.

2. After the children have had some time to explore the materials, discuss their observations. Ask, "What materials did you like to use for painting? Are there some that did not work?" Build the children's vocabularies by pointing out the names of the materials you used to make the painting sheets.

3. Encourage the children to talk about what happens to the paint on various surfaces. They might use words and phrases such as *puddle, runny, smear, it makes dots,* and *it messes up.*

4. Have the children sort their sheets by those paint adheres to and those it does not adhere to. Tell the children, "We can say that the materials that were easy to paint were alike and those that were not easy to paint were alike. We have classified them into two groups with different properties—*paintable* and *not paintable.*"

Alike and Different

Keep It Simple

● Choose two very different materials for the children to use. For example, you might try newspaper and waxed paper. As the children work, encourage them to talk about the differences they see and feel.

Add a Challenge

● Try to see if the children can tell by the feel of a material how it will work as a painting surface. Do they group the materials in the same categories that were created in the original activity?

Theme Connections
Colors

MaryAnn Kohl's book *Preschool Art: Painting* provides a wealth of ideas for a Painting or Colors theme. This activity could also enrich a theme on Water and Other Liquids.

Observing and Assessing the Child's Science Learning

● Does the child understand that some materials are better to paint on than others?

● Does the child identify some materials that do not work?

Connecting Science to the Curriculum

• **Language and Literacy**—In this activity, the children talk about what happens to the paint on various surfaces.

• **Mathematics**—The children group the painting sheets by those that paint will adhere to and those to which it will not adhere.

• **Taking It Outside**—Give the children water and paintbrushes. Have them "paint" on leaves, rocks, cement, bricks, metal, and other things they find outside and see how they can be classified as painting surfaces.

Family Involvement

Encourage families to visit art museums to observe a variety of paintings and the various surfaces that the artists have used. There also may be public murals or wall paintings that the children could visit.

Using Museums and Other Community Assets

Visit an art gallery or museum. Help the children focus on the various surfaces artists use for their paintings. Perhaps an artist could visit your classroom and demonstrate painting techniques.

Alike and Different

Science Process Skills

Focused observing

Observing to classify

Organizing and
communicating observations

Science Vocabulary

alike

collage

descriptive words, such as
rough, smooth, and *bumpy*

different

feel

same

touch

Materials

collection of materials with a
variety of textures, such as
sand, gravel, sticks, fabric,
and textured paper

glue

large box with a hole cut in
the side

large sheet of heavy paper or
tagboard (1 per child)

Children's Books

*That's Not My Puppy: Its Coat Is
Too Hairy* by Fiona Watt and
Rachel Wells is a short and
simple book that is another look
at using touch to identify things.

DK Publishing has a *Touch and
Feel* Library that includes *Pets,
ABC,* and several other titles.
Consider making a class touch-
and-feel book.

When You Feel This Art

When children create individual pieces of art, they can usually use
their eyes to find their own work among other pieces. Introduce this
tactile experience to make children aware of the sense of touch as
another way of observing and identifying differences.

Science Content Standards

The children will note and use similarities and differences among
the tactile properties of objects to separate them into groups; the
children will begin to use simple descriptive language when
discussing the objects' textures. (Science as Inquiry)

What to Do

1. Show the children how to make their tactile art projects by
   putting glue on the paper and then adding various materials. Let
   the children spend a lot of time on this very engaging and
   exploratory part of the activity.

2. Be sure the children's names are on their work. Allow the texture
   collages to dry thoroughly.

3. Working with a small group of children, say, "Can you tell which
   collage is yours? Our eyes help us know which artwork is ours.
   Now we are going to see if our fingers can help us find our work
   with our eyes closed."

4. Have the children feel their own texture collages until the
   children are confident they can identify them. Help the children
   talk about what they feel. Support their choice of words, and
   supply other words to expand their vocabularies.

5. Place two children's texture
   collages in the box. Have a
   child reach in and try to
   identify which is her
   collage. Lift the box to see
   if the child's choice is
   correct. As the children
   become more skilled, you
   may want to use more than
   two texture collages at a time.

Keep It Simple

● Make a collection of sandpaper or texture letters, numbers, and shapes for the children to explore. Some of the children may want to find the letters in their name. Encourage the children to describe and compare the textures they feel.

Add a Challenge

● Make a list of the texture words that the children use. Gather the children and their artwork and talk about the words they have used. Can the children find places on the collage where the texture words occur?

Observing and Assessing the Child's Science Learning

● Given two collages, can the child identify her own work without looking?

● Can she use descriptive language to talk about her collage?

Connecting Science to the Curriculum

• **Language and Literacy**—Encourage the children to describe what their fingers feel as they touch their texture collages.

• **Taking It Outside**—Create collages with natural objects collected from the schoolyard or a nearby park. Encourage the children to notice textures by thinking aloud about your own observations. Run your hand over a leaf and comment about how smooth or fuzzy it is. Notice a rough rock or the bumpy surface of a climber ladder. The children will soon join you in sharing their own observations. Bring out magnifiers and ask the children, "How do rough things look under a magnifier? Are they different than smooth things?" This is a fun way to help expand the children's awareness of how interesting the world is!

Family Involvement

Have the children bring natural objects from home to make collages. Do the children have an easier time identifying their collages because they are made of objects they brought from home?

Children with Special Needs

Children with sensory integration or autism spectrum disorder issues may need to look at an array of items and select those materials that they are comfortable touching for this activity.

Incorporating Technology

Take close-up photos of the children's collages. Ask the children, "Does this new perspective change the way the collages look?" Can the children tell which collage is theirs? Do they see something in their collages that they didn't notice before?

Art

The World in Different Colors

Make the world a different color! Children create their own color viewers with cardboard tubes, colored plastic wrap or cellophane, and rubber bands. They will begin to discover that things can be alike and different at the same time.

Science Content Standard

The children will note similarities and differences among colors; the children will begin to use simple descriptive language when discussing colors. (Science as Inquiry)

Before the Activity

Find colored plastic wrap or cellophane. Also, consider making a set of color lenses by cutting out circles from clear, colored notebook dividers and covers. Tape these into place on the tubes.

What to Do

1. Begin this activity by giving each child a cardboard tube, rubber bands, and different colors of plastic wrap. Show the children how to use a rubber band to hold the plastic wrap over the end of the tube. Suggest that the children work together. One child can hold the plastic in place and another child can put the rubber band in place. (Some of the children may still need help.)

2. Ask, "How does what you see in the room look different when you look through the colored tube?" Encourage the children to look at different-colored objects with and without the tubes. Have the children exchange tubes to see how the variously colored sheets alter what they see. Ask, "What does the red block look like through the blue tube? What happens when you look at it with the yellow tube?"

3. Now comes the fun part. Have the children use another rubber band or two and connect a pair of tubes so they resemble binoculars. (Some children may find it easier to use tape). Ask, "Now what color are all the objects in the room? Are they the same or different as they were before? Do the colors change?"

Science Process Skills

Focused observing

Organizing and communicating observations

Science Vocabulary

alike

change

color names, such as *red, blue, green,* and so on

different

same

Materials

cardboard tubes (2 per child) and rubber bands

large sheet of newsprint and markers (for a Discovery Chart)

plastic or cellophane wrap in different colors

rubber bands (3–4 per child), which are used for the second part of the activity

Children's Books

Leo Leonni's *A Color of His Own* explores color changing through the eyes of a young chameleon.

City Colors by Zoran Milich finds beautiful colors everywhere and could inspire young photographers to make their own School Colors book.

Keep It Simple

● Fill clear plastic bottles of various sizes with different colors of water. Talk with the children about how objects look through these viewers.

Add a Challenge

● Have the children draw or write their observations in their Discovery Journals. Possible entries include the following: a blue viewer makes a red block purple; a red viewer makes a yellow duck orange. Have children work in pairs and see if they get the same results.

Theme Connections
Colors

Use this activity with themes that explore Color, Art, and Light. What happens to crayon drawings when viewed through the color tubes? Do some colors seem to disappear? Cover flashlights in the same way that you covered the tubes and let the children play with colored light.

Dual Language Learners

Demonstrate and verbalize activity directions repeatedly to reinforce the children's understanding of the concepts of *alike* and *different*.

4. Encourage the children to try making binoculars from tubes with mismatched colors. Have the children look with one eye and then with the other eye. (If a child has difficulty closing one eye, model how to cover one eye with your hand.) Talk with the children about the similarities and differences in colors among the tubes. Also, talk about the differences in colors when they keep both their eyes open.

5. Have the children dictate lists of things in the room that are yellow, blue, or red. Put the lists on a Discovery Chart. Talk about how the color tubes change our perception of the colors of the items on the lists.

Observing and Assessing the Child's Science Learning

● When looking through different-colored viewing tubes, can the child describe the apparent changes in appearance of the objects she sees?

Connecting Science to the Curriculum

● **Art**—Have the children make window color collages by taping pieces of transparent colored term paper covers to the windows.

● **Language and Literacy**—Use a Discovery Chart to list the children's descriptions of how the color tubes change their perceptions of certain objects.

● **Taking It Outside**—Take the viewers outside. Ask, "How is using a viewer outside similar to using it inside? Are there ways that the experience is different?"

Family Involvement

Ask the children's families to send in collections of cardboard tubes and plastic bottles to use for this activity.

Block Sandwiches

Making sandwiches gives children a simple metaphor to work with as they explore the relationships between different block shapes. This simple building model can be used at various times as children begin making more complex structures. Children should refine their observation and classifying skills as they create their own sandwiches and compare them to the ones their friends make.

Science Content Standard

The children will note and use similarities and differences among size properties of objects to separate them into groups; the children will begin to use simple descriptive language with regard to specific objects. (Science as Inquiry)

What to Do

1. Engage the children in a discussion about their favorite sandwiches and what goes into those sandwiches. Let the children pretend to make sandwiches with the blocks. Talk about their favorite sandwiches. It might be fun to use some of the children's recipes to make some of the sandwiches for snack time.

2. Tell the children they will play a game making layered sandwiches. Place a block on the floor. Say, "This is the bread." Ask a child to cover it exactly with other differently shaped blocks. For example, with unit blocks, four triangles cover a standard rectangle. Invite the child to name this layer of the sandwich. The child might choose to call it "peanut butter."

3. Ask, "Can you make another layer for this sandwich? How about some 'jelly'?"

4. Continue to encourage the child to find out whether there are more possible ways to combine blocks to make the same shape as the "bread." The children will make the same shape again and again from different shapes.

5. Choose another shape to be the base, or "bread." How many possible sandwiches can be made with your set of blocks? Lay out the sandwich possibilities until the children cannot make any others.

6. Have the children play the sandwich game with several different sets of blocks. Ask, "Are there sets of blocks that will work when mixed together? Are there some sets that will not work together?"

Science Process Skills

Focused observing

Observing to classify

Organizing and communicating observations

Science Vocabulary

alike

different

fit

layer

match

mix

same

sandwich

shape words, such as *triangle* and *square*

Materials

pattern blocks or other sets of blocks with a variety of shapes

unit blocks

Children's Books

Sam's Sandwich by David Pelham takes creative sandwich making to new heights. It will inspire the children to see just what tasty or not-so-tasty morsels they can fit into their own make-believe sandwiches.

The appealing photographs by Ken Heyman in Ann Morris' *Bread, Bread, Bread* show how bread is both alike and different all over the world.

Keep It Simple

- Show the children a square block. Say, "We are going to pretend that this is the bread. How many pieces of bread are in a sandwich?" Collect another square block. Say, "We're going to pretend to make a bread and butter sandwich." Show them a yellow square and a yellow triangle of construction paper. Ask, "Which is the same shape as our pretend bread? Let's use that to make our bread and butter sandwich." Encourage the children to find shapes. When they are successful with that, begin to explore how to combine shapes to make other shapes.

Add a Challenge

- Make real sandwiches. Provide different shapes of bread: slices cut to make triangles, squares, or rectangles. Flat bread circles (tortillas or pitas) offer another shape to consider. Ingredients can be in many shapes as well. Lunch meats or cheese slices can make various shapes, while spreads such as peanut butter or hummus can fit anywhere. Talk about shapes as the children make their sandwiches. Some sandwiches will fit together "just right," while others will not, but any shape can make a tasty sandwich. Encourage the children to talk about whose sandwiches are like theirs and whose are different.

Theme Connections
Rocks

Bring in samples of sedimentary rock for the children to examine. Then, instead of making block sandwiches, make block sedimentary rocks.

This helps illustrate to the children that some sets of blocks are not compatible with others for this activity.

7. Have the children look at the different sandwiches that they have made and invite them to describe how the various sandwiches are alike and different.

8. Once the children understand the concept, they can play this sandwich game with each other independently.

Observing and Assessing the Child's Science Learning

- Given a set of blocks, can the child use a variety of combinations to cover the same area?

- Does the child understand that some blocks are proportionately related (fit together) and others are not?

- Can the child point out sandwiches that look alike or look different?

Children with Special Needs

Apply gripping materials to blocks for children with limited motor skills who have difficulty with gripping or grasping the blocks.

Connecting Science to the Curriculum

- **Healthy Foods**—Talk with the children about how healthy food comes in many forms. Bring in foods for the children to sample that are both alike and different. For example, corn, tortilla chips, and popcorn look different, but they are all made from corn. Green grapes and celery are the same color. What is different about them?

Science Process Skills

Focused observing

Observing to classify

Organizing and
communicating observations

Science Vocabulary

alike

build

construct

color names, such as *green,
blue, purple, orange*, and so on

different

model

same

shape names, such as *square,
rectangle, triangle*, and so on

size words, such as *big, small,
tall, short*, and so on

Materials

blocks

Children's Books

Michael J. Crosby and Steve
Rosenthal have created a
wonderful four-book collection
for children about the details of
architecture: *Architecture
Shapes, Architecture Colors,
Architecture Counts,* and
Architecture Animals. With
beautiful photographs, they help
children really look at buildings.

Roberto, the Insect Architect by
Nina Laden is a humorous look at
architecture that still manages to
include factual information about
architecture and construction.

Tower Builders

When children build block structures that differ from or are similar
to a sample structure, they are exploring the concepts of *alike* and
different. Such an activity also develops children's fine motor skills
and visual perception.

Science Content Standard

The children will note and use similarities and differences among
objects to separate them into groups by the properties of size and
shape; the children will begin to use simple descriptive language.
(Science as Inquiry)

What to Do

1. Build a simple structure using three or four blocks. Ask the
children, "Can you make a tower that looks just like mine?"

2. When the children finish making their own towers, talk with
them about how their towers and yours are alike. Are they
different, too? They may be if the children used blocks that were
the same shape but different colors.

3. Ask the children to build towers that are significantly different
from your sample tower.

4. Talk with the children about the differences in the various towers.
Ask, "Are there any ways they are like?" Encourage the children to
use color, size, and shape words as they talk about how their
structures are alike or different. This can be a real challenge for
many of the children. Use a think-aloud approach to model
language for the children. For example, say, "Hmm, I'm thinking
about colors. Both Dory and Ayisha have orange blocks in their
towers. That's something alike about them. I wonder what is
different. I have to look carefully. If I look from here I can see that
Dory's tower is taller than Ayisha's."

5. Encourage the children to continue this activity with each other.
Many children find it easier to focus on building similar and
dissimilar structures using blocks at a table rather than on the
floor in the block area.

Alike and Different

Keep It Simple

● Build structures that are simple enough for the children to duplicate successfully. Once the children can confidently build structures that are the same, challenge them to trick you by making a different structure.

Add a Challenge

● Have the children make two structures that are the same in every way but one. Then ask other children to look at the structures to see if they can find the one thing that makes them different.

Theme Connections

Snack

Give the children a slice of bread for snack and cut it in half. Provide them with a choice of spreads (cream cheese or peanut butter) and decorations (raisins, small carrot and celery pieces, radish slices). Let the children decide if they want to make snacks that are alike or different.

Dual Language Learners

Encourage the children to use their visual observation skills to successfully complete this activity. Provide the children with sample descriptive language and model how to use those terms. Encourage the children to listen to the words other children use to talk about their structures. Model descriptive terms and use gestures as you observe the children during this activity. For example, you might say, "Gregory, that's such a tall tower" as you simultaneously use hand gestures showing the structure's height.

Children with Special Needs

Apply gripping materials to the blocks for children with limited fine motor abilities.

Observing and Assessing the Child's Science Learning

● Given a set of blocks, can the child construct simple towers that are similar to or different from the towers that other children make?

● Can the child describe or show how the structures are similar or different?

Connecting Science to the Curriculum

● **Language and Literacy**—The children use color, size, and shape words as they talk about how their structures are alike or different and identify the similarities and differences.

● **Our Neighborhood**—Incorporate this activity and expand it during a theme on Our Neighborhood and Community. How are buildings in your neighborhood alike and different?

● **Taking It Outside**—Invite the children to collect sticks outside and then use them to build structures. When you use natural materials, can any two towers be exactly alike? What happens when you use rocks or bricks? Encourage the children to talk about what is alike and different about natural and manufactured materials.

Incorporating Technology

Download images of towers from around the world to show the children. Inspire some creative building by posting some of the photographs in the block area.

Looking at Critters

For this activity, children will observe small creatures. You can use pictures, but using live animals is not that much trouble and can be much more interesting. Using live animals will give children the opportunity to care for living things as they explore those creatures' similarities and differences.

Note: Before the children engage in any activities that involve live animals and creatures, be sure to discuss the importance of treating all creatures gently and with respect.

Science Content Standard

The children will note similarities and differences among animals by comparing them to other animals; the children will use simple descriptive language when discussing living things. (Life Sciences)

Before the Activity

Locate a place in the classroom to keep the animals. To house the animals, use viewing containers, clear jars, or inflated resealable plastic bags (though any live creature should be kept in plastic bags for only a very short time). Keep slow-moving animals, such as snails or slugs, in reusable containers, such as plastic margarine tubs. Write the name of the animal on the container.

What to Do

1. Share the collection of various species with the children. Use this experience to develop the children's descriptive vocabularies. Give the children plenty of time to touch, look at, and talk about the animals.

2. Ask the children if they can name any of the animals. Have the children note the names on animals' containers. Ask the children, "What is the same about all the animals? How are they alike?" Encourage the children to observe the animals carefully and talk about what they see. Talk with the children about the animals' various physical characteristics, such as legs, eyes, and bodies. Set out magnifiers if they are available. They can help the children look even more closely.

Science Process Skills

Focused observing

Organizing and communicating observations

Science Vocabulary

alike	animal names
animal	body part names
different	home
match	same

Materials

magnifiers (if available)

paper and crayons (for a Discovery Book)

several of the following species (or whatever you can collect): Pill bugs, slugs, snails, beetles, earthworms, houseflies, grasshoppers, fish, ants, and so on (Also consider using dead insects that you find.)

Children's Books

Ladybugs and Other Insects by Gallimard Jeunesse provides useful information about insects in an inviting way and also serves as a simple field guide for identifying common insects.

For another look at *alike* and *different*, read *Way Out in the Desert* by T. J. Marsh and Jennifer Ward. It is a retelling of the traditional song, "Over in the Meadow." There is one version of *Over in the Meadow* by Ezra Jack Keats and another by Olive A. Wadsworth and Anna Vojtech. Help the children compare how the animals and the books are alike and different.

Keep It Simple

● After the children examine the animals, read a book about animals' lives and what they eat.

Add a Challenge

● If the animals are in containers that have enough soil, leaves, and other necessary materials that will enable them to survive comfortably for several days, ask the children to continue to observe the insects and worms and record their observations in their Discovery Journals.

More Books

Eric Carle's *The Very Hungry Caterpillar, The Very Quiet Cricket,* and *The Grouchy Ladybug* take children into a fictional world of insects.

Bugs Are Insects by Anne Rockwell and Steve Jenkins and *Insects* by DK Publishing provide more factual information.

Dual Language Learners

Children who are just beginning to learn English may be more comfortable with pointing to the animals that are the same and different than with saying their names.

Children with Special Needs

For children with developmental delays, provide a few pictures of animals that visually illustrate the concepts *same* and *different* and demonstrate the essential aspects of this activity. Group the pictures accordingly before starting with the live creatures.

3. Discuss with the children how the animals move. Perhaps they can try moving the way animals do. This is especially fun if there are worms or grasshoppers in the container! Some of the children will want to hold a worm or other slow-moving creature, while others may not. For those children who do want to hold an animal, model how gentle they must be.

4. After the children carefully observe the animals, have each child draw a picture of one of the animals and dictate a caption for it. Assemble the pages into a Discovery Book.

5. With the children's help, return the animals to their habitats or to the Discovery Center for later observation.

Observing and Assessing the Child's Science Learning

● This activity encourages the child to observe animals to determine characteristics that make them alike or different.

● Can the child point out some of the animals' characteristics and say whether those characteristics are alike or different?

Connecting Science to the Curriculum

● **Language and Literacy**—The children use descriptive vocabulary as they touch, look at, and talk about animals. The children also draw pictures of animals and write captions that can be used to make a class book.

Just Like Me

Alike and Different

Science Process Skills

Focused observing

Organizing and communicating observations

Science Vocabulary

alike

build

construct

color names, such as *green, blue, purple, orange*, and so on

different

model

same

shape names, such as *square, rectangle, triangle*, and so on

size words, such as *big, small, tall, short*, and so on

Materials

crayons

paper for drawing

playdough or clay of different colors

tools to roll out the playdough

This activity typically takes place at the Art Center. It challenges children to make simple art projects that are alike or different than artwork the teacher has made. Make sure you select materials that are appropriate for the motor skills of the children.

Science Content Standard

The children will note and use similarities and differences among objects to separate them into groups by properties; the children will begin to use simple descriptive language to describe observations. (Science as Inquiry)

What to Do

1. Position yourself at the Art Center with several different-colored containers of playdough.

2. Invite the children to the Art Center individually or in small, manageable groups. Tell the children you are going to make something and you want them to make something "just like it."

3. Take a small portion of playdough and shape it into simple shapes, such as a small ball or a snake.

Close Observation

• **Show It**—Ask each child to make an object just like the one you made. Observe how the child works. Does she refer to the object you made? Does she follow your technique? Does she use the same color of clay? Does she compare her object to the one you made?

• **Tell It**—Ask each child to tell you how her clay figure is like the one you made. Listen to the descriptive terms she uses to make her comparisons.

• **Draw It**—Give each child markers and paper. Ask the child to draw an object that looks like the one she just made. Can the children point to specific elements of the drawing (such as shape, color, size, and so on) that are the same as the actual object?

• **Write It**—Ask a more advanced child to write about her picture, describing what makes her picture look just like the object she made. Review what the child writes, looking for accurate comparisons and appropriate terminology. The child may write no more than basic word labels.

Observing and Assessing the Child's Science Learning

- After you give the child an object to make from playdough, is she able to construct a similar-shaped object?
- Can the child describe how that object is the same?

Science Process Skills

Focused observing

Observing to classify

Organizing and communicating observations

Science Vocabulary

alike

descriptive words for the group of objects (color, size, whether it rolls, whether it has one, two, or three parts, and so on)

different

group

same

sort

Materials

collections of objects with similar and different members in the group: rocks, nuts, leaves, shells, twigs, or other natural materials

Children's Books

Grandma's Button Box by Linda Williams Aber introduces another kind of collection that is fun to sort.

How Do They Go Together?

Young children often begin to classify objects by themselves. They may group toy animals in the Blocks and Building Center, or arrange manipulatives by color. This activity capitalizes on that inclination by encouraging children to sort collections of objects from nature in a variety of ways.

Science Content Standard

The children will note similarities and differences among objects and use those similarities and differences to separate the objects into groups by properties; the children will begin to use simple descriptive language when discussing living things. (Science as Inquiry)

What to Do

1. Place all the objects in front of a small group of children. Begin to group the objects to capture the children's attention.

2. When the children are watching what you are doing, start moving the objects into sets of similar shapes, colors, textures, and so on.

3. Ask the children to help you group the objects. Use the words *alike* and *different* and describe the objects as you talk with the children about their selections.

4. Sort the same group of objects another way. Ask the children to suggest additional ways to sort the objects.

5. Repeat the activity with a variety of objects. Encourage the use of descriptive words as you and the children group the objects by shape, size, or some other attribute.

6. Place the collections in the Discovery Center for the children to use independently.

Observing and Assessing the Child's Science Learning

- Given a set of objects, can the child classify the objects into groups and use the words *alike* and *different* to explain her work?

Keep It Simple

● Make a collection of intriguing objects that have very distinct properties. For example, you might use a shoe, two shells, matching jingle bells, and a big rock. As the children's skills increase, introduce them to collections with more subtle differences.

Add a Challenge

● Encourage the children to use more complex approaches to classifying the materials. Can the children make three groups instead of two? What about including measurement? For example, are objects shorter or longer or about the same as three interlocking cubes?

Theme Connections

Art

Move some of the more interesting objects from the collections into the Art Center.

Blocks

Move some of the objects in the collections to the Blocks and Buildings Center so that children can add new and complex materials to their constructions.

Dual Language Learners

Working with real objects makes it easier for children to learn vocabulary related to the outdoor environment. It is especially helpful if you use materials commonly found in your area.

Children with Special Needs

Children with cognitive challenges may not understand subtle differences. Therefore, start by showing only two or three examples of pairs, some that are similar and some that are very dissimilar to be sure the children understand the concept of *same* and *different* before proceeding with the activity.

Connecting Science to the Curriculum

• **Language and Literacy**—Have the children use the words *alike* and *different* as they talk about which things belong in a group and which do not. Support their use of descriptive words to explain their selections.

• **Mathematics**—Work with the children to classify objects by a number of different attributes. Some of the children may want to count the number of objects in each group.

• **Taking It Outside**—What kinds of things can the children collect nearby? Do they find different materials on a walk through the neighborhood or on a field trip? Encourage the children to classify materials "on the spot" and look for more things to add to their collections. Children can begin to understand that each environment has its own unique characteristics.

Family Involvement

Invite families to contribute collections for the children to explore. They might bring things from home or things from a trip to another area.

Alike and Different

Lid Turn and Match

This sorting and classifying activity also develops fine motor skills. In it, children sort jars into groups with matching lids and talk about what makes the interchangeable lid groups alike or different.

Science Process Skill

Focused observing

Science Vocabulary

alike

different

fit

group

match

same

Materials

variety of jars of different sizes with screw-top lids to match; several jars should have interchangeable lids

Science Content Standards

The children will note enough similarities and differences among jars and lids to be able to separate them into groups by their properties; the children will use simple descriptive language when discussing the objects. (Physical Properties—Properties of Matter; Science as Inquiry)

What to Do

1. Place the jars, with lids removed, on a table or on the floor. Let the children predict which lids will fit which jars before they begin trying to match them to one another.

2. Have the children match the lids to the appropriate jars. After doing this self-correcting activity a number of times, the children will be able to show you which lids fit which jars.

3. Once the children are comfortable placing the lids on the jars, have the children group the jars by size of lid. The children will learn that a single lid can match multiple jars. This discovery may surprise some children, and they will want to prove it several times before they are certain it is true. With the children, count how many jars there are in each group.

4. Have the children test the lids to see if they are interchangeable with all the jars in a group.

Children's Books

Putting lids on jars is hard work for little hands. *Hands Can* by Cheryl Willis Hudson (photographs by John-Francis Bourke) shows children's hands doing all kinds of things.

Alike and Different

Keep It Simple

● Place easy-to-handle plastic jars, bottles, and lids in the water table with soapy water. The children will enjoy putting the lids on and shaking the jars to make bubbles.

Add a Challenge

● Have the children bring in plastic jars with lids to add to the collection. Place the jars on a table and challenge the children to order them by height or weight.

Theme Connections
Me and My Body

Consider making your own *Hands Can* book with digital photos. How many things can the children show you that their hands can do? What about a *Feet Can* book? It is a fabulous way to celebrate young children's capabilities.

Dual Language Learners

Verbalize and demonstrate the activity. Modeling will help the child grasp the concept.

Children with Special Needs

Apply gripping materials to lids and jars for children with limited motor skills, especially for those who might have difficulty gripping or grasping the various sizes of lids and jars.

If a child does not have the motor skills for this activity, use teamwork. Have one child be the matcher and another child the one who "puts on" the lids.

Observing and Assessing the Child's Science Learning

● Looking at the sets of jars, can the child explain how she chose to group the jars?

Connecting Science to the Curriculum

• **Taking It Outside**—Take a water table or large tub outside along with a collection of plastic bottles, jars, and tubs with lids. Then let the children match and splash.

Family Involvement

Ask the children to collect a variety of different-sized jars with lids to bring from home.

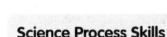

Science Process Skills

Focused observing
Observing to classify
Organizing and
  communicating observations

Science Vocabulary

alike
attract
different
group
magnet
same
sort

Materials

assorted objects, some that
  are attracted by magnets and
  some that are not, such as
  paper clips, small plastic
  toys, nails, washers, pennies,
  and aluminum foil; objects
  should not have different
  parts that are attracted and
  not attracted to magnets
  (For example, a ballpoint pen
  may have both plastic and a
  metal clip.)

large sheet of newsprint and
  markers (for a Discovery
  Chart)

magnets (1 per group)

paper bag (1 per group)

tape (optional)

Children's Books

Science with Magnets by Helen
Edom provides additional ideas
to share with the children.

Magnets Attract

Magnetism is a property of all matter. Magnets can be used to separate objects into two groups—those that are attracted to magnets and those that are not. This activity encourages children to identify ways objects in the two groups are alike and different and to find things to add to the groups.

Science Content Standard

The children will note the similarities and differences among objects that are attracted to magnets and those that are not attracted; the children will begin to use simple descriptive language when discussing magnets. (Physical Sciences—Properties of Matter)

Before the Activity

Place a wide variety of objects in the paper bags.

What to Do

1. Introduce the word *attract* to the children. Most of the children will continue to say such things as, "The magnet picked up the nail"; nonetheless, it is important to introduce them to a word they will continue to hear as they work with magnets. It will also give them a word to use when they feel the pull of a magnet on something that the magnet cannot pick up, such as a filing cabinet.

2. Show the children a magnet and two objects, one attracted to the magnet and the other not (such as a washer and a piece of cardboard). Point to a bag and say, "Some of the objects in this bag are like this washer. They are attracted to a magnet." Pick up the washer with the magnet, then say, "Some objects will be different. The magnet will not pick them up." Demonstrate with the cardboard.

3. Place the bags of objects on tables. Have the children work in groups to sort the objects into the two groups: magnetic and nonmagnetic.

4. As the children sort, they will discover that magnets will consistently attract metal objects (objects containing iron). The magnets always react the same way to those objects. They also react consistently to nonmagnetic objects.

Keep It Simple

● Make several collections for the children to sort in the Discovery Center. You can create answer containers by drawing a magnet on two plastic tubs. To indicate that one of the tubs is for objects that are not magnetic, draw a line through the image of the magnet you put on the front of the tub.

Add a Challenge

● Put a large collection of magnetic and nonmagnetic objects in a tub. Ask a child to go to the collection and choose 10 items that are not magnetic. Then ask the child to test her choices by holding them up to a magnet. With a little practice, the children will be right every time.

Theme Connections
Magnets

Use this activity to introduce a Magnet theme. Magnets enter children's worlds in a surprising number of ways. There are magnetic letters, numbers, and shapes; wooden puzzles with a magnet to move the pieces; and games that use magnets to put hair on a bald man, get a bee through a maze, or send cars along a street. Many classrooms have magnetic construction toys. How many different uses for magnets can the children discover?

Children with Special Needs

This activity enables children with fine motor challenges to repeat actions that support their wrist, hand, and finger manipulation development.

This is an especially good activity for children who have hearing or visual disabilities, as they can hold the objects and feel the magnetic attraction.

5. Talk about the two groups. Each group contains objects that are like each other, and the two groups are different from each other. Ask the children to find other things to add to each group.

6. Make a Discovery Chart. As the children dictate, list items attracted to a magnet on one side of the chart and those not attracted to a magnet on the other side of the chart. You may want to tape objects on the chart. Then count how many are magnetic and how many are nonmagnetic.

Observing and Assessing the Child's Science Learning

● Given a magnet and a set of objects, can the child test an item and place it in the correct group: magnetic or nonmagnetic?

● Can the child explain how objects in the same group are alike? (For example, some children may be able to explain how a washer and a nail are alike.)

Connecting Science to the Curriculum

• **Language and Literacy**—The children begin to use words that describe the phenomenon of magnetic attraction.

• **Mathematics**—The children classify objects into groups of items attracted or not attracted to magnets.

Family Involvement

Ask the children's families to send in items for your magnetic/nonmagnetic collection.

Science Process Skills

Focused observing

Observing to classify

Organizing and
communicating observations

Science Vocabulary

alike

different

fit

match

nut, bolt, screw

same

size

size relationship terms, such
as *smaller, too big,* and *the
same size*

turn

Materials

nuts and bolts, with a variety
of bolts that can be screwed
into the same nut

paper bags

Children's Books

*Old MacDonald Had a
Woodshop* by Lisa Shulman and
Ashley Wolff is a great book to
use with this activity. This book
offers a fun look at tools,
complete with sound effects. It
also allows you to talk about how
this version of Old MacDonald
is alike and different when
compared with the original song.

Nuts and Bolts

Using nuts and bolts gives children another experience with sorting
objects that fit together. A quick and easy way to build a collection
of nuts and bolts is simply to ask children's families to send some to
school. The more diverse the collection, the more interesting this
activity will be.

Science Content Standards

The children will note similarities and differences among nuts and
bolts and separate nuts and bolts into groups by properties; the
children will use simple descriptive language when discussing nuts
and bolts. (Physical Science—Properties of Matter; Science as
Inquiry)

Before the Activity

Ask families to donate various sizes of bolts and nuts or collect
them yourself. In each bag, place two nuts of two sizes. Also put in
4–10 bolts of two different diameters (but in a variety of shapes)
that will fit one or the other of the two nuts. The number of bolts
depends on your children's abilities. In addition, prepare more
challenging bags with three or more different sizes of nuts and bolts
in each bag.

What to Do

1. Have children pour their bags of nuts and bolts on the floor or
   table.

2. Tell the children to group the bolts by which nuts they will fit.

3. Have the children take one of the groups of bolts and screw them
   one at a time into the proper nut. Use comparative terms and
   phrases such as *smaller, too big, little,* and *the same size* as you
   work with the children.

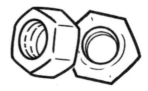

Keep It Simple

● Ask the children to order the nuts and bolts by size from smallest to largest.

Add a Challenge

● Provide the children with a more challenging set of nuts and bolts. You might want to include both metric and SAE (standard) American bolts. These bolts are not interchangeable with each other. As the children try to fit the metric nuts on the American bolts and the SAE American nuts on the metric bolts, they will discover that they are not alike and will not fit no matter how hard they try. After making this discovery, the children can continue fitting the nuts on the appropriate bolts.

Theme Connections
Tools, Construction, and Jobs

These themes are natural fits with this activity. Extend it by bringing in real tools for the children to explore.

Children with Special Needs

By doing this activity, children with fine motor challenges will repeat actions that support their wrist, hand, and finger manipulation and development. For children with more severe fine motor challenges, consider using very large nuts and bolts, as well as large plastic nuts and bolts.

Observing and Assessing the Child's Science Learning

● Watch as the child sorts the bolts. Is the child able to determine that the diameter of the bolt and the size of the opening of the nut are the criteria for predicting which will fit?

Connecting Science to the Curriculum

• **Language and Literacy**—The children use comparative terms as they match nuts to bolts.

• **Mathematics**—The children match the diameter of a bolt to the size of the opening in a nut. They may also find nuts and bolts that are the same shape and/or size. By ordering nuts and bolts by size, the children learn seriation, or how to order items in a series.

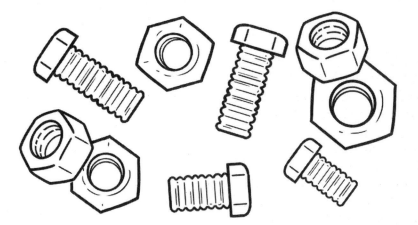

Science Process Skills

Focused observing

Observing to classify

Organizing and communicating observations

Science Vocabulary

alike

different

fruit

match

same

sight-related terms, such as *color, shape*

size relationship terms, such as *big, long, little, small*, and so on

smell-related terms, such as *sweet, strong, strawberry*, and so on

sound-related terms, such as *loud, tingle, soft, clack, click*, and so on

touch-related terms, such as *soft, hard, smooth, rough, mushy*, and so on

vegetables

This activity provides an excellent way for you to gauge how well the children are using all of their senses to make observations. It also tells you if the children understand the concepts of *alike* and *different*. Even more important, this activity gives children the opportunity to use a set of observations that they truly understand to make decisions. They will enjoy the novel objects you bring to the classroom.

Science Content Standards

The children will note similarities and differences in order to separate items into groups by properties identified by the senses; the children will begin to use simple descriptive language. (Physical Science—Properties of Matter; Science as Inquiry)

What to Do

This activity has five different sets of observations, one for each sense, for the children to perform. Consider doing them together or separately. Use your knowledge of your children to determine how complex these observation opportunities should be. For example, for skilled observers, you might show them an orange and a tangerine and ask them to tell you about how these two fruits are alike and different. For beginning observers, you might show them a coconut and an apple and ask the children how these foods are alike and how they are different. Then help focus the children's observations on the characteristics of the foods.

Listening

1. Have the children close their eyes tight and put their hands over their eyes for an additional check. Encourage the children to listen carefully because you are going to make some interesting sounds and you want them to say whether those sounds are alike or different from each other.

2. Make a pronounced sound, such as a clicking a metal clicker or blowing a small whistle. Pause and remind the children to be good listeners and to tell you if this next sound is similar to or different than the first sound. Repeat the same sound and have

Children's Books

My Five Senses by Aliki Brandenberg explores the five senses through the eyes of a young child.

Materials

foods with distinct differences to see, smell, touch, and taste (for example, coconut, artichoke, papaya, pineapple, citrus fruits)

herbs, spices, or flowers with scents

knife (adult use only)

noisemakers (for example, whistles, slide whistles, metal clickers, bells)

small containers to hold smelling samples

textured materials (for example, fleece and other textured fabrics, fake fur, sandpaper, scrubbers, feathers)

the children vote with their hands as to whether they thought the sounds were alike or different.

3. Now add a different sound, such as a bell ringing, and ask the children to vote if this sound is similar to or different from the last sound.

4. Repeat these steps, using as many different fun sounds as you have available. Sometimes use matching sounds. At other times, use very different sounds.

Looking

1. Show the children an interesting object, such as a coconut, and ask them to look at it carefully. In your other hand, hold up another coconut and ask, "Are these objects alike or different?"

2. Put your hand behind your back or under the table and bring out an artichoke. Ask, "Is this just like the coconut?" Now try a papaya and an orange, a lemon and a lime, and so on. Talk with the children about why they think the objects are alike. Ask, "What do you see that tells you they look alike?" If the children think the objects look different, ask them to describe the differences. Are some both alike and different? For example, lemons and limes are very similar in shape, but different in color.

Touching

1. Have the children feel a soft piece of fleece and then a different piece of fleece. Ask, "Do these objects feel alike?" Have the children feel other soft or smooth objects. Ask the children to talk about the objects they feel. Children can sometimes come up with better descriptions if they feel an object and think about it with their eyes closed. Suggest that the children try this.

2. Give the children some rough items, such as sandpaper or a coconut. Have the children explain how some of the objects feel alike and how some feel different.

3. Ask the children to group items according to how the objects feel. Encourage the children to think beyond the basic distinctions of *rough* and *smooth*. Let the children come up with their own categories, such as *bumpy*, *pointy*, or *scratchy*.

Smelling

1. Cut an orange or other piece of fruit in half and have the children smell both halves. Ask, "Do these fruit halves smell alike or different?"

2. Cut open a papaya, lemon, lime, or other fruits, place small pieces in containers, and let the children smell the pieces of fruit. Then add a rose or other scented material to the mix. Try having the children close their eyes before describing the smells they observe. This will ensure that the children are using their sense of smell to tell whether the fruit samples are alike or different.

Tasting

1. Explain to the children how it is fun to explore new flavors, particularly when someone gives you a food you have never tried before. Remind the children, however, that for their safety it is important that they only try foods given to them by someone they know and trust.

2. Use the fruits or other foods you have already worked with during smell test for the taste test. Provide small samples for the children to try. Encourage the children to think like scientists. Challenge them to taste two foods, observe their flavors, and then decide if the two foods taste alike or different, rather than tasting the foods to decide if they like the flavors.

Observing and Assessing the Child's Science Learning

- Given a set of objects, can the child provide simple descriptions that indicate careful observation?

- Can the child classify the objects into groups and use the words *alike* and *different* to explain her work? Some of the children may be able to identify objects as being alike or different, but at this point, they may not have the ability to give reasons for their choices.

Alike and Different

Keep It Simple

● Have the children draw and write or dictate their observations in their Discovery Journals.

Add a Challenge

● Some time in the future, bring back a few of the favorite items the children tasted for a quick encore performance. Do this to check the extent to which the children are focusing their observations. Try taking a few votes to see which foods the children think are alike and different before having the children explore the foods in sensory detail again. Do the children's decisions change after closer observations? Add some new and unusual objects and foods to the mix.

Connecting Science to the Curriculum

• **Taking It Outside**—Take the children outside and have them listen to see if they can hear sounds that are alike or different. Encourage the children to look for some things that smell the same or different. Ask, "Does the metal on the climber smell the same as the metal on the fence? What about when it is wet?" Ask the children to feel some of the textures of plants and compare how they feel to manufactured, out-of-doors objects. Can the children find things that feel the same or different?

Family Involvement

Challenge the children to bring from home pairs of objects that they think are in some way alike or different. Ask the children to describe to the rest of the children the similarities and differences they see in these objects.

Alike and Different

Digging in the Sand

In this activity, children use their sense of touch to explore in the sand table. As they burrow below the surface of the sand, children will discover pairs of objects. How do they feel? Are their textures very different or almost alike? When the children pull them out and look, they will see whether they were correct.

Science Content Standards

The children will note similarities and differences among objects by comparing pairs of objects with similar properties that are buried in sand; the children will begin to use simple descriptive language to compare how objects feel. (Physical Science—Properties of Matter; Science as Inquiry)

Before the Activity

Collect a number of objects that are alike and different and bury those objects in the sand.

What to Do

1. Say, "Put your hands in the sand. Use your fingers to feel for two objects, one for each hand."

2. Ask, "Have you found something? Do the objects you are holding feel alike or different?"

3. The children answer first and then pull up the objects, one in each hand, to immediately check their responses.

4. Ask the children to sort the objects they have pulled from the sand into pairs that are alike and pairs that are different.

Science Process Skills

Focused observing

Organizing and communicating observations

Science Vocabulary

alike

buried

different

pairs

same

sort

touch words, such as *rough, smooth, curved,* and *sharp*

Materials

box of sand or a water table filled with sand

pairs of small objects, such as washers, marbles, plastic animals, toy cars, coins, pieces of paper, blocks, rocks, and sticks

Children's Books

Beach Day by Karen Roosa brings a day at the beach into your classroom. Digging in the sand takes on a whole new meaning with an ocean nearby.

Alike and Different

Keep It Simple

● Have the children take two objects that match and bury them in the sand. Then have them reach into the sand and find the objects—one in each hand.

Next, have them place two different objects in the sand. Mix them up and have them find the two objects with their hands—one for each hand. Before they uncover the objects, have them say whether they are alike or different. Children can pull them out of the sand to confirm their observation.

Add a Challenge

● Make up a very difficult set of objects that will require very fine touch to sort, such as two each of pennies, dimes, nickels, washers, tokens, and magnetic tokens.

Theme Connections
Animals
Bury plastic animals for the children to find during a Zoo or Farm theme.

Shapes
Bury shapes in the sand during a Shapes theme.

Dual Language Learners

Model the use of the terms *alike* and *different* for the children. Each time the child pulls out a pair, say the appropriate word and encourage the child to repeat it.

Children with Special Needs

Some children with sensory integration issues may avoid this activity as it involves some messy play. Try substituting confetti for sand.

Observing and Assessing the Child's Science Learning

● Working with objects buried in the sand, can the child feel to discover whether the two buried objects are alike or different?

● Can the child describe characteristics that make the objects alike or different?

Connecting Science to the Curriculum

• **Language and Literacy**—The children learn comparative language as they talk about the objects that feel alike and different.

• **Mathematics**—The children sort objects into pairs that are alike and pairs that are different.

• **Taking It Outside**—If you have an outdoor sand area, have the children collect both natural and manufactured materials to bury and find.

Alike and Different

Science Process Skills

Observing to classify

Organizing and communicating observations

Science Vocabulary

alike

different

graph

group

same

shortest

longest

Materials

Children's Books

Hats, Hats, Hats by Ann Morris—the title says it all. Photographs by Ken Heyman show how hats are the same—for example, soft—yet different all over the world. Ann Morris' other titles, such as *Houses and Homes* and *Loving*, are equally appealing.

You and Me Together: Moms, Dads, and Kids Around the World by Barbara Kerley is a vibrant celebration of how families are alike and different everywhere.

What's Alike About Us?

Children are often aware of ways in which they are alike or different from other children. "Look, we both have stars on our shirts," or "We have the same shoes, but mine are black" are the kinds of comments children share with their friends or teachers. This activity uses these observations to form groups. It may surprise the children to find that they can belong to more than one group.

Science Content Standard

The children will note similarities and differences among themselves in order to separate themselves into groups; the children will begin to use simple descriptive language when discussing living things; the children will organize information by creating a graph. (Life Sciences)

What to Do

1. Begin the activity by having the children explore what is the same and different about the ways they look. Encourage the children to talk about how they are alike and different. Capitalize on commonalities that you see or hear the children talking about. Take this opportunity to discuss how all people are all alike in many ways and yet each person is special and unique.

2. Place some of the children in a group according to a shared characteristic without telling the children what that characteristic is. At this age, it is usually best to group by just one attribute, such as children wearing shoes with laces and children wearing shoes without laces.

3. Once the groups are formed, line up the children to make a living model of a bar graph. This will help the children compare the relative size of the two groups. One of the easiest ways to form a human bar graph is to have two groups of children face each other. Starting at the same point, the children form two lines and sit cross-legged. This naturally spaces the children fairly evenly, and they can see which line is the longest.

4. Have the children try to discover what is the same about everyone in the group.

Keep It Simple

● On the sidewalk or blacktop, draw squares with different colors that correspond to eye and hair colors (blue, green, brown, black, and so on). Ask the children with black hair to move to the black square, children with brown hair to the brown square, and so on. Discuss why the children went to the group that they did. Then have them look for differences within their group. For example, if they went to the group with those with the same hair color, the eye color may not match. Repeat the activity with a focus on eye color. Then compare the eye group with the hair color group.

Add a Challenge

● Give the children squares of paper. Help the children write their hair color on the squares, or mark the paper with that color in some way. Challenge the children to group the squares that have the same color on them, and then make a graph out of those squares to see what is the most common and the least common hair color. Repeat the activity for eye color, shirt color, shoe color, and more.

Theme Connections

All About Me and My Body, Caring for Others, Getting to Know Each Other, and Families are just a few of the themes that this activity will enrich. Bring in mirrors and help the children really look at themselves and each other. Encourage the children to talk about and draw what they see. Ask them to write captions for their drawings. Provide help as needed.

Observing and Assessing the Child's Science Learning

● Can the child identify a common characteristic within a group?

Connecting Science to the Curriculum

● **Language and Literacy**—The children describe how they are alike and different.

● **Mathematics**—The children learn about common characteristics by dividing themselves into groups. The children also make a living model of a bar graph; this helps them compare the sizes of the groups.

● **Taking It Outside**—Go outside with the children and look for things that are alike and different. To get them started say, "Look at the trees. How are they alike? How are they different? What other things can we see out here that are alike in some ways and different in others?" Draw their attention to leaves, animals, windows, or buildings.

We both have stripes.

Alike and Different

In the Circle or Out of the Circle?

Science Process Skills

Focused observing

Observing to classify

Organizing and
  communicating observations

Vocabulary

alike

characteristics

different

descriptive words for colors,
  shapes, textures, and so on

matter

properties

This simple little game helps you evaluate how well the children understand the concepts of *alike* and *different*. It also provides a clear indication of how well the children are developing their visual observation and classification skills. Finally, this activity provides an illustration of the level of critical detail at which the children are able to observe. Play this assessment game with individual children or in small groups. You can easily adjust the challenge level to the abilities of individual children.

Science Content Standards

The children will note similarities and differences in order to separate items into groups by their properties; the children will begin to use simple descriptive language. (Physical Science—Properties of Matter; Science as Inquiry)

What to Do

1. Spread out an array of interesting objects within easy reach of the children playing the game. You will need two objects per child, plus a few extras. Select objects that the children should be able to classify based on your previous observations of their grouping skills. For example, for some children you might select identical items, while for others, the items will be very dissimilar. Challenge more skilled children with more complex sets of materials.

2. Say, "Look at all these things. Some of them are things we've observed and classified lots of times. Other things are new. When I say 'go,' take two things, one for each hand. Ready, set, GO!"

3. Once the children have their items, say, "Look at what you have in your hands. Are they alike or different?" Listen to the children's responses and encourage them to communicate their observations. You might say, "So you think your two blocks are

Materials

1 meter (or 1 yard) length of rope or yarn

cardboard box big enough to contain manipulatives for this activity and clearly labeled *Alike and Different Check Point*

variety of interesting materials that are both safe for children to handle and will fit easily into the assessment box for easy storage and access **Note:** These might include: rocks of different colors and shapes; acorns and other natural materials; plastic toys, pictures, pattern blocks, and unique household gadgets. Be sure to include some items that are exactly the same, such as pairs of blocks or counters.

alike. What is alike about them? They are both red? You're right. They are both red. What else is alike? Is there anything different about them or are they just the same?"

4. Have everyone return their items, then mix them up and have the children select two more objects. Setting a quick pace will make the game more exciting. Continue with several rounds of the game until you have a clear understanding of the children's abilities to identify items as alike or different, as well as their abilities to communicate their observations.

5. Use the rope or yarn to create a large circle in front of you. Go through a large production of describing the attributes of an object you select from the available set. For example, pick up an acorn and say, "Let me look carefully at this acorn. Let's see. It's brown. Part of it is rough and part of it is smooth. It's round and rolls around in my hand. I wonder what it smells like. Hmm, not much of a smell." Then place it in the circle.

6. Explain that you are now looking for other objects that are similar to the object in the circle so those objects can join the circle, too. Ask a child to select an object that can join the circle. The key to this is to have the child tell you why the object can join the circle. Ask the children to explain what it is about this object that makes it like the one in the circle. Make sure the children understand that the new object doesn't have to be the same exact object; it just has to have a characteristic that is similar. The new object might be a brown button or a round marble.

7. Talk with the children to make sure they make their decisions based on valid comparisons.

Observing and Assessing the Child's Science Learning

- Given a set of objects, can the child provide simple descriptions that indicate careful observation?

- Can the child classify the objects into groups and use the words *alike* and *different* to explain her work? Some of the children may be able to identify objects as *alike* or *different*, but may not yet have the ability to explain their reasoning.

- Can the child make observations that allow her to accurately select an object that is like the object in the circle in some way?

Chapter 3

Exploring Motion

Exploring Motion

Science Concepts

This chapter explores the following science concepts:

- Motion occurs when force is applied to an object.

- A change in motion occurs when the amount or direction of force applied to the moving object changes.

- All moving objects in the everyday world eventually stop.

Introduction

From birth on, motion plays a crucial part in people's lives. As soon as children start to wave their arms and legs, a natural fascination with movement begins. This chapter is designed to help children understand more about the phenomenon of movement. They explore different aspects of movement, including how to control motion as well as how movement affects them and their surroundings. By understanding what motion is, what causes motion, and what alters motion, children can begin to understand why objects in nature behave the way they do.

Getting Ready

Place the following materials, along with any other interesting objects, in the Discovery Center or other appropriate places in your classroom for the children to explore during Free Discovery:

- 2" plastic pipe 1–1½ meters long, along with an elbow connector and a T connector

- air pump

- assortment of handheld fans

- beach ball

- marbles and golf balls

- plastic foam pipe insulation tubes or cardboard tubes
- spinning toys, such as tops
- things that can be used to move air, such as a dustpan and pieces of cardboard
- toy vehicles
- toys and other items that show movement, such as a jack-in-the-box or a marble maze

Free Discovery

Begin Free Discovery by talking with the children about how different things move and what the children can do to make those objects move. Have some interesting things with you that will help illustrate movement, such as a jack-in-the-box or a marble maze. Ask the children to think of other things that move. Ask, "Do they roll, jump, or fly? Do you have toys that move?" As the children share their thoughts, add them to an Exploring Motion Discovery Chart. You may also want to list all the ways the children can think of to make their own bodies move.

Allow the children ample opportunity to investigate the new materials in the classroom. While the children may need some guidance or suggestions when they first begin to explore these movement materials, it is important to let the children explore freely, so be careful not to overdirect their exploration.

Now is the time to begin the class Discovery Books for this chapter. You may want to make several books, each focusing on a specific activity, or you may want to make a general book with drawings and captions showing what the children are learning about motion. Either method works, as does making both types of Discovery Books. The children can also draw and write or dictate about what they do and observe in their own Discovery Journals.

As the children do the activities in this chapter, add their discoveries to the Exploring Motion Discovery Chart.

Exploring Motion

Track the Marble Roll

Marble painting is a common activity in many early childhood classrooms. It expands beyond art to science by using the paintings to make a record of how objects move. Use paint to track a marble as it moves up, down, and all around!

Science Process Skill

Focused observing

Science Vocabulary

across
curve
direction
motion words
stop
straight line
track
trail

Materials

cardboard boxes
marbles or golf balls
papers cut to the size of
   the box
paper towels (for cleanup)
shallow cups to hold paint
tempera paint

Science Content Standard

The children will learn that changing the amount or direction of an applied force results in a change in motion. (Physical Science—Position and Motion of Objects)

What to Do

1. Place a sheet of paper in the bottom of the cardboard box. Drop one marble in the box and have the children watch it move around and change direction as you move the box. Then let them try it. Talk with the children about what they should do to stop the marble's movement and how to make it change directions.

2. Say, "We want to make a picture that helps us remember how the marble moved in the box." Cover the marble in paint and drop it in the box. Move the marble by moving the box until the marble stops leaving a track. Repeat with another color of paint to show the different tracks each marble made.

3. Encourage the children to create as many marble-track paintings as they like. With practice, the children will learn how to control where the marble moves, resulting in more complex paintings.

Children's Books

In *The Funny Little Woman* by Arlene Mosel (with illustrations by Blair Lent), a woman chases a rolling dumpling down under the ground in this beautifully illustrated Caldecott Award winner. This funny little woman has an incredible adventure, all because of gravity and a round object that rolls!

Keep It Simple

● Give the children other objects that roll and see what kind of motion tracks they leave behind. Try toy cars or balls with different textures. Wrap foil or rubber bands around a golf ball for interesting tracks. There are many small balls made of a variety of materials—suction cups, rubbery fibers, foam—so try them all. Provide paints of various thicknesses and encourage the children to explore the different ways they affect the marble. What do they think is the best paint for the job?

Add a Challenge

● Put chart paper or newspaper into a very large box and let several children work together to move marbles or balls to make a big painting. Can the children predict where the ball will go when they tip the box a certain way?

Theme Connections
Colors

This activity provides a great way to explore mixing and layering colors, as well as experimenting with round objects. Given time to experiment, the marble paintings the children create become more complex.

Children with Special Needs

Children with sensory integration issues may avoid dipping the marbles into the paint. Consider encouraging these children to try pushing the marbles with a spoon or some other object they are comfortable with.

Those with severe motor delays may need assistance to raise and lower the box.

Use pizza boxes or shoe boxes with lids to minimize problems with the marbles coming out of the boxes.

Observing and Assessing the Child's Science Learning

● Looking at the paper, can the child locate where the marble changed direction in the picture?

● Can the child make the marble go to a certain corner or side of the box?

Connecting Science to the Curriculum

● **Mathematics**—Challenge the children to identify shapes the marble tracks create.

● **Taking It Outside**—Go outside and have the children make a giant painting. First, the children should put on smocks. Then make a large paper square 12' across or bigger by taping several pieces of mural paper together. Place about ½" of paint in a rimmed tray or dishpan. Cover a playground ball or basketball in plastic wrap (for ease of cleanup). Have the children sit around the edges of the paper, dip the ball in paint, and push it back and forth across the paper to make a huge "marble painting."

Exploring Motion

One Moves Many

Have you heard of the domino effect? Of course! Many children, however, may not have experienced how one thing can start a chain reaction, as properly set-up dominoes can do. Dominoes or blocks allow children to experience multiple motion and chain reactions.

Science Process Skill

Focused observing

Science Vocabulary

fall

line

pattern

push

space

Materials

at least 10 rectangular blocks of various sizes (Use large unit blocks or smaller blocks, depending on the children's motor skills.)

Children's Books

The Balancing Girl by Berniece Rabe is the story of Margaret, who wears leg braces and sometimes needs to be in a wheelchair. She is an expert at balancing things. In this book, she carefully sets up a domino pattern on the floor at school and then sells chances to knock over the first domino at a school fundraiser.

Science Content Standard

The children will observe that motion occurs when force is applied to an object. (Physical Science—Position and Motion of Objects)

What to Do

1. Show the children how to arrange 10 or more blocks vertically in a line with a small space between each block.

2. Have the children gently push the first block in the line toward the second block.

3. The first block will fall as the energy from the push to the first block is transferred from block to block. Ask, "What must happen for all the blocks to fall?"

4. Each child should have a turn touching a block and watching the rest of the blocks in the row fall.

5. Repeat the activity, this time having the children count the blocks they have set up. Then, just for fun, have them try to count the blocks as fast as they fall. Can the children keep up with the falling blocks?

6. Let children set up the blocks in other configurations and let them fall where they may. Have them arrange the blocks in a pattern, such as big, little, big, little. Encourage the children to explore this fascinating process on their own.

Keep It Simple

● Can the children find other blocks or objects that will work as well? Are there some blocks (such as semicircles) that do not work?

● Give the children dominoes of various sizes to use.

Add a Challenge

● Give the children pattern blocks to make intricate or long shapes. Do some pattern blocks work better than others?

Theme Connections
Blocks

Engage children with blocks in some new ways. "How many different kinds of blocks do we have to explore? How many different ways can we find to use them?" Create a photo and video gallery to document and display the results of the class' investigations. You might even create a block museum.

Dual Language Learners

Repeatedly demonstrate and verbalize the steps of the activity to help the child grasp the concept related to motion as well as the new terms.

Observing and Assessing the Child's Science Learning

● Does the child understand that he has to set up the blocks close enough to each other to touch in order for all the blocks to fall down?

● Does the child understand that he provides the initial force that causes the blocks to fall?

Connecting Science to the Curriculum

● **Mathematics**—Challenge the children to count the blocks they have set up.

● Point out to the children that when they arrange the blocks, they are establishing patterns.

Family Involvement

If the children's families have collections of dominoes or blocks at home, they can use them to reinforce what they are learning about motion.

Incorporating Technology

● Locate a video clip online for domino-building contests. Most of these feature huge collections of dominoes that, when pushed, fall to create a variety of complex patterns.

● Use a digital camera to record video clips of the blocks as they fall. Discuss similarities and differences in how various blocks fall. Are some blocks better for this activity than others? If so, why?

Using Museums and Other Community Assets

Someone in the community may have a hobby of creating elaborate domino designs. That person may be willing to come to the classroom and set up a demonstration.

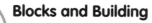

Exploring Motion

Children's Books

Big Wheels by Anne Rockwell and
Don't Let the Pigeon Drive the Bus
by Mo Willems are both books
that involve wheels and rolling.

Consider reading the children's
book *Bicycles,* a nonfiction book
by Kate Petty.

*Rolling Along: The Story of Taylor
and His Wheelchair* by James
Riggio Heelan and Nicola
Simmons is a book that increases
children's awareness and
sensitivity to children with
special needs.

Ramps

Ramps can be found many places in the real world. Examples
include driveways, wheelchair access ramps, slanted floors in
buildings, and sliding boards on playgrounds. Once the children
investigate the ramp, they will begin to see it everywhere.

Science Content Standard

The children will observe whether an object moves down a ramp
when force is applied and classify the objects as rollers or sliders.
(Physical Science—Position and Motion of Objects)

What to Do

1. Build an inclined plane with a small group of three or four
   children. Use blocks to adjust the height of the ramp and make
   it stable.

2. Pour out your collection of materials for the children to
   investigate. Get the children thinking by saying something like:
   "Take a look at all of this stuff. I want you to pick one thing you
   think will roll down our ramp and one thing you think will slide.
   We'll each get a turn to test our guesses."

3. After the children test their guesses, have them put those objects
   that roll in one pile and those objects that slide in another pile.

4. Send the children off on a hunt to find other *rollers* and *sliders.*
   Ask the children, "Are some things both rollers and sliders?" For
   example, a toy car on its wheels rolls, but slides when upside
   down. In what ways could a checker or a spool come down the
   inclined plane?

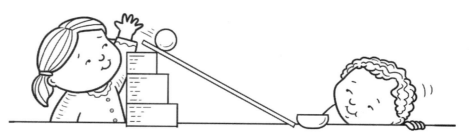

Keep It Simple

● Have the children race a collection of objects. Emphasize comparative words such as *farthest, faster,* and *slow.* Have the children collect the objects that traveled the farthest or fastest and place them in a winners' circle. Encourage the children to draw pictures of their favorite objects, write labels or captions if they are able, or dictate to you a label or caption for the objects. The children can measure the distances traveled and create a graph of the results.

Add a Challenge

● Using a simple measuring unit (for instance, a hand or a shoe), measure the distances objects travel from the end of the ramp. For example, a marble may travel the length of eight shoes, while a toy car may travel the length of only five shoes. Also, consider using standard measuring tools, such as a ruler or a meter stick. Explain to the children how and why to use each tool. For instance, because most people are familiar with measurements such as meters and inches, these measurements can be used to describe to our families the distances the objects traveled.

Theme Connections
Ramps

There are ramps all around us for work and play. Explore the ramps in your world. Create your own ramp book with photographs of all the ramps you can find.

Dual Language Learners

Repeatedly model and demonstrate the activity; be very specific about the names of each of the objects the children send down the ramp.

Children with Special Needs

Putting objects on the ramp and releasing them is helpful for children who have small motor challenges.

Observing and Assessing the Child's Science Learning

● Can the child distinguish between the attributes of objects that roll down the ramp and the attributes of those that do not?

Connecting Science to the Curriculum

• **Language and Literacy**—In this activity, the children use comparative words such as *farthest, faster,* and *slow.*

• **Mathematics**—This activity gives children an opportunity to measure the distance that objects travel from the ramp.

• **Taking It Outside**—Either make a ramp outside or use a sliding board on the playground. See how many rollers and sliders the children find outside to test on the ramps.

Incorporating Technology

Take photos of ramps that are located around the community. Show these to the children and discuss how ramps make it easier to get items or people in and out of buildings.

Exploring Motion

Science Process Skills

Focused observing
Linear measuring

Science Vocabulary

hill
ramp
roll
slope

Materials

blocks
marbles
masking tape
standard pieces (4'–6') of
   flexible foam pipe insulation,
   cut in half lengthwise

Children's Books

Roller Coaster by Marla Frazee
begins with everybody standing
in line, waiting for a roller
coaster ride. The illustrations are
fun—all sizes and shapes of
people are waiting. The roller
coaster looks huge, intricate, and
daunting. Fun pictures and text!

In *Ira Says Goodbye* by Bernard
Waber, Ira's best friend Reggie is
moving to a new town...with a
thrilling roller coaster! That is
just one of the reasons Reggie
says he is happy about going
away.

Roller Coaster Ride

It's roller coaster time! With a few simple materials, children can
experiment with the slopes of inclined planes, getting marbles to
move up and down hills and maybe even around curves. If the slope
is too steep, the marbles may jump the track. If the slope is too level,
the marbles may not go up the next hill. What kinds of roller
coasters can the children make?

Science Content Standards

The children will observe that motion occurs when force is applied
to an object; the children will observe that changing the amount or
direction of an applied force results in a change in motion. (Physical
Science—Position and Motion of Objects)

The children will compare heights and angles of portions of the
ramp. (Measurement—Linear)

What to Do

1. Show the children how to make various pathways for the marbles
   using pipe insulation and how to use blocks to create inclines
   along the pathway. Construct a high incline and a low incline and
   compare how the marble rolls on each incline.

2. Help the children tape the structures to blocks, chairs, or other
   props to make the structures semipermanent. The children might
   create a path that ends with the marble splashing into a cup of
   water. Ask, "Can you make a roller coaster with one tube? Can
   you connect two tubes to make a longer roller coaster?"

3. Observe as the children roll marbles down their roller coasters
   and listen as the children describe what happens. Did the marble
   make it to the end? If it did not, can the children find a way so
   that it does?

Exploring Motion

Keep It Simple

● Ask the children to look carefully at their roller coaster and talk about what they see. How many blocks did they use to hold it up? What else did they use to hold it up? Have the children draw their roller coasters. Some children's drawings will include details, such as the number of blocks supporting each hill, while other drawings might be simple curvy lines indicating a slope. Encourage the children to write captions for their drawings or dictate to you so you may write down their words for them.

Add a Challenge

● Challenge the children to make a longer, more complex system, using curves and loops. Test this system to see if a marble will roll long distances.

Theme Connections
Summer Fun

Since families sometimes go to fairs and amusement parks during the summer, add this activity to a Summer Fun theme. With a little adult help, these marble roller coasters can make the same kinds of loops that children's race-car tracks make. There are also commercial marble tracks that go from simple to very complex. A project on Track Toys could explore ways to move marbles, cars, and trains.

Children with Special Needs

Children with motor challenges may enjoy being the marble releaser or catcher.

Observing and Assessing the Child's Science Learning

● Given the roller coaster apparatus, can the child describe how a marble will behave as it rolls down the slope?

● Can the child point out where in the slope the marble may slow down or stop and compare distances the marble moves before it stops?

Connecting Science to the Curriculum

● **Language and Literacy**—Make a class Discovery Book from the children's drawings and the written descriptions of their roller coasters.

● **Mathematics**—In this activity, the children count the number of insulation units they use to make their tracks. The children also compare how the height and angle of the structure affect the speed of the marble.

Family Involvement

Ask families to share family photographs of experiences the children have had on roller coasters or at amusement parks.

Incorporating Technology

Download images of roller coasters and marble runways from around the world to show the children. These images may inspire the children to make some creative designs of their own.

Exploring Motion

Turn Right, Turn Left

This activity puts the children into the action: They observe and then experiment with movement control as they learn to use balls in a new way.

Science Process Skills

Focused observing
Observing to classify

Science Vocabulary

control
move
pipe
release
roll
turn

Materials

1 elbow connector
1 T connector
2 boxes
piece of plastic pipe, 2" (about 5 centimeters) in diameter and 3'–4' (1–1½ meters) long
several marbles or golf balls

Science Content Standard

The children will learn that changing the amount or direction of an applied force results in a change in motion. (Physical Science—Position and Motion of Objects)

What to Do

1. Put the elbow connector on a piece of pipe. Place the box on the floor on its side.

2. Show the children how they can lay the elbow end of the pipe on the floor a few inches from the box and roll a ball down the pipe. The ball will come out the elbow and possibly roll into the box.

3. Give the children time to experiment with rolling the balls and trying to get them in the box. The children should soon realize that if the elbow connection is facing the box, the ball consistently rolls out of the elbow connection toward the box and not in any other direction. Ask the children to count how many balls roll into the box and the how many balls miss the box.

4. After the children have had sufficient time experimenting with the elbow connection, give them the T connector. Let them discover for themselves the difference in the predictability of the outcome. With a T connector, the children never know which side the ball will emerge from or how frequently the ball will roll toward the box.

5. Have the children count how many balls roll into the box and how many balls miss the box.

Children's Books

In *Alberto the Dancing Alligator* by Richard Waring, Alberto accidentally gets flushed down the toilet while he and his friend, Tina, are dancing in the bathroom. The story follows his journey through the underground world of pipes until he finally makes it home to rejoin his dancing partner.

Keep It Simple

● Ask the children if they think the height or angle that the pipe is held will have an effect on which side the ball will emerge. Test their theory.

Add a Challenge

● Show the children how they can use tally marks or a graph to record how many balls go into the box and how many miss the box.

Theme Connections
Games

• Young children enjoy the challenge of honing their physical skills, especially if they can do it their own way. This activity is a simple game of skill. The children must aim and practice using the elbow to get the ball in the box. As their abilities improve, children typically challenge themselves by moving farther from the target.

• When the children are ready for the next challenge, give them boxes and beanbags and balls or pinecones to throw through hoops, and squirt bottles to squirt at the shapes on the blacktop. What other great games can you think of that relate to motion?

Dual Language Learners

Show the children the materials. Then be sure to verbalize and repeat the instructions and demonstrate the procedure to ensure that the children understand.

Observing and Assessing the Child's Science Learning

● Does the child understand that he can control the direction in which the ball will roll with the elbow connector and that it is much more difficult to influence the outcome with the T connector?

Connecting Science to the Curriculum

• **Mathematics**—In this activity, the children count how many balls roll into the box and how many miss the target.

Using Museums and Other Community Assets

● Invite a plumber to visit the classroom to give the children a demonstration on how pipes function in their homes and school. This plumber may be a resource for a pipe and connector donation.

What Rolls?

Exploring Motion

Children witness motion every day. In fact, children themselves are excellent examples of motion in action. This activity lets children observe and predict items they think will roll or not roll. As a final exercise, the children will get into the act.

Science Content Standard

The children will observe that motion occurs when force is applied to an object. (Physical Science—Position and Motion of Objects)

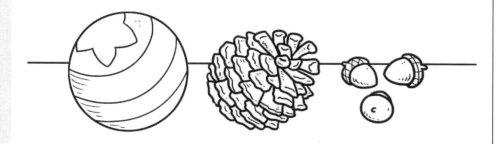

What to Do

1. Talk with the children about all the things they have made roll recently. For example, say, "Who can remember some rolling things? You're right, Phillip. We did lots of things with marbles. We've used beach balls and things with wheels. Now we're going to try some new things."

2. Dump a collection of materials on the floor and say to the children, "Let's see what rolls." Encourage the children to try pushing the objects, pulling them, or trying to find other ways to

exert enough force to make the objects roll. Comment on their efforts: "Hmm, no matter what you do, that frozen dinner tray doesn't seem to roll. I noticed you turned the bottle on its side and it rolled a long way. Can you make it roll if it's standing up? I wonder what you could do to the newspaper to make it roll?"

3. Challenge the children to explore around the room to see if they can find other objects they think might roll and gather them up. Keep in mind that the children may find some unusually shaped rollers. Remember that even cubes such as dice will roll when you toss them.

4. Ask the children if they themselves can roll. Show the children how to do body rolls, and suggest that they pretend they are wheels that roll across the room. Can the children find other ways to make themselves roll?

Close Observation

• **Show It**—Have the child show you which things rolled and which did not. Ask the child to put the things that roll in one place and to put the things that do not in another place.

• **Tell It**—Talk with the child about why some things roll and some do not. Does the issue of shape come up in the discussion?

• **Draw It**—Ask the child to select one "roller" and draw a picture of it. On another sheet, ask the child to draw one of the non-rollers. Does the child capture the idea of shape in the drawings?

• **Write It**—Ask the child to dictate words or labels for his drawing or write using his own words and spelling. The child can label the two drawings as *rollers* and *non-rollers*, write about the shapes of the rolling objects, or list the rollers he likes best.

Observing and Assessing the Child's Science Learning

● As a result of your observations and the child's performance, have you seen evidence that the child understands that shape has an effect on how things move?

Exploring Motion

Science Process Skills

Focused observing
Observing to classify

Science Vocabulary

bounce
down
find
test
up

Materials

variety of objects, some that bounce and some that do not bounce

Children's Books

Bounce by Doreen Cronin is a simple book with a bouncing bunny and other bouncy things.

Things That Bounce

From infancy, children enjoy watching things that bounce. This activity lets the children move beyond balls to explore and investigate many things in their world that bounce.

Science Content Standard

The children will learn that changing the amount or direction of an applied force results in a change in motion; the children will learn that in the everyday world, all objects eventually stop moving. (Physical Science—Position and Motion of Objects)

Before the Activity

Gather several bouncing and non-bouncing objects. Select a few bouncing objects that are not shaped like balls so the children can observe that not all objects that bounce are balls. These might include corks, pet squeaker toys, or irregular pieces of foam rubber. Make sure there are plenty of things in the room the children can collect for the bounce test.

What to Do

1. Talk with the children. Ask, "Who knows how to bounce? Can you make your whole body bounce? Look, David's shirt is bouncing with him. Ann Marie's braids are, too. Can you sit down and bounce? Can you bounce your hands on your knees? What else can you think of that bounces?"

2. Bring out your collection of objects and tell the children: "Let's investigate! Let's find out what bounces. That piece of foam bounces, but the feather just kind of lies there. So does the paper. What did you find out about the mustard bottle?"

3. Send the children on a search through the classroom for objects they think might bounce. Have the children bring the objects they collect to the group for testing. Make one pile of objects that bounce and another pile of objects that do not bounce.

Keep It Simple

- Line up the collections of bouncing and non-bouncing objects side by side to make a simple graph. Did the children find more of one kind of object than the other?

Add a Challenge

- Help the children make more detailed classifications. The children might make subgroups such as *really good bouncers, little bouncers,* and *no bouncers.* Help the children record their findings in their Discovery Journals using both pictures and words.

Theme Connections
Rhymes

Many children's rhymes, fingerplays, games, and books involve jumping and bouncing. Today's children need all the active play they can get. Spend some time exploring and acting out "Five Little Monkeys," "Jack Be Nimble," and more.

Dual Language Learners

Say the name of each object that the children handle as they determine which objects bounce and which do not.

Observing and Assessing the Child's Science Learning

- Can the child sort a variety of materials into groups of things that bounce and things that do not bounce?

- When given new objects, how well can the child predict whether the objects will bounce?

Connecting Science to the Curriculum

- **Mathematics**—This activity gives the children the opportunity to sort objects into two groups: those that bounce and those that do not bounce.

Exploring Motion

Sailboat Races

With a water table and some lung power, children can explore the world of pretend sailboats and wind-powered machines. Let the children find things that float and show how wind power can move objects across water. Children will explore whether some objects move better with the wind than others.

Science Content Standard

The children will observe that motion occurs when force is applied to an object and that changing the amount or direction of that applied force results in a change in motion. (Physical Science—Position and Motion of Objects)

What to Do

1. Place in the water table a few objects that float and show the children how they can blow on one of the objects to cause it to move across the water. Say, "Let's pretend these floating things are boats. We're going to be the wind that makes them sail across the water."

2. Cheer on the children as they try blowing the boats "across the pond." Can the children blow together on one boat to make it move faster? Ask one child to blow from one direction and another from the opposite direction. What happens? Can the children try different tools, such as fans and air pumps, to move the objects? Are some boats easier to move than others?

3. Say, "Tell me about all the different ways you've found to move the boats. Try some of your friends' ideas and see how they work."

Science Process Skill

Focused observing

Science Vocabulary

across
air pump
blow
fan
float
move
sail
sideways
wind

Materials

objects to create wind, such as fans and air pumps

pieces of plastic foam, wood, or other floating materials

water table or large, flat container filled with water

Children's Books

Boats on the River by Marjorie Flack features a lot of different boats, including sailboats.

Sail Away, Little Boat by Janet Buell (Jui Ishida, illustrator) follows a toy boat on a journey to the ocean.

Keep It Simple

● Make simple sailboats using plastic foam for a base, a craft stick for a mast, and paper or an index card for a sail. Ask the children, "Are these easier or harder to move than the floating objects?"

Add a Challenge

● Have the children group the materials in order based on how easy or difficult it is to move them.

Theme Connections
Water Table

Boats, Machines That Work on Water, and People and Waterways are all intriguing themes that can begin with this simple experience. What sources of water are near you? Ponds, lakes, rivers, an ocean? How do people interact with that water? Do they swim, fish, or boat? Finding out the answers to these and other questions can become a wonderful "close to home" project.

Dual Language Learners

It may be helpful for children to make their bodies move like the objects are moving when wind is applied: *fast, faster, slow,* and *slower.*

Observing and Assessing the Child's Science Learning

● Watch to see if the child can anticipate where his object will go. Does the child adjust the direction he is blowing to get an object to move a certain way?

Connecting Science to the Curriculum

• **Mathematics**—In this activity, the children group the objects according to how easy or difficult they are to move.

• **Taking It Outside**—Bring the water table outside and let the children find their own objects to float and blow through the water. Or have the children find objects outside and then bring them back inside to try them out on the water table.

Family Involvement

Children can use their wind power at home in the bathtub when they take a bath.

Can You Move Me?

It requires a certain amount of force to push a child sitting on a scooter board. It takes even more force to push two children—or one teacher—on the scooter board. Put in children's terms, it is a lot harder to push the teacher than a friend.

Science Process Skill

Focused observing

Science Vocabulary

move
pull
push
stop

Materials

scooter boards, a wagon, skateboard, or other wheeled vehicles

Children's Books

Roller Skates by Stephanie Calmenson is easy to read and has many pictures of people (dogwalkers, delivery men, shoppers, commuters) using roller skates to get where they need to go.

In *The Little House* by Virginia Lee Burton, the little house is jacked up and put on a trailer and moved to the country. Wheels can even move heavy things like a house!

Science Content Standard

The children will learn that changing the amount or direction of an applied force results in a change in motion and that in the everyday world, everything that moves eventually stops. (Physical Science—Position and Motion of Objects)

What to Do

1. Sit on the scooter board in the middle of the classroom. Ask the children, "Why am I not moving? Can you help me move? What can you do to make me move?" Let the children try to move you.

2. Now ask the children if they can help you stop moving. Move, and let them try to stop you. Talk with them about what happens when they try to stop you. Ask, "Can you feel the scooter pushing you?"

3. Have the children take turns pushing you on the scooter board. Ask, "How many children does it take to move me?"

4. Divide the children into pairs. Have the pairs of children take turns pushing and stopping each other on the scooter boards.

Exploring Motion

Keep It Simple

● Have the children bring in toys that will hold materials (for instance, a large toy truck). Have the children pull or push the truck when it is empty and then place bricks in the truck to make it heavier. Ask the children to explain the difference in pulling or pushing the loaded and unloaded vehicle.

Add a Challenge

● Bring in a furniture dolly that will allow a number of children to climb on and be pushed or pulled. Compare the force required to move the loaded dolly and the force or distance required to stop it.

Theme Connections
Movement

Toys with Wheels, Moving Machines, and Moving Day are themes that allow children to explore how wheels make our lives easier. Think of all the problem-solving that goes on when the children are in charge of figuring out how to pack and move the dramatic play area from one side of the room to the other. It requires some real teamwork!

Dual Language Learners

Demonstrate and verbalize the procedure to start and stop the movement of the scooter. Have the children listen to others talk about what actions they are taking to move and to stop the scooter.

Observing and Assessing the Child's Science Learning

● Observe pairs of children as they work together pushing and stopping each other. Ask each child to tell you what his role is.

● Can each child tell you whether he is pushing the scooter (making it move) or stopping the scooter?

● Can each child say which person was hardest to move or when it required more force?

Connecting Science to the Curriculum

● **Mathematics**—In this activity, the children count how many of them it takes to move the teacher on the scooter board.

● **Taking It Outside**—It is best to use wheeled scooters, scooter boards, and skates outdoors in wide open spaces. Have the children experiment with pushing and pulling each other on scooters and skates. Use inclined planes when you can find them.

Family Involvement

Ask families to join in by emailing photos of tools they see that are being used to move things in the community.

Incorporating Technology

Use a digital camera to take pictures of all the wheels the children can find in their school.

How Far Can You Jump?

A standing jump takes a lot of energy, and a child can jump only so far. When a child runs or adds the energy of running (force), he can jump much farther. Let's explore just how much farther!

Science Content Standards

The children will observe how changing the amount or direction of an applied force results in a change in motion. (Physical Science—Position and Motion of Objects)

The children will measure the lengths of their jumps using nonstandard measurements. (Measurement—Length)

What to Do

1. Place a short piece of masking tape on the floor. Talk to the children about jumping. Say, "Can you jump? Show me! How far can you jump? Let's find out. We can use this yarn to measure our jumping distance."

2. Have each child place both feet at the tape mark and jump from a standing start. Use one color of yarn to measure the child's standing jump distance. Cut the length of yarn and give it to the child (adult-only step). Repeat for each of the children.

3. Repeat the procedure, only this time let the children have a running start of 1½ –2 meters (4'–6'). (**Safety Note:** Some children may have difficulty landing without falling when they jump after getting a running start. Consider setting out cushions to protect the children should they fall.) Measure the children's jump distances using the second color of yarn. Then give the measurement yarns to the children.

4. Help the children compare the measurement strings from their standing jumps and their running jumps. Ask, "Which of your jumps was the farthest? What do you think helped you to jump farther? If you want to make the farthest jump, should you jump when standing still or should you run and then jump?"

Science Process Skills

Focused observing
Linear measuring

Science Vocabulary

compare
far, farther, farthest
force
graph
jump
measure
motion
move
run
start

Materials

masking tape
scissors (adult use only)
yarn in 2 different colors

Children's Books

Anna Banana: Jump Rope Rhymes by Joanna Cole doesn't have to be read with a jump rope in hand! Everybody can jump up and down to the poems included inside this book . . . and there are lots of them!

Exploring Motion

Keep It Simple

● Use a standard meter stick to measure the children's jumps.

Add a Challenge

● A person who is physically fit should be able to jump the length of his own height. Have one of the older preschoolers in the class do this as the other children watch. Such a jump may require physical coordination that younger children do not have at this point but will acquire later on. Measure the children's heights and then compare that measurement to the lengths of the children's jumps. **Note:** Athletes measure a jump from the back of the heel standing to the back of the heel after landing.

Theme Connections
I'm Special/All About Me

Have an "Everybody Wins" Olympics. Work with the children to think of all kinds of events to try. For example, make an obstacle course with reusable materials.

Dual Language Learners

If the teacher does not understand the child's home language, use gestures to explain what the child should do in this activity. Also, demonstrate and verbalize repeatedly as you make the gestures.

Children with Special Needs

For children who are unable to jump, consider trying a similar comparison by doing an overhand, underhand, or sidearm throw.

Observing and Assessing the Child's Science Learning

● Listen to the child's comments when comparing standing jumps to running jumps.

● When asked to jump as far as possible, does the child use running jumps or standing jumps and can she explain why?

Connecting Science to the Curriculum

● **Mathematics**—In this activity, the children learn how to measure their jumps using a nonstandard unit of measurement. Also, the children compare lengths of jumps that begin from a standing position with those that had a running start.

Using Museums and Other Community Assets

● Visit a local high school track meet or practice to watch the athletes who are jumping.

● Bring in a volunteer (high school, college student) who does broad jumping in track to show the children interesting ways to jump.

Incorporating Technology

Take pictures of each child's jump to record in a personal journal.

Rocket on a String

Children love watching objects move, particularly when those objects appear to move on their own. This activity will introduce children to the concept of propulsion and helps show that an object does not simply move on its own; rather, there is a force behind any movement.

Science Process Skills

Organizing and communicating observations

Science Vocabulary

air	inflate
blow	motion
distance	move
farther	shorter
force	

Materials

2 chairs

5-meter-long (or 5-yard-long) piece of string or fishing line

plastic drinking straws

several balloons of the same size and shape

tape

Children's Books

Emily's Balloon by Koko Sakai is an award-winning toddler book with beautiful illustrations. Some older preschoolers might be able to read this book by themselves.

Balloons, Balloons, Balloons by Dee Lilligard and Katya Krenina is a fun story about children whose town is inundated with balloons. The children can choose their favorite colors.

There are lots of surprises in *The Blue Balloon* by Mike Inkpen, a story about a little boy, his dog, and a balloon.

Science Content Standards

The children will observe that motion occurs when force is applied to an object and that changing the amount or direction of an applied force results in a change in motion. (Physical Science—Position and Motion of Objects)

The children will measure the distance an object travels. (Measurement—Nonstandard: Length)

Before the Activity

Cut approximately 5 centimeters (2") from the plastic drinking straw and thread it onto the length of string. Tie the ends of the string to the backs of two chairs. Pull the chairs apart to make the string taut.

Safety Note: Do not leave balloons unattended as they can be a choking hazard. Be aware of any latex sensitivity among the children.

What to Do

1. Blow up one of the balloons. Have the children hold their hands out and let them feel the air as you release it a little at a time. Talk about blowing air into the balloon using the force of your lungs and letting it come back out. The air coming out has a force that the children can feel. Blow up the balloon again and let it fly around the room. Talk with the children about what happened when the balloon was released.

2. Blow up the balloon again with just a little air. Tape the partly inflated, untied balloon to the straw on the string. Pull the straw to one end of the string. Discuss with the children what will happen if you release the balloon now.

3. After the children make their predictions about what the balloon will do, let it go and talk with the children about what they see happening. Keep a record of how far the balloon went by laying it on the floor under the string at the distance it traveled on the string.

Keep It Simple

- Attach different sizes and shapes of balloons to the straw. Observe how these differences affect the distances that the balloon travels.

Add a Challenge

- Sit with the children and go over the process that has just been completed. Throw out the challenge to the children that you want to raise one end of the string clear to the ceiling. See if the children want to join you in making the balloon rocket to and hit the ceiling. Have them think through what needs to be done and then complete that task.

Theme Connections
Bubbles

Provide the children with the materials necessary to blow bubbles. Blowing bubbles gives children another way to explore how air takes up space and can make things move.

Dual Language Learners

Children learning English can expand their vocabularies significantly when they listen to others talk about their common experiences.

4. Repeat the process two more times, blowing up a balloon about half full. Then repeat the activity with the balloon completely filled with air. Again, place each balloon on the floor to mark where it stopped.

5. Talk with the children about what they observed. Refer to the balloons on the floor. Ask, "Did this balloon go farther than this one? How do you know? Why do you think that this balloon went the farthest? Why did this balloon only go a little way?" Use the words *force* and *motion* to explain the movement of the balloon along the string. For instance, you can say that the more air the balloon has in it, the more force it can give, which makes it move farther along the string.

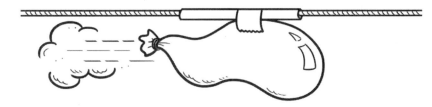

Observing and Assessing the Child's Science Learning

- Can the child identify which balloon traveled the farthest?
- Can the child make a connection between the amount of air in a balloon and the distance that it travels?
- Does the child use the words *force* and *motion* to describe what happened during the activity?

Connecting Science to the Curriculum

- **Mathematics**—In this activity, the children use a nonstandard unit of length to measure the distance the balloon travels.

The Rolling Beach Ball

Children use a beach ball to explore the way motion occurs through the application of force. Because a beach ball is so light, many different forces can cause it to move. Encourage the children to be resourceful and creative as they find new ways to make the ball go.

Science Content Standard

The children will observe that motion occurs when force is applied to an object; the children will observe that changing the amount or direction of an applied force results in a change in motion. (Physical Science—Position and Motion of Objects)

What to Do

1. Place the beach ball in the center of the room. Explain that gravity is holding the ball to the spot. Someone has to apply force to make it move.

2. Ask one child to come forward, select a way to provide force and attempt to move the ball, and then try out his idea. It is likely that the child will try kicking or throwing the ball. Share your observations: "Mario used force from his foot to move the ball. Gaia stopped it with her legs. What's another way we can move the ball?"

3. Have another child select a new way of moving the ball. Can the children guess which way the ball will move when the force is applied?

4. Repeat this activity, always encouraging the children to think of new ways to move the ball. Let the children try using air pumps, paper fans, and anything else you all can think of to use.

Science Process Skills

Focused observing

Science Vocabulary

direction
force
stop

Materials

beach ball

devices to make the ball move, such as an air pump, a plastic bat, a large piece of cardboard to wave, or various kinds of fans

Children's Books

Beach Ball by Peter Sis is about an imaginative little girl with a wind-blown beach ball. This book is suitable for older children, and the illustrations are wildly colorful.

The Beach Ball by David Steinberg is a board book for younger children. All of the creatures at the beach wait for the people to leave, and then they have a dance!

Keep It Simple

● Give the child a plastic bat to use to move the ball from one spot to another. Talk about how the child used force to move the ball from one place to another. Encourage the children to use force and motion terms as you talk together. For example, ask, "Did you use a lot of force to move the ball or just a little?"

Add a Challenge

● Have the children practice making marbles instead of a ball move in different directions. Can the children apply what they have learned about motion to make the marbles move great distances or in a particular direction?

Theme Connections
Beach

This activity is great to use during a Summer or Beach theme.

Gear for Games

What do people use to play active physical games? Think about all the different kinds of balls people use for games, as well as the things people use to make those balls move. People use their heads and feet, bats, rackets, clubs, and many other objects to make balls move. For safety purposes, people use helmets and other protective gear. Make a collection, including uniforms for dress up, and gear up for some active outdoor time.

Dual Language Learners

Say the name of each strategy or device the children use to move the ball. If the child points to the device, say the device's name again and encourage the child to repeat the name, using both his native language and English.

Observing and Assessing the Child's Science Learning

● Does the child select materials that will move the ball easily?

● Does the child correctly indicate the direction in which the ball will move?

Connecting Science to the Curriculum

• **Taking It Outside**—Bring the children and the beach ball outside on a windy day and encourage the children to play with the beach ball in the wind. Talk with the children about how the ball moves through the air. Explain how wind is a kind of force applied to the ball, much like their legs and hands.

Swing High, Swing Low

Exploring Motion

Science Process Skills

Organizing and
 communicating observations

Science Vocabulary

heavy
light
pull
push
swing

Materials

duct tape (optional)

plastic bucket with handle

twine or lightweight rope to
 suspend the bucket

variety of objects with
 different weights that will fit
 in the bucket, such as blocks,
 toys, pieces of sponge foam,
 and shoes

This activity uses a simple pendulum to provide the teacher with an
opportunity to assess children's understanding the following two of
the three major science concepts from the Exploring Motion chapter:

1. Motion occurs when a force is applied to an object.

2. Changing the amount or direction of an applied force results in
   a change in motion.

Both of these concepts come from classic Newtonian physics and
are absolutely essential for children's understanding of how their
world works.

Science Content Standard

The children will observe that motion occurs when force is applied
to an object and that changing the amount or direction of an applied
force results in a change in motion. (Physical Science—Position and
Motion of Objects)

What to Do

1. Tie the twine to the bucket and suspend it over the edge of a table
   so that it can swing back and forth freely. Secure the twine to the
   table either by tying it or with a few pieces of duct tape.

2. Spread out all of the different items on the table in front of the
   children.

3. Select a child push the bucket, letting it swing a few times, and
   then ask the child to catch the bucket. Give everyone a chance to
   swing and catch the bucket.

4. To test each of the children further, ask them to describe what
   they did to make the bucket swing. Ask, "Would the bucket swing
   if you didn't push it?" Have each child take one of the objects

from the top of the table and put it in the bucket. Then ask the children what they will have to do to make the bucket move. If the children know that they have to push it, say, "That's right, it needs to be pushed to move."

5. Have the children take turns pushing the bucket and catching it on the returning swing. Ask, "Was harder to push the bucket with something in it? Was it harder to stop?" Give everyone a chance to swing and catch the bucket. Ask the children what they think about the experience, and how it differed from the first time they swung the bucket. Wonder aloud: "Some things seem to make it harder to swing and catch the bucket. I wonder why that is?"

6. Pile several objects in the bucket. Ask the children if adding all these items will change how hard they have to push the bucket to get it to move. Let everyone try it and see what they think.

7. Next, take all of the objects out of the bucket. Show the children a light piece of plastic foam, and pass it around for each child to handle. Ask the children what they think will happen when the foam is in the bucket. Let the children push the bucket with the foam, then ask them to describe how pushing and stopping the bucket with the foam in it compared to pushing and stopping the bucket when it was full of the other objects.

8. Be sure that all the children in the group get a chance to try pushing the bucket with each of the different items in it. Listen carefully to the children's conversations about which objects are easier to push and which are more difficult. Have the children put the objects on the table and arrange them in order from easiest to push and stop to hardest. Talk with and observe the individual children as they work to be sure you assess each child's level of understanding.

9. Finally, ask the children what they need to do to get the bucket to swing sideways. If they have trouble answering the question, help them discover that they will need to start swinging the bucket from a different point.

Observing and Assessing the Child's Science Learning

- The child indicates that he has a clear understanding of force and momentum when he can consistently make connections between the weight of the objects in the bucket and how difficult it is to make the bucket start and stop swinging.

Chapter 4

Exploring Change

Exploring Change

Science Concepts

This chapter explores the following science concepts:

- Some changes are reversible; some changes are not.
- Some change is fast; some change is slow.
- Some change occurs naturally; some change is caused by humans.

Introduction

Scientists categorize change into two basic groups: physical change and chemical change. Physical changes are changes that modify the appearance of an object, whereas chemical change alters the chemical makeup of an object. Most of the changes that children will come in contact with during the science activities described in this chapter are physical changes.

Encourage children to investigate all aspects of change. Children should explore the events and objects in their immediate world that are undergoing change. How those objects change, what the new characteristics are like, and how long the process of change takes are just a few of the essential elements of change that children can easily observe.

Getting Ready

Place the following materials and any other things you think are interesting in the Discovery Center or in other appropriate places in your classroom so the children can explore them during Free Discovery:

- blocks of various kinds
- cardboard paper rolls
- clear plastic jars with lids
- eyedroppers
- flashlights
- interlocking cubes

- magnets

- seeds of various kinds

- toys that can be changed, such as dolls with different clothing, puppets that fold open to reveal a different character, pieces that can be assembled into different figures, magnetic drawing toys that can be erased, and so on.

Free Discovery

Begin Free Discovery by talking with small groups of children about how things they are familiar with go through changes. Have one or more examples with you to share with the children. Consider having a balloon that you can change by blowing it up, or consider showing the children a cup of water and then pouring food coloring into it.

Talk with the children about other changes they know about. The children used to be babies, but now they are not. Did anyone ever make water change by adding juice or a drink mix? Did anyone ever change her bathwater by adding bubbles?

Then discuss how things in nature bring about changes. How does the rain make the sidewalk change? Talk with the children about current seasonal changes. Are flowers growing or are leaves changing color?

Another kind of change the children are familiar with happens in the classroom. Point out how the classroom changes every day when you get things out, play, and then clean up. Then encourage the children to think of what they might be able to do to objects to change them. Ask, "How could you change a piece of paper? How could you change a peanut butter sandwich? How can you change what your body is doing?" As the children share their thoughts, write them on an Exploring Change Discovery Chart.

Allow the children ample opportunity to investigate the new materials in the classroom. While the children may need some guidance or suggestions when they first begin to explore these materials, it is important to let the children explore freely, not to overdirect their exploration.

Exploring Change

Science Process Skill

Focused observing

Science Vocabulary

after
before
change
color names
melt
mix
shape

Materials

crayons with paper removed
  (a good way to use old
  broken crayons)
electric skillet or toaster oven
muffin tins
paper

Children's Books

From Wax to Crayon by Michael H. Forman is a book that actually shows the process of making crayons.

The pictures are fascinating and colorful in *The Art Lesson* by Tomie dePaola. Tomie cherishes his box of 64 Crayola Crayons® because of the beautiful colors, such as gold, silver, and copper.

Crayon Muffins

Physical changes are the easiest for young children to observe. For example, when crayons are melted, they just change shape; their other qualities remain the same. It is possible to melt the crayons into new shapes that perform the same function—making colored marks on paper. In addition, it is just plain fun breaking up and melting crayons.

Science Content Standard

The children will observe how objects change when heat is applied. (Physical Science—Properties of Objects and Materials)

What to Do

1. Have the children break the crayons into small pieces and put the crayon bits into muffin tins. Consider challenging the children to sort the crayons pieces by color or let them mix the colors to make rainbow crayon muffins.

2. Talk with the children about how heat often changes things. For example, you might talk about how heat changes bread to toast. Say, "Usually, the more heat we use, the more something changes. Can you think of other things that heat changes?"

3. Tell the children that you are going to use heat to change the crayons. Set the muffin tins in an electric skillet containing about 2 centimeters of water or in an oven. Set the skillet on 350 degrees or medium heat.

   (Adult-only step) **Safety Note:** Do not leave crayons unattended in the oven or skillet. Make sure the children do not touch any hot surfaces.

4. When the crayons have melted, remove the tins and set them aside to cool. Talk with the children about how the smell of hot crayons indicates a change.

5. Pop the crayon muffins out of the tins. Show the children the new crayons. Ask, "How did we change our crayons? How are they still the same as the other crayons?"

Keep It Simple

● Do a simple experiment to compare crayons that are heated with crayons that are not heated. Melt some crayons of one color. This is the experimental group. Set some crayons of the same color aside to compare with the crayons that are changed with heat. This is the control group. How are the two groups the same? How are they different?

Add a Challenge

● Change crayons yet another way. Place more broken crayons in a heavy plastic or paper bag. Have the children hit them with a hammer to break up the crayons. Sprinkle the resulting crayon crumbs on waxed paper. Top the crayon sprinkles with another piece of waxed paper and press the paper with a slightly warm iron (adult-only step) to make the two pieces adhere to each other. This will make a translucent picture to hang in the window.

Theme Connections
Colors and Shapes

Use heavy-duty aluminum foil to make molds of crayons in a variety of shapes.

Construction

Include Crayon Muffins in a Construction theme. It is a good example of something that the children made themselves that works quite well.

Dual Language Learners

Support children's language development by repeatedly saying in English the names of the colors of the crayons as the children place the crayons into the muffin tins.

6. After the crayons have cooled, let the children enjoy making pictures with the new round crayons. Talk with the children about how these crayons are different from their usual crayons. Ask the children to show you how they can draw with these crayons and make different kinds of marks.

Observing and Assessing the Child's Science Learning

● Having watched the crayons being heated, can the child describe how the old crayons have changed?

● Can the child describe some of the differences while using the new crayons?

● Can the child describe how heat was involved in the change?

Connecting Science to the Curriculum

• **Language and Literacy**—Talk with the children about what the crayons used to look like and how they look now. This is a good opportunity to use the words *before* and *after*.

• **Mathematics**—In this activity, the children sort the crayons by color.

Lumpy, Bumpy Playclay

Science Process Skills

Focused observing

Organizing and
communicating observations

Science Vocabulary

change
half a cup
ingredients
measuring cup
mix
mixture
texture words

Materials

large sheet of newsprint and
markers (for a Discovery
Chart)
playclay
spoons
textured material, such as
sand, gravel, and so on

Children's Books

Chocolate Chip Cookies by Karen
Wagner is delicious book that
guides children through the step-
by-step process of making
cookies. A real treat!

Tony's Bread by Tomie dePaola is
the tale of a baker who makes
special breads that have all kinds
of tasty textures.

Children don't get many opportunities to make their own mixtures.
By allowing them to see what happens when they add a mix of
materials to make their own lumpy, bumpy playclay, the children
can make something fun by themselves.

Science Content Standards

The children will communicate observations about change in the
physical property of objects when other materials are added.
(Science as Inquiry)

The children will describe how some change occurs naturally while
other changes are caused by humans. (Physical Science—Properties
of Matter)

Before the Activity

Make the playclay, using the following recipe:

Ingredients

250 ml (1 cup) flour

125 ml (½ cup) salt

30 ml (2 T.) vegetable oil

water added in small amounts to a maximum of 125 ml (½ cup)

Directions

No cooking is required.

Mix the flour and salt and pour the oil into the mixture.

Add water a little at a time until the clay has a workable consistency.

Store the clay in a plastic bag or an airtight container.

What to Do

1. Give each child a half cup of playclay. Talk with the children about
   how clay feels. Let the children take a spoonful of one or more
   substances and mix it in with their playclay.

2. Ask, "What does your clay feel like now? Does it feel *bumpy*,
   crunchy, or *sandy*? Can you say some more words to describe
   how the clay feels? Close your eyes and talk about what you feel."

Keep It Simple

● Encourage the children to use the playclay to construct simple forms.

Add a Challenge

● Bring in some of the many commercial playdoughs and challenge the children to find ways to compare them to the playclay.

Theme Connections
Making Things

This is a good activity to include in a theme that focuses on construction and making things. What can the children make with their homemade playclay?

Senses

Incorporate playclay into an exploration of the five senses. Change how the playclay looks, smells, and feels by adding scent, color, and texture. Does the children's playclay make any sounds?

Children with Special Needs

Children with sensory integration issues may feel uncomfortable touching and mixing the clay. However, they can still be involved as helpers, using spoons to add the various materials to the mixture.

Adding materials to the clay and mixing using fingers and hands can help children with developmental delays improve their fine motor skills.

You may need to continue to supply words for the children's experimentation, because at this age children are just beginning to use descriptors.

3. Ask the children to trade playclay with a friend. Say, "Does your friend's clay feel the same? How does it feel the same? How does it feel different?"

4. Write down the words the children use on a Discovery Chart. It is okay if the children use many of the descriptive words you supplied. When the list is complete, read it back to the children. Can they think of any more texture words?

Observing and Assessing the Child's Science Learning

● Can the child describe what was done to change the clay?

● Can the child use descriptive words to describe the change?

Connecting Science to the Curriculum

● **Language and Literacy**—In this activity, the children use lots of descriptive language when describing the playclay. Provide additional words for the children to use and encourage them to come up with their own words.

● **Taking It Outside**—Have the children collect objects from nature to add to their clay to change its texture. Show the children how to make mud pies from the clay.

● **Language and Literacy**—On the Discovery Chart, list the words the children use as they make and discuss the playclay.

Using Museums and Other Community Assets

Visit the school cafeteria so the children can see the cooks mixing ingredients as they make the day's meals.

Science Process Skill

Focused observing
Measuring—nonstandard: time

Science Vocabulary

bigger
build
change
compare
construct
higher

Materials

digital camera and printer
several different block sets

Children's Books

The Construction Alphabet Book by Jerry Pallotta and Rob Bolster has complex illustrations and explanations for everything children and teachers want to know about building, starting with aerial lifts!

In Pat Hutchins' wordless picture book, *Changes, Changes,* little wooden people live in a block world. When their house catches on fire, they build a fire engine. When there's too much water, they build a boat, and so on. It's a book about blocks in action that children can read by themselves.

Change in Action

A block structure goes through changes in the same way a building does as it is built. Taking pictures allows the children to view the different stages of construction and make comparisons. While construction requires slow, observable change, knocking down structures is a whole different story.

Science Content Standards

The children will observe changes in objects placement over time. (Science as Inquiry; Measurement—Nonstandard: Time)

What to Do

1. Gather a small group of children and talk with them about building something big together. Tell the children you are going to take pictures of the structure as they build it. Begin by taking a picture of the empty construction site and the building materials: the blocks.

2. Once the children begin building, ask them to pause from time to time so you can take pictures of the various stages of construction. Talk with the children about each of the stages of construction and how the new stage compares to the previous stages. If time allows and if the builders are patient, have several periods of construction, picture taking, and discussion of the changes taking place.

3. Print the pictures of the construction from start to finish (black and white is fine). Have the children work together to put the photos in sequence from start to finish. Can they describe the changes from photo to photo? Use the children's comments to add captions to the photos to create a book documenting the children's progress.

4. The final big change is dismantling the structure. Challenge the children to think of different ways of taking down the structure.

Keep It Simple

● Instead of developing complex structures, have the children make tall structures using only one block shape. What is the maximum number of a type of block that can be stacked before the structure collapses? Try to capture the moment of collapse with a video camera. Do the structures all change (collapse) in the same way or do they fall in different ways?

Add a Challenge

● Take the children to various home-building construction sites to see progressive stages of construction as the homes are built. If no sites are readily available, consider taking or finding photographs of construction and showing them to the children. Many sites have numerous buildings in various stages of construction: the building of foundations, the pouring of basements, walls going up, and roofers and painters applying their skills. Show the images to the children and challenge them to order the photos to make a book showing the progress of the construction.

Theme Connections
Blocks and Construction

Add some "heavy equipment" vehicles to the construction site and incorporate this activity into a theme on Construction. Add sticks, bamboo and reed placemats, rocks, and other materials to add challenges to the construction process.

Children with Special Needs

Building and construction actions support the development of visual perceptual and motor skills for children who have developmental impairments in those areas.

Observing and Assessing the Child's Science Learning

● As you share the pictures of the construction site during and after the child's building efforts, does the child identify some of the ways it changes?

● Can the child describe how some of the changes occurred?

● Can the child show an awareness of time by sequencing the photos in order from beginning to end?

Connecting Science to the Curriculum

• **Language and Literacy**—In this activity, the children use descriptive words to talk about the changes they make to their block structure.

• Challenge the children to try making homes for the characters in books such as *Three Little Pigs* or *Animals in the Wild.* Can the children make a cave for a bear?

• **Mathematics**—The children compare pictures of the structure to observe changes made over a period of time.

• **Taking It Outside**—Challenge the children to build structures outside using donated scrap lumber from some of the construction sites they have visited. Logs and stones add interest to outdoor building.

Bubble Jars

The bubble jar is a way to introduce the children to the idea that some changes are reproducible. Collect several different bottles and jars with lids, and then make bubble jars for the children to use and reuse. After a few hours, the bubbles will settle enough to be ready for the children to change them again.

Science Content Standards

The children will observe changes in the property of objects that are mixed; the children will compare sizes of bubbles that are made in various jars. (Physical Science—Properties of Matter; Measurement—Nonstandard: Linear)

What to Do

1. Show the children how to make bubble jars. Place a teaspoon of dish soap in one of the jars, fill the jar half full with water, and put on the lid.

2. Say, "Look at the water and the soap in this jar. What do you see?" The children should be able to see both the soap and the water.

3. Ask, "How can I change this soap and water to bubbles?" After you shake the jar, ask the children to describe what they see.

4. Let the children use the variety of containers to make their own bubble jars. Encourage the children to talk about how the liquid changes when they shake the jars. Ask, "Where else have you seen bubbles?"

5. With the children, compare the sizes of the bubbles. Ask, "Are the bubbles in the jars all the same? Do the bubbles in the bigger jars look the same as the bubbles in the smaller jars?"

6. Set the jars aside for a while. Ask the children to observe the jars periodically and to comment on the changes they see. After the bubbles settle, ask, "Can you make the bubbles come back?"

Science Process Skills

Focused observing

Measuring—nonstandard: linear

Science Vocabulary

alike

bubbles

descriptive words for the bubbles

different

repeat

round

Materials

dish soap

plastic jars and bottles with lids, in a variety of sizes and shapes

teaspoons

water

Children's Books

POP! A Book About Bubbles by Kimberly Brubaker Bradley and Margaret Miller shows that everybody loves bubbles. It also provides a scientific explanation for the properties of bubbles.

Keep It Simple

● Make bubble paintings by adding paint to the bubble solution, dipping bubble wands into the solution, blowing bubbles, and catching the bubbles on paper.

Add a Challenge

● Place soluble powders, such as sugar, salt, and baking soda, in the experimentation area so that the children can add these materials to the bubble solution. Note how adding these powders changes the bubbles that are formed.

Theme Connections
Seasons/Summer Fun

• Take water tables or tubs outside and fill them with soapy water for bubbly outdoor play.

• If you blow bubbles outside when it is below freezing, the bubbles will immediately float upward because of the warm air inside. They will also freeze and shatter when you touch them.

Dual Language Learners

To help children understand the procedure and concept, verbalize each step and demonstrate repeatedly.

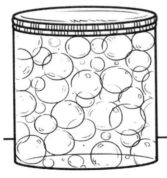

Observing and Assessing the Child's Science Learning

● Can the child describe how the liquid changes when she shakes a jar?

● Can the child describe the difference in the bubbles in terms of size?

Connecting Science to the Curriculum

• **Language and Literacy**—In this activity, the children describe how the liquid changes when they shake the jars.

• **Mathematics**—The children can compare the sizes of bubbles and can compare the number of shakes necessary to fill each jar with bubbles.

• **Taking It Outside**—Make a bubble solution and let the children blow bubbles outside. The children can make their own bubble tools (pipe cleaners, straws, and paper cups with the bottoms removed, for example) and discover which ones make big bubbles and which ones make small bubbles. Can anyone figure out a way to make a bubble that is not round?

Family Involvement

● Ask children's families to collect and send a variety of clear plastic jars with lids to use with this activity.

● Encourage families to work with their children to make an array of bubble-blowing tools that the children can use at home. Berry baskets, pipe cleaners, straws, and paper cups with their bottoms removed all work well. Discuss which tools make big bubbles and which make small ones.

Exploring Change

Dunk a Pair

Water is an excellent medium for creating change. This activity asks the children to place one of a pair of identical objects in water to discover how the water changes the objects. The change made by contact with water may be quite obvious, as with crepe paper; minimal, as with a penny; or take a long time, as with cardboard.

Science Content Standards

The children observe changes in the physical property of objects; the children observe that some changes are reversible and some changes are permanent. (Science as Inquiry; Physical Science—Properties of Objects and Materials)

What to Do

1. Show the children two objects that are alike. These objects should be something that will change when placed in water, such as tissue or crepe paper. Ask the children to describe how the objects are alike.

2. Show the children how to place one object of the pair in a cup of water to test what water will do it. The dry object is for the children to make easy comparisons.

3. Hold up the wet object. Discuss the change. Ask, "Was the change a big one or not much of a change?" Lay the pair on the table.

4. Now select a pair that will show little change, such as pennies. Put the object in water, and observe the change (if any) with the children.

5. Compare the two changes. Then start two piles on the table: one for objects on which water has a significant effect and one for those objects on which water has little or no effect.

6. Have the children experiment with their own pairs of matching objects by placing one of them in water and leaving the other of the pair out of the water.

Science Process Skill

Observing to classify

Science Vocabulary

alike
compare
different
group
same
wet

Materials

clear plastic cups

pairs of objects, such as sponges, rocks, shells, paper of various kinds, sugar cubes, cotton balls, coins, magnets, chalk, dirt, sand, and cloth

water

Children's Books

"The Bath" is a funny story in Arnold Lobel's book *Mouse Tales.* It tells the story of a mouse who keeps bathing and bathing. The bath water runs out of his window and into the street. His neighbors beg him to turn off the water. Everyone is relieved when the mouse is finally clean!

Water by Frank Asch is a beautifully illustrated book about our precious natural resource.

Keep It Simple

● Dry out the pairs and determine whether the changes the water made on the objects is permanent or reversible.

Add a Challenge

● Have the children bring in their own sets of objects and challenge the children to predict how water will affect each set of objects.

Theme Connections

All About Me

During this activity, ask the children to observe what happens to their fingers and toes when they are in water a long time.

Sand and Water

Talk with the children about how water affects sand and dirt.

Dual Language Learners

Model and encourage all the children to use descriptive words as well as gestures and nonverbal language.

Children with Special Needs

Children who have visual impairments may not be able to see the changes in the objects. Emphasize the use of touch to help these children assess the changes in the objects caused by the water.

For children with sensory integration issues, do the activity in a quiet place, where the children can interact with an adult or experience the activity on their own.

7. After the exploration, have the children share their observations with the group and place their pairs of objects in the "easy to change by water" group or the "not easy to change by water" group.

8. Ask, "Are more object pairs in one group or the other?" With the children, count how many pairs are in each group.

Observing and Assessing the Child's Science Learning

● Can the child describe the changes taking place when placing the objects in water?

● Can the child classify the pairs by placing them in the correct groups?

Connection Science to the Curriculum

● **Mathematics**—In this activity, the children receive matching pairs of objects. The children form two groups of objects based on their tests, and then count the number of objects in each set.

Incorporating Technology

Have the children use a timer to determine how long it takes for some of the objects to be changed by being placed in the water.

Rainbow Water

Exploring Change

Science Process Skill

Focused observing

Science Vocabulary

change
color names
fast
mix
slow

Materials

food coloring (red, blue, and yellow)

medicine droppers, eyedroppers, pipettes, or spoons for mixing the colors

several containers to hold colored water (such as margarine or whipped topping tubs)

small plastic cups or white foam egg cartons for color mixing

sponges or paper towels

water

This activity provides a quick way for you to assess the children's understanding of change as they mix colored water and then observe the changes that occur. This can be a messy activity, so have sponges or paper towels on hand.

Science Content Standard

The children will observe quick changes in the properties of materials and see how people can cause change. (Physical Science—Properties of Objects and Materials)

Before the Activity

Fill the containers with water. Add one of the colors of food coloring to each cup of water. Ask families to save reusable medicine droppers and send them in for the activity.

What to Do

1. Do this activity in an area where spilled water will not be a problem. Place the containers of the primary colors—red, blue, and yellow—near the children. Give the children several empty plastic containers or egg cartons for mixing the food coloring into the water, along with droppers or spoons with which to transfer and stir the color mixtures. Have plenty of absorbent paper towels or sponges available for cleanup.

2. Let the children mix the colored waters to create new colors. Start by mixing only two colors to prevent all the mixes from turning a muddy brown. Eventually, let the children mix as many colors together as they like. Ask, "How many colors of water can you count in your cups? How many colors of water did you start with?"

3. Talk with the children about the speed with which the color changes take place. Ask, "Do the colors change quickly or slowly?"

4. Talk with the children about their previous experiences mixing colors. Discuss the differences between mixing fingerpaints and colored water, and the speed with which the different changes take place.

Close Observation

• **Show It**—Take an empty plastic container and add some of the yellow colored water to it. Ask the child how she might change this yellow water to green. Though the child might even know that if she adds blue to the yellow it will make green, what is most important is that the child knows that a change will take place when she mixes one color with another color.

• **Tell It**—Listen to the child as she talks about color mixing. Do her comments show that she realizes she can make a new color by mixing two colors together?

• **Draw It**—Talk with the child about the color mixing and help her think through what she did. Pour three containers of water like those you began with. Say, "Can you draw what you see?" The child may just make three color splotches, or she may draw fairly accurate representations of what she sees. Ask the child to look at the colors she made and try to draw what she sees. This activity gives the child many ways to illustrate her understanding of how mixing colors quickly creates other colors.

• **Write It**—Encourage the child to write about her drawings. Also consider offering to record the child's ideas and observations for her.

Observing and Assessing the Child's Science Learning

● Does the child understand she can mix colors to create new colors?

● Can the child name the colors made by mixing the primary colors?

Exploring Change

Science Process Skill

Observing to classify

Measuring—nonstandard: time

Science Vocabulary

iron

metal

names of rusting and non-rusting objects

rust

Materials

dishpan or other container

objects that will rust, such as nails, washers, and springs

objects that will not rust, such as plastic buttons and plastic paper clips

salt

white paper towels

Children's Books

Micah wonders why his grandpappy keeps his old tractor in Jay Cowley's *The Rusty, Trusty Tractor*, but soon Micah learns that under the rust and age is a reliable old friend.

Rusting happens to objects throughout the world, usually to objects created by humans. When an object rusts, it is being acted upon by oxygen. Wetting an iron surface and adding salt speeds up the rust process. Through this activity, children will find that some objects—those not made of iron—do not rust. Children will sort objects into groups—those that rust and those that do not.

Science Content Standards

The children will classify changes in the physical property of objects. (Science as Inquiry; Physical Science—Properties of Objects and Materials)

What to Do

1. Place several layers of paper towels in the dishpan. Have the children scatter the various objects on the paper towels.

2. Add enough water to saturate the paper towels. Sprinkle the objects with salt to accelerate the rusting process. Keep the towels wet over the next several days.

3. When the rust appears, ask the children to describe what they see happening. What color do they notice appearing? Is rust always the same color? Have the children note the rust stains surrounding some of the objects. Do they see any changes in the other objects?

4. Have the children divide the objects according to those that rusted and those that did not.

5. Make a simple chart with either the names of the objects that rusted or drawings of them on one side and objects that did not rust on the other side.

Keep It Simple

● Take the children on a rust walk. How many rusty objects can the children find? Make a list of all the rusted objects the children find.

Add a Challenge

● Test everything with a magnet. The things that rust will also be attracted to a magnet. That is because objects that rust usually are made of iron, which is also attracted to magnets.

Dual Language Learners

Name each of the objects that the children handle. Repeatedly describe the changes that the children observe in the rusting objects, and describe the differences between those objects that rust and those that do not.

Observing and Assessing the Child's Science Learning:

● Does the child understand that some things rust (iron) and others do not?

● Can the child divide the objects into two groups based on the objects' tendency to rust?

● Does the child recognize that rusting is a process that takes time?

Connecting Science to the Curriculum

● **Mathematics**—In this activity, the children count the objects that rusted. The children also sort and classify the objects into two categories.

● **Taking It Outside**—Find a piece of rusted iron on the schoolyard and invite the children to clean the rusted object with a wire brush or sandpaper. Remind the children to look at the object from time to time to see whether the rust returns and how long it takes for this to happen.

Family Involvement

Ask the families to take their children on a rust hunt at home. They can compile a list of the rusted items that they find or take digital photographs and send them to school to share with the rest of the class. How many rusted things can the children and their families find?

Exploring Change

Mixing Things with Water

Most young children enjoy mixing materials, such as salt, sugar, and sand, in water. That is because the procedure yields consistent results: salt and sugar always dissolve, while sand never does. The children can repeat the activity again and again, and the results of the experiment will always be the same. **Hint:** Before you start, make sure the children have containers with lots of water and little spoons to transfer the materials.

Science Content Standards

The children will observe the changes that occur when substances dissolve in water; the children will observe that some forms of matter do not dissolve in water. (Science as Inquiry; Physical Science—Properties of Matter)

What to Do

1. Working with a small group of children, give each child two cups of water and a spoon. Tell the children to put a spoonful of salt in one cup and a spoonful of sand in the other cup. Ask, "What do you see?"

2. Now have the children stir the water in each cup. Ask, "What changes do you see?"

3. Talk with the children about the change that occurred. The salt dissolves in the water and the sand does not.

4. Have the children repeat the dissolving activity by adding sugar to another cup. Ask the children to compare what happens with the sugar in water to what happens with the salt and the sand in water.

5. Provide cups of warm and cold water, and have the children mix the same three substances in each of the cups. Ask the children to describe the ways the temperature of the water alters the way the materials mix with the water. Specifically, discuss whether the materials dissolve more quickly or slowly in the warm and cold water.

Science Process Skill

Focused observing

Science Vocabulary

dissolve

mix

mixture

salt

Materials

clear plastic cups or small plastic jars

labeled container of salt

labeled container of sugar

labeled container of white sand

spoons

water

Children's Books

In Stuart J. Murphy and Julia Gorton's *Super Sand Castle Saturday*, the children are at the beach. They rush to build sand castles for a sand castle contest and they have to finish their castles before the tide comes in.

Keep It Simple

● Place the materials out one at a time and repeat the procedure for each material several times. Make a chart of those that dissolve and those that do not.

Add a Challenge

● Give each child a spoon and a piece of black paper. Show the children how to scoop out a small amount of each of the solutions and spread it on a separate portion of the paper. Talk with the children about what they see after the water evaporates. Discuss how the spots of white powder left by the sugar and salt look different from the little bits of sand. Then have the children put a few drops of plain water on each spot. Ask the children to describe what happens. Once again, the salt and sugar dissolve, but the sand does not.

Theme Connections
Sand and Water

This activity is great for any theme that involves water. For more explorations with dissolving, help the children make their own summer drink with either powdered drink mix or with lemons and sugar.

Observing and Assessing the Child's Science Learning

● Can the child describe what happened to the salt, sugar, and sand in both warm and cold water?

Connecting Science to the Curriculum

• **Language and Literacy**—In this activity, the children describe what they see happening. This activity also introduces children to the scientific term *dissolve*.

• **Taking It Outside**—Go outside and encourage the children to collect some sand or dirt. Provide plastic jars full of water for each child to use to try to dissolve the sand or dirt they brought in from outside. Do these materials behave differently from those that the children mixed with the water before?

Science Process Skill

Focused observing

Science Vocabulary

cold
cool
freeze
freezer
ice
melt
temperature
warm

Materials

2–3 cups of water
food coloring
freezer
glitter or sequins
ice cube trays
pitcher
potted plants

Children's Books

Angelina Ice Skates by Katharine Holabird and Helen Craig is the story of a little mouse who wants to dance on ice. Children will discover why ice dancing is tricky.

From Cow to Ice Cream by Bertram T. Knight tells another liquid-to-solid story with interesting photographs and a delicious array of ice-cream treats.

Sparkle Ice

The children have probably been introduced to water freezing and forming ice. This activity is a simple review of the process, but this time the children should focus on the change taking place. The water changes into ice because of the cold temperature. When the temperature warms up, the ice can change back to water. A little glitter provides evidence of the change.

Science Content Standard

The children will observe how objects change when placed in a freezing environment; the children will observe how some changes are reversible. (Physical Science—Properties of Objects and Materials)

What to Do

1. Talk with the children about what they know about ice. Encourage them to share things they know in addition to their classroom experiences. Perhaps someone knows about icicles. Someone else might ice skate. Another child might talk about snow cones.

2. Fill a pitcher with water. Have the children feel the water and talk about its temperature. Tell the children that you are going to use the water to make ice. Talk about what you need to do to make ice. Most children at this age will know you can put water in the freezer to make ice.

3. Tell the children that you are going to do something special with this ice so that when it melts, it will be easy to find where the ice once was. Set out several ice-cube trays. Provide some food coloring, glitter, and sequins and invite the children to put these materials into the water they put in the trays.

4. Place the trays in the freezer. Say, "Tomorrow we will look at the trays to see if the ice is ready." Let the children observe the freezer to see how cold it is.

5. The next day, remove the trays from the freezer and show them to the children. Encourage the children to talk about how the water looks now. Point out that the water changed because it was very cold in the freezer. Ask the children how the water is different from the water they touched yesterday.

Keep It Simple

● Place pieces of fruit in the freezer and encourage the children to observe how the pieces of fruit change when they freeze. Compare the frozen fruit to frozen water.

Add a Challenge

● Place water in one compartment of an ice tray, powdered drink mixture in another, orange juice in another, milk in another, and so on. Compare the results when you freeze these different liquids.

Theme Connections
Seasons/Weather

Take Sparkle Ice outside in both the summer and winter and let the children see how different kinds of weather affect the ice.

Snack and Cooking

Make frozen treats as part of a summer or cooking theme. Bring in an ice-cream freezer and help the children make ice cream. Make frozen juice, yogurt, or pudding pops for the children to try. Frozen bananas and grapes are delicious, too.

Dual Language Learners

Make this a collaborative project by pairing children who are learning English with fluent English-speaking buddies. Encourage each of the children to help one another describe what they see.

6. Tell the children they are going to let the ice change back into water. "We are going to find lots of places to watch it happen. When the ice cubes disappear, the glitter, sequins, and some remaining water will tell us where the ice cubes used to be."

7. With the children, walk around both inside and outside and find places to put the ice so it can melt. Remind the children that ice turns into water, so they need to find places where the ice can melt without hurting anything. Suggest putting one cube in a cup where everyone can see it, and putting others in potted plants around the room. Another possibility is to put one on the counter by the sink and another in an empty paint cup. Go outside and find more places to put the ice. Ask, "Could one go at the end of the bench? How about in a few spots on the sidewalk?"

8. Ask the children to observe the ice periodically. The glitter or colored water will mark the spots where the ice changed back to water.

Observing and Assessing the Child's Science Learning

● Can the child describe the different states of water she observed?

● Can the child explain that ice forms when water freezes and that when ice melts it changes back to water?

Sprouts Galore!

Seeds produce sprouts. They change from seemingly inanimate objects into living, growing things. Sprouts from the same type of seed look the same, but sprouts look similar even if they are from different seeds. The change from seed to sprout is slow for many plants, but some will sprout overnight.

Science Content Standards

The children will observe changes in growing seeds; the children will observe that some changes occur quickly and other changes occur slowly. (Science as Inquiry; Life Sciences—Characteristics of Organisms)

What to Do

1. Have the children line the bottom of a container with paper towels three or four deep. Show the children how to use a small watering can to pour enough water into the container to saturate the towels, but not enough to leave standing water.

2. Let the children sprinkle a variety of seeds on the paper towels. Talk with the children about what the different seeds look like.

3. Over the next several days, keep the towels moist. Ask the children to look at the seeds periodically and to describe any changes they observe.

4. Talk with the children about the changes they see as the seeds begin to sprout. Ask the children to describe the differences they see among the various sprouts. Some sprouts, such as the lima bean and radish sprouts, will initially produce two leaves, while corn and grass seeds will produce one. Ask, "How does watering the seeds change them?"

5. When the sprouts have grown sufficiently, bring the children to a spot outside and help them transfer the sprouts into the soil or into pots filled with soil. Explain to the children that the sprouts need nutrients from the soil in order to continue growing.

Science Process Skill

Focused observing

Science Vocabulary

plant
seed
seed names
sprout

Materials

assorted seeds, such as radish, grass, zinnia, lima bean, corn, and peas

dishpan, aquarium, or water table

paper towels

small watering can

water

Children's Books

A Seed Is Sleepy by Dianna Hutts Aston and Sylvia Long is beautifully illustrated and makes seeds and the study of seeds a fascinating topic.

Jack's Garden by Henry Cole is a variation on an old favorite. Children and teachers will love the sing-song quality of the text.

Keep It Simple

● Give the children some more seeds and have them sort the seeds by similarities and differences.

Add a Challenge

● Have the children draw images of the various seeds in their Discovery Journals, and then draw images of the sprouts at various stages of development.

Theme Connections
Seasons

This activity connects well with themes on the seasons, farms, and the environment. Lettuce seeds are quick to sprout. Plant some in a large dishpan or plant tray. In a few weeks, you will have enough lettuce for everyone to have a taste of salad.

Dual Language Learners

Demonstrate and repeatedly verbalize the steps in the activity to ensure that children understand the process and concept.

Observing and Assessing the Child's Science Learning

● Can the child use words or pictures to describe how the seeds and sprouts looked at various points in the sprouting and growing process?

Connecting Science to the Curriculum

● **Taking It Outside**—Collect some dandelion seeds or other seeds you find and plant them in a resealable bag for the children to observe the sprouting and growing process.

Using Museums and Other Community Assets

Arrange for a visit to a greenhouse or neighborhood garden so the children can watch or help the gardener plant seeds. Occasionally return to these places so the children can observe the plants' growth over time.

Science Process Skill

Focused observing
Measurement—linear

Science Vocabulary

grass
grow
lawn
measure
plant
potting soil
sprout

Materials

child-safe scissors
grass seed
interlocking cubes or other
   items for measuring
   (optional)
potting soil
small paper cups and small
   spoons (1 for each child)

Children's Books

In the Tall, Tall Grass by Denise
Fleming is a backyard tour of
what is really happening in the
grass that we typically only walk
on. This book inspires a closer
observation of grass.

Don't forget *And The Green
Grass Grew All Around: Folk
Poetry From Everyone* by Alvin
Schwartz and Sue Truesdell. This
book contains lots of fun rhymes
and songs about grass that keeps
on growing.

Keeps on Growing

The first change children observe in this activity is how the seeds
sprout and grow into grass. The second change children observe is
one they make themselves: They cut the grass. What happens next?

Science Content Standards

The children will observe changes in the growing grass seed.
(Science as Inquiry; Life Sciences—Characteristics of Organisms)

What to Do

1. Ask, "Do you know what grass looks like? Where have you seen
   it?" The children may respond by saying "in the yard" or "in the
   park" or "on the ground." Ask the children to describe how they
   have seen people take care of grass at their house or at a park.
   Then show the children the grass seed. Explain that the seed will
   grow into grass. Say, "For the grass seeds to grow, we must plant
   them and water them."

2. Let the children prepare containers to plant their grass seed. Give
   a paper cup to each child. Have them fill their cups almost to the
   top with the potting soil. They can do this with their hands or
   with small spoons.

3. Give each child a small amount of grass seed. Show them how to
   plant the seed by sprinkling it on top of the soil and stirring it into
   the surface a bit. (**Note**: Seeds don't need to be completely buried.)

4. After they plant the seeds, ask the children what they think the
   seeds will need to grow. Some children may know that the seeds
   will need water. The importance of creating a proper environment
   for growth can be discussed further, but do this only after the
   children have contributed their thoughts. Be sure the children
   understand that water is an ingredient the seeds need in order to
   sprout. Once the seeds sprout, they will also need sunlight.

5. Observe the containers over the next two weeks and watch the
   grass begin to grow.

6. After the grass has grown to a height of 1"–2" (3–5 centimeters),
   ask the children, "What change would happen if we cut a bit off
   the top of the grass? Do you think it will grow tall again or change
   in some other way? Do you think it will stay the same size?" Let

Keep It Simple

● Allow the grass to grow without cutting. Talk with the children about the changes they observe in the grass.

Add a Challenge

● Have the children make "Grass Growing Journals" with observational drawings every few days, including drawings of when they plant the seeds, cut the grass, and days after they cut the grass.

Dual Language Learners

Focus on the conceptual understanding of this activity. Clearly state the name of each of the materials with which the children will interact.

the children make guesses about what they think will happen. If they have observed grass being cut before, they may be able to actually predict that the grass will grow tall again.

7. You may want the children to measure the height of the grass with interlocking cubes or another unit of measurement. Then the children can measure the height again after it is cut.

8. Let the children cut their grass using child-safe scissors.

9. Continue to water the grass and give it sunlight. Observe it over the next several days. Ask, "What is happening? What happens to the grass that grows outside? Have you ever seen grass being cut?"

Observing and Assessing the Child's Science Learning

● Can the child describe how the seeds changed?

● Can the child use measurement terms to describe how the grass changed when she cut it?

Connecting Science to the Curriculum

● **Language and Literacy**—The children use expressive language to describe grass, where they have seen grass, and ways to care for grass.

● **Mathematics**—In this activity, the children measure the height of the grass before and after cutting it.

● **Science and Nature**—Make Egg Heads. Place half an eggshell in a lump of playdough or clay so it will stand upright. Have the children draw or glue paper cutouts or other materials on the eggshell to make a face. Fill the eggshell with soil; plant grass seed and wait for the "hair" to grow.

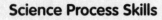

Exploring Change

Science Process Skills

Focused observing
Classifying

Science Vocabulary

change
environment
litter
recycle
responsibility

Materials

3 containers large enough to hold the three groups of sorted trash

3 pieces of cleaned trash items per child (a combination of plastic, metal, and paper items that children can handle safely)

large piece of paper and some colored markers

large trash bag, partially split down the side so it is easy to "accidentally" spill

Children's Books

The Man Who Didn't Wash His Dishes by Phyllis Krasilovsky is a funny book about a little man who is too tired at the end of the day to clean up his dishes. The dirty dishes pile up until they are all over the house. There are no dishes left except dirty ones! What a mess. How does the man solve his dirty dish problem?

Wow, What a Mess!

Imagine children's dismay when they see their play area littered with trash. Although the cause is a staged "litter spill," it should encourage the children to have a sense of ownership over the space, thus generating a desire to take responsibility for and clean up their space. This activity also provides a way to categorize their observations of the litter they find.

Science Content Standards

The children will observe the natural environment of an area outdoors for signs of change; the children will make observations about natural and human-made objects and change that has occurred in their play area. (Science as Inquiry; Life Sciences—Organisms and the Environment)

Before the Activity

Clear this activity with your administrator as well as the people responsible for outdoor maintenance.

What to Do

1. Take the children outside the day before this event and talk with them about the importance of the little piece of Earth surrounding their school. Is there a nice piece of asphalt that is kept clean for playing ball games or riding wheeled toys? Maybe you have pretty flowers or shrubs. Every place for children has some special features. Help the children discover the features of this outdoor space that makes it special to them. Take crayons, markers, and paper outside and have the children draw something they like about this special place. If you have a digital camera, let the children decide what to photograph to document their special place.

2. The next day, set the stage. Choose the approach that works for you.

   • Choice 1—When taking the children out to play, take the bag of trash with you. (You may want to provide a reason that fits your setting.) "Accidentally" stumble and scatter the trash across as much of the play area as you can.

Keep It Simple

● If there is a nearby recycle center or a store that sells items for reuse, consider taking the children to see how their trash can be reused or recycled.

Add a Challenge

● Encourage the children to think of some ways they could use some of the materials. For example: Could yogurt containers become paint cups or sand scoopers?

Theme Connections
Our Neighborhood/Caring for Our Environment

Use this activity as part of a theme on your neighborhood and community, or about caring for the environment.

Dual Language Learners

Encourage children whose home language is not English to discuss the work they are doing with the other children in the class.

• Choice 2—Before taking the children outside, spread the trash throughout the play area and create the illusion that the trash or recycle containers accidentally spilled into the area.

Give the children a chance to comment about the mess. If they do not immediately react, prompt them to describe what they see. Do they see how messy their play area is? Remind them of how it looked the day before. Show them some of their drawings or photographs from earlier.

3. Ask, "Do we want to leave our play area like this or is everyone willing to help clean it up?" Have the three containers ready for them to sort the different trash items into the correct boxes.

4. Before the children clean up the trash, have them lay out the items in three different lines to demonstrate graphically the percentage of different trash types. Count and record the number of trash items in each box. Talk about which type of trash is most common, which is least common, and which type of trash takes up the most space.

5. Ask the children to pick up all the materials. When the children finish picking up all the trash, talk with them about how it feels to have made a positive change. Help the children focus on their sense of pride and how they feel good about the work they did to take care of their play area.

Observing and Assessing the Child's Science Learning

● Does the child realize that she can do things to change the way a place looks?

● Can the child sort the items into the three categories (paper, plastic, metal)?

● Listen to the child's reaction when she sees and cleans up the trash: Is the child developing a sense of environmental responsibility?

Family Involvement

Encourage families to discuss what they can do at home and around the community to stop littering.

What Happened to This Place?

Exploring Change

Science Process Skills

Focused observing

Classifying, organizing, and communicating observations

Science Vocabulary

change

flowers

grass

grow

weeds

Materials

clipboards (or pieces of cardboard with a paper clamp to keep paper from blowing away)

drawing paper and drawing materials

scrap yarn (preferably green)

water-based, powdered paint (a bright color) or flour

This activity will help your children develop their observation skills and give you insight into their understanding of the three science concepts addressed in this chapter: Some changes are reversible, some are not; some change is fast, some change is slow; some change occurs naturally, some change is caused by humans.

Science Content Standards

The children will observe how objects change; the children will observe and describe changes that are fast and those that are slow; the children will distinguish between changes that are human-made and changes that happen naturally; the children will observe how some changes are reversible and some are not. (Science as Inquiry; Life Sciences—Characteristics of Organisms)

Before the Activity

Talk with the maintenance staff and find out the mowing schedule so the children can see the outdoor space before and after the staff cuts the grass.

What to Do

1. Take your children out to observe the lawn **two days before** it is to be mowed. Have them walk through the grass and talk about how high it is on their feet. Take out pieces of yarn and demonstrate how the children can use the yarn to measure the height of the grass. Cut a piece of yarn to the height of the grass and tape it to a piece of paper to save.

2. Encourage the children to draw what they see. Do they see plants that are not grass? Find a weed or maybe even a flower such as a dandelion. Study what it looks like and mark its location with small circle of tempera paint or flour. Again, cut a piece of yarn to measure how tall it is and tape it to the piece of paper.

3. **One day before** the lawn is to be mowed, take the children back outside to observe again. Check to see that the weed they marked is still there. Help them see that little has changed from the day before.

4. Mowing Day! Right after the lawn is mowed, take the children out to observe the changes. (**Note:** If possible, ask the maintenance staff to cut some of the grass and leave another portion uncut so the children can have a clearer sense of the differences between the two.) Talk about how different their observations of the setting are now. Use yarn to measure the grass. Tape the yarn beside the pieces you cut previously. This creates a simple graph that allows the children to see how much shorter the plants are now.

5. Use a large piece of paper and make a list of all the changes the children observe. Then record all the things that are the same.

Observing and Assessing the Child's Science Learning

- Can the child identify some of the ways the lawn changed because of mowing?

- Can the child identify what caused the change?

- Can the child identify mowing as a sudden change and the grass growing as a gradual change?

Chapter 5

Exploring Tools

Exploring Tools

Science Concepts

This chapter explores the following science concepts:

- Tools and materials are made for specific purposes.

- We can manufacture tools and materials to accomplish certain tasks.

Introduction

In exploring tools and materials, children begin to unravel answers for such important questions as, "What can we do with this? How does it work? Why is this shaped the way it is?" In this activity, children also have the opportunity to devise special tools for specific tasks. Imagine how a child feels when he invents the perfect gadget for accomplishing a feat or for helping in the classroom.

Getting Ready

Place the following materials, along with other interesting objects, in the Discovery Center or other appropriate places in your classroom for the children to explore during Free Discovery:

- balance scales
- basters
- brooms
- dustpans
- egg beaters
- funnels
- measuring cups and spoons
- meterstick, measuring tape, and other measurement tools
- mop

- plastic plumbing pipe and connectors
- tongs
- toy tools
- tweezers

Free Discovery

Begin Free Discovery by talking with the children about what they know about tools. Explain that tools are objects designed to serve a specific purpose. Have some tools available to share with the children. Ask, "Do you have any tools at home? What have you used tools for at home? What tools do people in your family use for cooking? Do you know anyone who uses tools to fix things? What do they do with them? Did you ever see someone make something with tools?" As the children share their thoughts, write them on a "Working with Tools" Discovery Chart.

Allow the children ample opportunity to investigate the new materials in the classroom. While the children may need some guidance or suggestions when they first begin to explore these materials, it is important to let the children explore freely, not to overdirect their exploration.

Now is the time to begin the class Discovery Books for this chapter. You may want to make several books, each focusing on a specific activity, or you may want to make a general book with drawings and captions showing what the children are learning about tools. The children can also draw and write about what they do and observe in their own Discovery Journals. As the children continue to discover new tools and uses for them, encourage them to share their discoveries with you and add them to the Working with Tools Discovery Chart. Consider having the children cut out pictures of tools to add to the chart, or help the children compile a list of tools and their uses.

Exploring Tools

Glue Tools

Most children love to use glue. Give the children three tools to use with glue to make their own creations. Which tool works best? Or perhaps their fingers make the best tools?

Science Process Skills

Focused observing

Organizing and communicating observations

Science Vocabulary

construct

creation

craft sticks

medicine dropper

paintbrush

paper tubes

pipette

spread

tool names

used

work

Materials

assorted collected materials, such as wrapping paper and empty food boxes

collection of items to be recycled or reused, such as egg cartons, wrapping paper, used greeting cards, cardboard boxes, wood scraps, foam packing peanuts, paper cups, and straws

craft sticks

glue

paintbrushes

pipettes (medicine droppers)

small containers for glue

Science Content Standards

The children will interact with tools to determine which tools are best for dispensing glue while reusing products to make new items. (Science as Inquiry; Science and Technology)

What to Do

1. Put some of the collected materials out on the table and begin to chat with the children about them. Talk about what the various materials are made of and what their original uses are. Wonder aloud: "This box looks like it used to have food in it. What do you think was in it? I wonder where this cardboard tube came from. Destiny, you brought in this wrapping paper. Was it from your mommy's birthday? Who brought these little Styrofoam pieces? I got a present in the mail once that had them in the box." Tell the children that they are going to reuse some things they have collected by gluing them together to make something interesting.

2. Show the children three tools (a medicine dropper, a craft stick, and a paintbrush), and explain that the children can use these tools to spread the glue. Encourage the children to decide for themselves which tools work best for them.

3. Allow the children to work independently to make their own creations.

4. Talk with the children about how the different tools work. The children might say things such as: "The glue plugged up the dropper, but the paintbrush really worked." Children this age are just beginning to understand what relative terms such as *better* and *best* mean. For them, the best one may be the one another child they admire chooses. That is all right. It is a start.

Exploring Tools

Keep It Simple

● Provide materials that are easy to use and give the children a choice between only two glue tools. Perhaps they can make something long or something tall.

Add a Challenge

● Challenge the children to use the glue tools to build props for the block area. With your guidance, the children can work together to create child-sized vehicles or buildings for dramatic play. Some children may find the liquid glue too messy or hard to handle. They may be more comfortable with different materials, such as glue sticks or tape.

Theme Connections

Art

There are many artists who create with recycled materials, perhaps in your own community. Search the Internet for photographs of recycled art to share with the children to inspire new creations.

Tools

Many of the activities in this chapter are good additions to themes on Tools, Machines, and Community Helpers.

Children's Books

Mrs. Toggle's Zipper by Robin Pulver is a story about a teacher who cannot take off her coat because of a stuck zipper. Everyone in the book tries to help solve the problem in creative ways until Mr. Abel, the custodian, comes into the room wearing a work apron. The apron is FULL of tools and he has the right tool for doing the job! This book also introduces some new words for children's fun use: *thingamajig, whatsit, doodad,* and *whatchamacallit* would make excellent word-wall words!

Observing and Assessing the Child's Science Learning

● Can the child indicate which tools worked best or which he most liked to use?

● Can the child explain his choices?

Connecting Science to the Curriculum

● **Taking it Outside**—Have the children find outdoor materials to make outdoor sculptures. Do different glue tools work better with outdoor materials? Talk with the children about the differences between the materials they used to create their indoor sculptures and the materials used for the outdoor sculptures. What would happen to their sculptures if they were left outside? Show the children how they can use string as a tool to hold sticks together. Can the children make temporary sculptures without using any tools?

Family Involvement

Ask the children's families to bring reusable materials, such as egg cartons, boxes, paper tubes, and plastic foam, to school for the children to use to make sculptures.

Using Museums and Other Community Assets

Take photographs of sculptures in your community and share them with the children. Talk about how people made the sculptures as well as the materials the artists used to create them.

Exploring Tools

Playclay Pancakes

Science Process Skills

Focused observing

Organizing and communicating observations

Science Vocabulary

change

flat

flatten

tool

tool names

Materials

assorted devices for flattening clay, such as rolling pins, children's wooden hammers, and other unbreakable objects

interlocking cubes

playclay

Children's Books

Pancakes Pancakes by Eric Carle walks children and adults through the process of making pancakes. The book contains and describes the uses of a variety of tools, such as a scythe, a flail, a millstone, a butter churn, a spoon, and a ladle, all the while making everyone who reads it crave pancakes.

What is the best tool to use to make playclay pancakes? Allowing children to select different tools to try and then discussing the results helps children focus their attention on tools as a variable to consider when preparing to make something. At the same time, they can enjoy some pretend play!

Science Content Standards

The children will use and describe what tool worked best for them to make playclay pancakes. What else can that tool be used for? (Science as Inquiry; Science and Technology)

Before the Activity

Make the playclay (see recipe on page 104) or use commercially available children's clay. Roll the clay into balls about the size of tennis balls. Make at least one clay ball per child. Flatten one of the clay balls into a pancake.

What to Do

1. Show the children the two forms of playclay you created: the round ball and the flattened ball. Explain that you had to work to make the ball into a pancake. You might ask, "Can you guess what I used to make my pancake?" The children might say you used the rolling pin or you smashed it with your hands. Respond that these are good guesses; both rolling pins and hands can be tools to make pretend pancakes.

2. Show the children the tools you have collected, and give each child a ball of playclay. Tell the children it is their turn to flatten playclay. Tell them that they must use these tools or others they find in the room to flatten their clay balls into pancakes.

3. After the children make their pancakes, talk about how they did it. Can the children show you or tell you what they did? Ask, "Can you make it a ball again and think of another tool to use to make a pancake? Try it!"

Keep It Simple

● Measure the width of each pancake with a tool, such as interlocking cubes. The children can measure the balls as well. Can the children tell which are wider?

Add a Challenge

● Combine all the playclay. Can the children use their tools to make the world's biggest pancake? How many cubes wide is the pancake? How many different tools did the children use to make the pancake?

Theme Connections
Snack and Cooking

Cooking pancakes and making the experience as authentic as possible (for example, grinding wheat in a coffee mill or grinder and shaking jars of cream to turn them into butter for the pancakes) helps create a rich learning experience for the children.

Observing and Assessing the Child's Science Learning

● Can the child describe the tools used and how they helped flatten the clay?

● Can the child indicate which tools worked best?

Connecting Science to the Curriculum

● **Language and Literacy**—Talk with the children about other kinds of flat breads; tortillas, chapattis, sandwich wraps, and pita breads might be familiar to some of the children.

Exploring Tools

Stampers Galore

Stores are not the only place to find stamping tools. The children can find all sorts of things to use for this purpose. With some time to experiment, the children should be able to group the stampers into those that work and those that do not.

Science Content Standard

The children will observe that tools are made for specific purposes; the children will observe that we can manufacture tools to accomplish certain tasks. (Science as Inquiry)

What to Do

1. Show the children the materials you collected for them to try out as "stampers" with the stamp pads. Say, "Look at all this stuff I found. Instead of throwing it away or recycling it, I have an idea. Let's try using them as stampers. We are going to try stamping with these things to find out which ones are good ink stampers and which ones are not."

2. Encourage the children to share their observations as they work. For example, say, "Look, you made a big square with the foam. What do you notice about the rock?" or, "Hmm, I can't figure out how you made that mark. Could you tell me about it?" Some children may be more comfortable showing you, rather than telling you. You can then provide the language: "Oh, I see. You stamped all over your page with the crumpled foil. You must have used both stamp pads because I see blue here and green here."

Science Process Skills

Focused observing
Observing to classify

Science Vocabulary

absorb
group
print
stamp

Materials

paper (for a Discovery Book)
paper towels (for cleanup)
variety of items that can be used to attempt to stamp with ink on paper, such as pieces of clay, plastic berry baskets, plastic foam, wood, brick, crumpled foil, rocks, wax, and cardboard
washable stamp pads

Children's Books

Leo Leonni's *Swimmy* is beautifully illustrated, and the artist's technique actually involves using stampers! Check out this book and talk to the children about how the artwork was created.

Exploring Tools

Keep It Simple

● Let the children use their favorite stampers to make a class Discovery Book. They can label the stamp marks with what they used to make them at their own writing level if they like. Provide help as needed.

Add a Challenge

● Have the children make stamp pictures with assorted items. Have their friends try to match which stampers were used to make the pictures.

Theme Connections
All About Me

Manufactured stamping tools are identical. This experience gives children the opportunity to create their own unique stamp that is special to them.

Illustrators

Who are the people who make pictures in our books and how do they make them? These questions can launch an exciting exploration of the world of illustration.

3. Talk with the children after they spend some time experimenting with their stampers. For instance, say, "Tell me what you decided about all this stuff. Did they all make good stampers? Let's put them into two piles. We'll put the ones we liked here. We can use them again. We'll make another pile for the ones that didn't work so well." Have the children compare the two piles and decide which pile has the most objects. To verify, either count the objects in each pile or line them up side by side to create a simple "real object" bar graph.

Observing and Assessing the Child's Science Learning

● Is the child able to separate materials into good ink stampers and ones that do not work as well and describe the differences between them?

Exploring Tools

Little Home Builders

A pretend home for a favorite animal or doll provides an ideal outlet for creative building. The children can use the tools and materials at the Art Center and items from your pile of plastic foam, cardboard, plates, and paper cups to create homes for their toys. While the children are building their homes is a great time to reinforce the concept of reusing materials.

Science Process Skills

Focused observing

Organizing and communicating observations

Linear measuring

Science Vocabulary

build

construct

home

house

reuse

tool

Materials

cardboard tubes

cups

egg cartons

glue

paper

child-safe scissors

small boxes (one for each child)

string

tape

yarn

Science Content Standards

The children will reuse collected materials to build a home for their favorite toy or doll. During the building, the children will determine the best tools to use and discuss which tools are best suited for which tasks. (Science as Inquiry; Measuring—Nonstandard: Linear)

Before the Activity

Ask the children to bring a small toy, such as a doll, a robot, or a stuffed animal to school, for which they would like to build a home.

What to Do

1. Gather a few children together so that they can show each other their toys. For example, say, "Look at all the different kinds of toys we all like. Baleek's and Tony's are about the same size. Ayoon's is really tiny. We're going to make houses for each of our toys." Some of the toys will need houses that are kind of big, while others can be quite small. Show the children all the materials they have available for making houses for their toys.

2. Let the children, working alone or with a partner, select their own materials from the collection you provide. Encouraging teamwork in the design and construction of the toys' homes promotes cooperation and may be a successful approach with some of the children.

3. As the children build, they will be experimenting with balance, stability, form, and function. Ask the children questions about their work: "Can you find a box big enough for your bear? What do you think she would like in her house? How can you find a bed that is the right size?"

4. Talk with the children about what they would do without certain building tools, such as tape and scissors.

Exploring Tools

Keep It Simple

- Encourage the children to construct tunnels and bridges for the block area. Talk with the children about what size they need to be for the vehicles you have.

Add a Challenge

- Have the children draw their houses in their Discovery Journals. Encourage them to make careful observations in order to draw what they see. Have the children label their drawings, providing assistance as needed. The children might also want to draw pictures of the toys for which they built the houses.

Children's Books

Building a House by Byron Barton actually walks the reader through construction of a house, beginning with digging a hole in the dirt.

A House for Hermit Crab by Eric Carle and *A House is a House for Me* by Mary Ann Hoberman are beautifully illustrated books that will prompt conversations about how some creatures have houses that fit them perfectly.

Begin a discussion about the diversity of homes by using Ann Morris' book *Houses and Homes*. The book features homes from all over the world and also discusses types of building materials found in regional areas.

Observing and Assessing the Child's Science Learning

- Can the child describe and compare the tools he used to build the houses? What tools helped him complete the job?

- Can the child describe or show how he measured or compared the toys to make the houses the right size?

- If two children worked together, can each of the children talk about how they made the home suitable for both of their toys?

Connecting Science to the Curriculum

• **Mathematics**—In this activity, the children use simple measuring skills to compare the sizes of their toys to the houses they are making.

• **Taking It Outside**—Many children spontaneously build pretend homes for toys, elves, or animals if they have the materials to use. Provide baskets or tubs of sticks, logs, rocks, shells, and other natural materials for the children to use if such materials are not readily available in your outdoor space. If the children are not familiar with this kind of imaginative play, help them get started by building the base of a structure, then asking the children what should go on the structure next.

Family Involvement

Request that families send a variety of materials from home that the children can use for building—small boxes, egg cartons, cardboard tubes, cups, and so on.

Using Museums and Other Community Assets

Encourage families to take their children to visit a construction site and see community builders in action.

Exploring Tools

Science Process Skill

Focused observing

Science Vocabulary

down

heavy

lift

pulley

up

wheel

Materials

assorted objects

pulley

rope or clothesline and a small bucket

Children's Books

What Is a Pulley? by Lloyd G. Douglas is one in a series of books on simple machines that gives children a look at real pulleys in action.

Pulleys

This experience with a pulley introduces the children to a simple but important tool of physics. Later in their scientific training, they will learn more complex ways of using pulleys to do increasingly difficult jobs. Now is the time to explore ways to use a single pulley to do work in the block area.

Science Content Standards

The children will observe the actions of pulleys to do work for them and observe the motion being created by forces on the rope or string. (Physical Science—Position and Motion of Objects; Science and Technology)

Before the Activity

If you do not have access to pulleys, you can purchase inexpensive ones at a hardware store.

The easiest way to suspend the pulley is to find a board that you can place between two book shelves. Screw in a hook where you will attach the pulley. This gives enough room below for the children to bring in trucks to load and objects to lift.

What to Do

1. Tie the rope to the bucket and secure the pulley in such a manner that the children can pull down on the pulley's rope and raise the bucket off the floor.

2. Let the children discover how they can use the pulley system to lift blocks and other things. As the children work with the pulley, reinforce the concepts *up* and *down*. Encourage the children to talk about whether picking up the bucket by hand is different from picking it up with the pulley.

Keep It Simple

● Invite the children to lift a bucket full of blocks by hand and then use the pulley. Talk about which was the easiest to lift.

Add a Challenge

● Have the children write shipping labels for the packages being moved by the pulley by drawing on labels or pieces of paper. Place a balance on the floor near the pulley. Have the children take two objects and place them on the balance. The heaviest object should be pulled up first on the pulley.

Theme Connections

Opposites

Using a pulley gives the children meaningful experiences with the concepts of *up* and *down*.

Simple Machines

Let children use simple machines to move things outside. They can use a pulley, a wagon (the wheel), a lever, and an incline plane to move rocks, jugs filled with water, or each other.

Observing and Assessing the Child's Science Learning

● Is the child able to manipulate the pulley successfully?

● Does the child understand that in order for the pulley to change direction, he must apply force to move it and that he has to pull down to move something up?

Connecting Science to the Curriculum

● **Taking It Outside**—If you have access to a real pulley or block and tackle, tie the apparatus to the crossbar of a piece of playground equipment and find some heavy objects to pick up. Try lifting a concrete building block. The children will be amazed at how they can lift heavy objects with the help of a pulley system. **Safety Note:** Be sure the children stay a safe distance from any heavy objects elevated by the pulley. Also, do not leave the pulley unsupervised.

Using Museums and Other Community Assets

High-school science teachers often have many different types of pulleys. A teacher might be willing to demonstrate these pulleys, and possibly even let your children try some of the more elaborate configurations.

Science Process Skills

Observing to classify

Organizing and
  communicating observations

Science Vocabulary

balance
higher
stack
support
unbalanced

Materials

unit blocks

Children's Books

Margaret Wise Brown's *Two Little Trains* comes to life with illustrations by Leo and Diane Dillon. A toy train makes a long journey, just like the real train, with some help from bridges and block constructions.

The Balancing Girl by Berniece Rabe is a story about a little girl in a first-grade classroom whose special talent is the ability to balance objects. She develops a clever idea for using her expertise to make extra money at a school carnival and becomes a hero.

T 'Em Up

Building-block Ts offer another way for young children to explore balance. Ts are tools that allow children to make simple bridges and other kinds of structures. Encourage the children to experiment with bigger and taller constructions. Can the children talk about what makes a structure fall? Can the children sort the blocks into groups that stack well and those that do not?

Science Content Standards

The children will be able to construct a tower using the T structure and describe how that structure functions in a purposeful way. (Science as Inquiry; Science and Technology)

What to Do

1. Join the children in the block area and begin building— unsuccessfully. For example, place a semicircle block on the floor and try to put a long rectangle upright on it. So far, so good. Now place another block on top, but off center. Say something about the trouble you are having, such as, "Hmm...that didn't work so well." Try again with another set of blocks. You might say, "I am trying to build something tall, but this doesn't seem to work. What else could we try?" Encourage the children to try their ideas. If the children have trouble coming up with their own ideas, show them how to balance different shapes of blocks using an upright block as a support or a T. Model building using this strategy and invite them to join in.

2. Have the children experiment with different shapes of blocks, maybe even two or three blocks at a time.

3. Encourage the children to try supporting the blocks with two, three, or more Ts. Ask, "Is it easier to add more blocks to the stack when you have more Ts?" Encourage the children to build as big a structure as they can. They may want to count how many Ts they used.

Exploring Tools

Keep It Simple

● Repeat the activity with other types of blocks. Use a variety of measurement tools to see how tall the structures are.

Add a Challenge

● Once the children have experience building using the T structures, have the children classify the blocks into groups according to how easy or difficult they are to build with. For example, the children might group rectangles, squares, and cylinders together as blocks that make good uprights. They might put triangles and semicircles in a group as blocks that are good toppers, but are hard to use if you want to make your building higher. After the children group the blocks, have them draw or trace their block groups in their Discovery Journals. Have the children look at each other's journals. Have different children created different groups of blocks?

● Domino sets can balance on their ends if the people who place them are very careful. Children can make domino trails and curves and watch what happens when they tap the first one in the line.

Theme Connections
Exploring Bridges

Collect books and photographs about bridges, including images of local bridges. Wonder with the children about why we need bridges. Encourage the children to think of reasons why bridges are necessary.

Construction and Building

What are the different ways we construct things? What can we use to construct things in addition to blocks? Make a class book or display of photographs of the children's constructions.

Children with Special Needs

Apply gripping materials to the blocks for children with limited fine motor abilities.

Observing and Assessing the Child's Science Learning

● Is the child able to group the blocks consistently based on specific characteristics?

● Is the child able to construct a block structure using the special T design?

● Can the child show or describe how the T design is helpful?

Connecting Science to the Curriculum

● **Language and Literacy**—After children build their elaborate structures in the Blocks and Buildings Center, encourage them to show their creations to you. Showing genuine interest and using questioning techniques that allow the children to focus on the building process helps the children put their thoughts, actions, and the sequence of those actions into words.

Family Involvement

Suggest that families continue this activity at home. Using cereal boxes and cardboard of various sizes and shapes, families can make their own Ts to continue to build with their children.

Science Process Skills

Focused observing
Measuring—mass

Science Vocabulary

balance
color names
compare
heavy, heavier, heaviest
level
light, lighter, lightest
weigh

Materials

crayons
double-pan balance

Balancing Crayons

This activity provides a good way to use that big bin of old crayons that sits in most classrooms. Challenge the children to determine which set of crayons weighs the most—the reds or the blues. The science tool, the balance, will help the children find out.

Science Content Standards

The children will use the balance as their tool to determine which color of crayons weighs the most. (Science as Inquiry; Measurement—Mass; Science and Technology)

What to Do

1. Show the children the tub of crayons and say, "Look at this tub of crayons! I think there's every color in it. I wonder if the red ones or blue ones weigh more. Do you think the green ones or brown ones are heavier? I can't tell, can you? I bet our tool, the balance, can help us figure it out." With the children, select two colors of crayons to compare using the balance.

2. Have the children sort the two colors of crayons, putting one color on each side of the balance. The level of the balance will change as they place more crayons in the pans. Watch as this happens. Say, "Now the red side is going down. The reds are heavier. What happens when we put some more crayons on the blue side?"

3. When the children cannot find any more red or blue crayons, have the children determine which side is heavier.

4. Three- and four-year-old children are beginning to use comparative language. You will often hear them say, "I'm the biggest," whether they are or not. As you work with this activity, verbalize your observations of their actions. Say, for instance: "You made the red side go down. That means the reds are heavier right now. I wonder which color will be lighter. Our balance is a tool that can help us find out."

Keep It Simple

● Let the children find items throughout the classroom to place on the balance to continue to explore how the balance works as a tool for comparing the mass of objects.

Add a Challenge

● Encourage the children to repeat the activity with other colors. Some children may be able to find which color set is the heaviest of all. Have the children grab a handful of a color of crayons and place them in the balance. Then do so with another color. Which is heavier? Do this with all the colors. See if the children can make sense of why this is not a way to see which color has the most crayons.

Theme Connections
I'm Me, I'm Special, or Friends

The children sort themselves, just as they sorted the crayons. Take turns choosing how to sort—shoelaces or no shoelaces; T-shirt or button shirt; walk, drive, or bus to school. Graph the results, or simply count the numbers with the children.

Dual Language Learners

Demonstrate the use of a balance as a tool and repeatedly use key vocabulary words, such as *heavier, lighter, even,* and *balance.*

Children with Special Needs

It may be easier for children with motor challenges to use a bucket or pan balance that will hold the crayons instead of a balance with no containers.

Observing and Assessing the Child's Science Learning

● Can the child identify which side of the balance contains the color that weighs the most?

● Can the child show or describe how the balance is a useful tool to find out about the weight of objects?

Connecting Science to the Curriculum

• **Art**—Set out books containing photographs of artists' work. Encourage the children to talk about the materials the artists used, and encourage the children to try using those materials themselves.

• **Mathematics**—In this activity, the children sort crayons by color, initially just looking for two colors. With experience, the children will be able to make piles of several different colors at the same time.

Using Museums and Other Community Assets

Many grocery stores and produce stores still provide balances or scales for customers to use to determine the weight of their purchase. Encourage families to use them so the children can see another weighing tool in action.

Science Process Skills

Focused observing

Organizing and
communicating observations

Science Vocabulary

branches	real
build	tool
leaves	tree
limbs	trunk
pretend	

Materials

4' piece of a 1" × 2" wood or
mop or broom handle for
the tree trunk

cardboard tubes

glue

hammer (adult use only)

nails (adult use only)

natural materials, such as
leaves and twigs

paper

stand for the tree "trunk" (a
Christmas tree stand works
well, as does placing the
"tree" in a bucket of sand or
gravel)

string

tape

yarn

Children's Books

Caldecott Medal Winner *A Tree
Is Nice* by J. M. Udry is a
beautifully illustrated classic
about trees.

Build a Tree

A tree is wonderful. It responds to gravity and the environment to
stand strong and upright. Is making a tree easy? Let's find out!

Science Content Standards

The children will build at tree that resembles an actual tree they
have observed outside. (Life Science)

The children will use tools of construction to accomplish the
project; the children will select the tools that helped them the most.
(Science and Technology; Life Science—Characteristics of
Organisms)

Before the Activity

Set a piece of wood in a tree stand so that the wood stands upright.
Hammer several nails along the length of the wood.

What to Do

1. Take a walk outside to look at a nearby tree. Point out the
   branches and limbs. Say to the children, "Can we make our bodies
   into tree shapes? Some branches spread out. Some branches grow
   up. How do your trees grow? What happens when the wind
   blows? Who can move in the wind?" If there are no trees nearby,
   share your own experience with trees and encourage the children
   to do the same. For example, describe a tree you saw on your way
   to work or one near your home. Encourage the children to share
   their experiences. "Does anyone have a tree where they live? Did
   anyone ever climb a tree? Who has a swing in a tree?" Bring out
   picture books about trees for the children to examine.

2. Show the children the materials you have collected. Work with
   them to make the tree, using cardboard tubes as branches.
   Through the building process, the children are experimenting
   with balance, stability, form, and function. Problems will develop
   as the children try to make the branches stay on the main trunk.
   They may have to use more tape.

Keep It Simple

● Provide paper and have the children design leaves to hang on the tree. They can draw their own leaves or do leaf rubbings to cut out and hang. Have the children draw their own trees.

Add a Challenge

● Bring in an artificial Christmas tree and have the children help put that tree together. How is this tree different from the one that they built? How is it similar?

Theme Connections
Trees or Plants

Make a field guide of the trees and/or plants in your neighborhood with digital photos you or the children take. Laminate the photos, hole-punch one corner, and put the photos on a ring. Make a tree for each season during a theme on The Four Seasons.

3. Talk with the children about what they would do without a building tool, such as tape. Ask, "Would the absence of the nails make a difference?"

Safety Note: Remind the children to be careful so they do not scratch themselves on the nails.

4. Discuss how the children's tree is similar to and different from a real tree. The children may want to collect some natural materials to add to the tree. Talk with the children about the differences between what is real and what is imaginary.

Observing and Assessing the Child's Science Learning

● Can the child show or describe what he used to build the tree and what materials became what part of the tree?

● Ask the child what tools or materials made the job easy. What was difficult to do?

Connecting Science to the Curriculum

• **Taking It Outside**—Collect additional leaves, sticks, and other materials to attach to the tree.

Family Involvement

Ask the children's families to donate materials to use for this activity, such as tubes, nails, broomsticks, and natural materials.

Exploring Tools

Help Me If You Can

Science Process Skills

Focused observing

Organizing and
    communicating observations

Science Vocabulary

choose

draw

show

tell

tool names

volume

Materials

assortment of different tools,
    some that are good water
    movers, such as cups or
    turkey basters, and that are
    poor water movers, such as a
    wooden spoon or a flat
    board

large bowl or pitcher

water table

This is a great activity to do to determine whether or not children grasp the concept that tools are useful devices that help people accomplish various tasks. It is also a fun assessment that you and the children should enjoy.

Science Content Standards

This activity is a review and check on the ability of the children to use the tools that have been introduced during the previous activities. The children should be able to indicate:

● If a tool is made for a specific purpose.

● Whether people can manufacture tools to accomplish certain tasks. (Science as Inquiry; Science and Technology)

What to Do

1. Start this activity by laying out an assortment of different tools for the children to select from and use in the activity.

2. Invite a small group of children to join you at the water table. Hold up a container and challenge the children to select and use any of the available tools to fill the container with water from the table.

Close Observation

• **Show It**—Let the child proceed in his own way using the tools he selects. How successful is the child? Observe the tools the child selects initially, noting any changes or corrections he makes in tool selection or use. Thank the child for showing you one way to fill your container. Ask the child if he could do it faster with different tools. Dump out the water and repeat the activity. What tools does the child choose, now that he has some experience with them? Does he ignore the ineffective tools and quickly choose those that work best or are the most fun?

• **Tell It**—Ask the child why he chose a particular tool. If the child change tools during the process, ask him why he decided to change. Ask the child to talk about tool shape or size and how that affects the water-moving process.

• **Draw It**—Give the child a piece of paper divided in half. On one side ask the child to draw a tool that really worked for this job; on the other side of the paper, ask the child to draw a tool that did not work so well.

• **Write It**—Look at the child's drawing with the child. Have the child label his drawing with the proper names of the tools. Ask the child to write or dictate to you his ideas about what made one tool better than the other.

Observing and Assessing the Child's Science Learning

• This activity provides ample opportunity to observe each child using different tools to transport water. Encourage the child to talk about why the tools he selected were useful. If the child changed to tools that worked better or moved more water, ask him to explain why he decided to make that change. Choose from the above strategies to determine if the child understands the appropriate use of the various tools.

Exploring Tools

Exploring Tools

Plumber Apprentices

The plumber apprentices you will train during this activity will discover the complexities of a water line. These little plumber apprentices use the plumber's most important tools—plastic pipes and connectors—to create working water lines. The children will soon discover that interesting shapes do not always make the best waterways.

Science Process Skill

Focused observing

Science Vocabulary

connector
names of connectors
pipe
plumbing

Materials

collection of plastic pipes in assorted lengths
containers to hold water
funnels
toolbox for connectors
variety of connectors
water table or large, flat container filled with water

Science Content Standard

The children will explore the complexities of constructing a plastic pipe that will, upon completion, allow water to flow through it; the children will be able to use all the various connectors and pipes to complete the task and discover how these various objects were created to serve a certain function. (Science and Technology)

Before the Activity

Help yourself out by making a trip to a construction site or a plumbing store to ask for pieces of cast-off plastic pipe. Most people will be happy to save pieces for your class. You will probably have to purchase fittings and connectors.

What to Do

1. Encourage the children to pretend to be plumbers or pipe fitters and to use the pipes and connectors in the Block and Dramatic Play Centers. Children typically enjoy constructing various configurations. Talk with the children about the different lengths of pipe, the types of connectors, and how they work together.

2. After the children spend some time working with the pipes, encourage them to test their connections in the water table or outside. The children can use funnels to help them pour water into the pipes.

3. Does the water come out where the children expect it to? Are there leaks or surprises? Ask, "How could you make the water travel a different way? Is there a way you could attach more pieces? What is the longest distance you can make the water travel?"

Children's Books

Mark Thomas' *A Day with a Plumber* tells children all about what real plumbers do. You may want to check out other books in his series about people at work.

"The Bath" is a funny story in Arnold Lobel's *Mouse Tales.* It tells the story of a mouse who is so dirty that he just keeps bathing and lets the water run out of his window and into the street. Everyone in the town begs him to turn off the water!

Keep It Simple

- Give the children cardboard tubes to use as pipes and let them connect them together with masking tape. Have them place a marble or small car in one end and observe it as it rolls out the other end. Can they make it roll out and hit a block or other target?

Add a Challenge

- Expert plumbers make plans before they begin. After the children are familiar with the pipes and fittings, challenge them to draw and then build a simple plan. Can the children draw plans for other little plumbers to execute?

Theme Connections
Community Helpers

Who are all the people who build our buildings and take care of them? You may have some of them in the families of your children. Bring in props so the children can pretend to be electricians, carpenters, and so on.

Water

With the children, track the water in your building. Where does it come into the building? Encourage the children to think of the many places in the building that have water—toilets, sinks, spigots, pipes, drains, and any other places unique to your setting.

4. Give the children plenty of opportunities to make all kinds of configurations. There is real value in helping them understand that there are many ways to make connections and many ways to get water from here to there.

Observing and Assessing the Child's Science Learning

- Is the child able to construct working lengths of plumbing with the pipes and connectors so that water flows through the pipes?

Connecting Science to the Curriculum

- **Mathematics**—In this activity, the children compare the various lengths of pipe and the types of connectors.

Using Museums and Other Community Assets

Invite a professional plumber to talk with the children about plumbing and to share and demonstrate some of the tools that plumbers use.

Exploring Tools

Help Me Fill This Up

Water, water everywhere! How do we get water from here to there? Let children splash and slosh their way to figuring out which tools work best to get the job done.

Science Process Skill

Focused observing

Science Vocabulary

best
better
fill
names of tools used
tool

Materials

basters
eyedroppers
funnels
measuring cups and spoons
plastic reusable containers of varying sizes with a range of openings, from large to very small: yogurt cups, water or juice bottles, jars, small medicine bottles, and so on
sieves
sponges (for cleanup)
water table or large, flat container for water play, filled with a few inches of water

Children's Books

Water by Frank Asch is a beautifully illustrated book about our precious natural resource.

Dr. Seuss' *McElligot's Pool* is a fantasy story about what just might be caught if a patient person tries to fish in a puddle.

Science Content Standards

The children will observe the functions of various tools that move water and be able to describe how they work to move water from one container to another. (Physical Sciences—Properties of Matter; Science and Technology)

What to Do

1. Play is the order of the day. Fill the water table or tub and put out the materials. Children enjoy pouring and filling and emptying containers and learning how to use the various tools. Basters and eyedroppers squirt, so plan for it. Give the children targets to squirt at as they figure out how to make them work.

2. Challenge the children to fill the various containers using the tools instead of just dunking them under the water. For example, say, "Figure out which of these tools is best to put water in the jar. Do you want to do this job by yourself, or do you want some help?"

3. Allow time for all the children to have a chance to play using the various tools to fill up the containers. Encourage them to try a variety of tools and containers.

4. Talk with the children as they work. For example, say, "That funnel fits right in the top of the water bottle. You are pouring water right in. I wonder if that tool will help get water into this little medicine bottle? Hmm, it does not fit. I bet you can find something that will. You are right, the baster works."

Keep It Simple

● Add one tool each day during a day devoted to tools, called "See What This Tool Does." Encourage the children to try out the tool at any station. After the day is over, review what the children say about the tool.

● Have the children draw pictures of their favorite water mover in their Discovery Journals.

Add a Challenge

● Add plastic tubing to the mix. The children can make water go uphill and downhill by moving the tubing up and down.

Theme Connections
Water

Make a book of all the ways the children use water, and all the tools and containers that make it possible. For example, what do the children need to take a bath? The children should mention pipes, a faucet, a bathtub, and a drain.

Dual Language Learners

Encourage children who are learning English to listen to others as they discuss the variety of tools they use. This will help the children learn the names of the tools. This activity also models descriptive language when children describe the efficiency or inefficiency of the tools.

Children with Special Needs

If children are hearing impaired, be sure they can see your lips clearly as you explain the activity.

Observing and Assessing the Child's Science Learning

● Does the child select a tool that is appropriate for the size of container?

● Can the child talk about how the tool he chose works?

Connecting Science to the Curriculum

• **Language and Literacy**—Have the children draw pictures of various tools. Encourage them to write or dictate their ideas about which tools are best for specific tasks.

• **Taking It Outside**—This activity can be a cooling experience when taken outside on warm days.

Science Process Skills

Organizing and
  communicating observations

Measurement—nonstandard:
  linear

Science Vocabulary

measure

plant

plant names

shortest

tallest

tool

Materials

crayons

graph paper

interlocking cubes or other
  measuring devices

Children's Books

In "The Garden," a story in *Frog and Toad Together* by Arnold Lobel, Toad plants some flower seeds and tells them to start growing. Toad tries everything to make them grow. Finally, Toad is exhausted and stops looking. That's when the flowers sprout.

Oliver Pig, the hero of *More Tales of Oliver Pig* by Jean Van Leeuwen, plants a "Surprise Seed" and waits for it to grow. It is a squash seed, and it takes a long time, but in the end of the story the whole family enjoys the squash that Oliver has grown.

The Measurement Walk

There is an array of plants available outside that children can observe and measure. Interlocking cubes are useful tools to introduce children to the skill of measurement. Put plants and interlocking cubes together and you have a fun and active introduction to measurement.

Science Content Standards

The children will discover how to use measuring cubes as a tool to see how tall a plant grows. (Life Science; Characteristic of Organisms; Science as Inquiry)

What to Do

1. Take a group of children on a measuring walk.

    Safety Note: Consult families regarding any allergies children may have to outdoor plants.

    Find a plant and measure it using interlocking cubes or another similar measuring tool. Help the children place the cubes on the ground and build the stack to the height of the plant. Keep the cubes together and find another plant to measure.

2. When the children finish measuring several plants, help the children use the stacks of cubes to determine the tallest and shortest plants they measured. If they can, let the children count the number of cubes used. Ask, "Are some plants the same height? How can you tell?"

Keep It Simple

- Measure inside! Use yarn to measure both children and adults. Then measure adult and child chairs. Compare the differences.

Add a Challenge

- Using graph paper, challenge the children to take turns coloring one square for each cube used to measure the plants. Use yarn as a tool to measure the various plant heights. Then make a graph showing the different yarn lengths.

Theme Connections

All About Me

Use this activity to enrich any theme in which the children learn and share information about themselves and their world.

The Seasons

Simple measuring activities such as this one invite the children to observe closely. This activity also helps the children become aware of changes over time.

Dual Language Learners

This activity does not require proficiency in English. Put a pair of children together that have well-matched math skills. Interaction between the two of them can strengthen their communication skills.

Observing and Assessing the Child's Science Learning

- Can the child use the cubes to measure the plants?
- Can the child identify the tallest and shortest plants?
- Does the child understand how to use the cubes as measurement tools?

Family Involvement

This activity can be fun for families to do at home to reinforce measurement skills.

Exploring Tools

Science Process Skill

Focused observing

Science Vocabulary

cleanup
names of tools
spill

Materials

basters
brooms
dust pans
measuring cups
scoops
sponges
squeegees
towels

Children's Books

Phyllis Hoffman and Sarah Wilson's *We Play* is a simple book that some preschoolers might be able to read by themselves. The children in the "story" build block structures with the blocks balanced upon one another, and they also use a variety of tools for cleaning up their own messes.

Small Pig by Arnold Lobel is about a little pig that runs away from home when his owner cleans up his favorite mud hole with her vacuum cleaner.

Clean Up a Spill

When children play with water, water gets spilled. The same thing happens with sand, birdseed, or anything else they use in the messy materials area of the classroom. Let them be in charge of cleanup. They will reach their own conclusions as to which tools work best for the job.

Science Content Standard

The children will use appropriate tools to clean up a spilled mess; the children will decide which tools work the best for specific purposes. (Science and Technology)

Before the Activity

Put out something for the children to play with that typically requires cleaning up. You might use water or birdseed in the sensory table. Playdough play almost always means playdough crumbles on the floor. Provide something that will create a real reason for the children to use cleaning tools.

What to Do

1. When children finish their messy play, say, "Whew, you were busy. It looks like we have a mess to clean up. What do you think we should use?" Show the children the collection of clean-up tools. Let them choose the tools they want to use for cleaning.

2. Talk with the children about the different tools. Are there some tools they don't choose? Why not? What happens when they try using the sponge to clean up birdseed? Is there something that works better? Encourage the children to see what happens when they use a broom and dustpan to clean up spilled water.

Exploring Tools

Keep It Simple

● Ask the children what kinds of tools their families use at home to clean up spills. The children may describe shop vacuums and other power tools.

Add a Challenge

● Have the children dictate a story about the clean-up tools that they have seen being used to clean up messes at the center or school. What tools does the teacher use? What tools have they used? Have a short field trip to the janitor's station for a demonstration of the clean-up equipment that is used to keep the classrooms clean.

Theme Connections
Art

Spend some time investigating messy fun. Try fingerpainting, making mud, playing squirting games, playing with confetti, and anything else you can think of. Challenge the children to think of the best clean-up tools for each experience.

3. When the children finish cleaning the space, talk with them about how the different tools worked. With the group, decide which of the tools did the best job cleaning up the mess. Encourage the children to describe how the various tools work. You may need to provide words for their actions.

4. Repeat this activity frequently, varying the materials the children use as they play. Give the children the chance to clean up water, dry materials, things that are sticky, and anything else they might use. Talk with the children about how different tools work better for different jobs.

Observing and Assessing the Child's Science Learning

● Can the child describe the tools that are most useful for cleaning up a certain type of spill?

Exploring Tools

Hammer, Hammer, What Do You Do?

This small-group activity gives children a playful way to share what they have learned. Be sure the groups are small enough so that each child can participate.

Science Process Skills

Focused observing

Organizing and communicating observations

Science Vocabulary

action words, such as *hit, screw, turn, pick up, move, place, pinch*

names of tools

purpose

tools

work

Materials

assorted tools (basters, bottles, chopsticks/tongs, eyedroppers, forceps, forks, funnels, hammers, measuring cups, pliers, rags, rolling pins, child-safe scissors, screwdrivers, and so on)

Science Content Standards

The children will be learning the names of common tools from the classroom by playing the rhyme game. (Science as Inquiry; Science and Technology)

What to Do

1. Sit with the children with a collection of the tools they have been using. Talk with the children about how they have used the tools in the activities they have done. For example, you may say, "Remember how we used the eyedropper and the measuring cup to pick up water and move it from one place to another? What about the sponge and cloth? Did anyone use the rolling pin for something?" Show them the hammer. What do they know about this tool? Ask, "Has anyone ever used one or seen someone use one?"

2. Share the following chant, practicing it with the children until they can join you:

"Hammer, Hammer, what do you do?

I bet (child's name) can tell you."

With that, the child named should pick up the hammer, and say, for example, "A hammer is used to hit things." The child might also pantomime how to use the tool. As the child is doing this, say, "Look, Jake is showing us how to hit with a hammer." The child then returns the hammer to the pile.

Children's Books

Cave Boy by Cathy East and Mark Dubowski is about a boy who likes to invent things that people have never seen before. Among his fun inventions, he actually creates a tricycle and what he calls a "bammer" with a stick and a rock. Then he demonstrates its use.

Keep It Simple

● Ask the children to name the tools they use the most at school. Print the names of all the tools used frequently on cards. Have the children take pictures of each other using the tools. Match each picture to the tool card and the tool.

Add a Challenge

● Create a tool museum. Ask family members, friends, school janitors, and others to lend tools for the museum. How do the children think they should group the tools to create the displays? Museums often have signs and labels. Put the children in charge of making everything they need. After the children finish making the museum, invite their family members or another class to take a tour.

Theme Connections
Making Things, Tools, or Inventions

What tools and machines can children create that no one has ever seen before? What names can children give the inventions they come up with? Children can brainstorm about things that are needed that they have never seen before, then draw and label their ideas for creations. Give the children a variety of collage and reusable materials and invite them to create models of their inventions.

Dual Language Learners

The children may enjoy sharing their home language with all the children as they engage in this activity.

Children with Special Needs

By doing this activity, children with motor challenges will get practice in arm, hand, and finger manipulation.

3. Go through all the tools in this way, giving each child a turn. This activity encourages the children to use language to show how to use the tools. If necessary, help the children think of words to describe the tools' actions.

Observing and Assessing the Child's Science Learning

● Can the child describe or show how to use the various tools?

Knock It Over

Reusable materials are perfect for child-sized bowling. Give the children the job of finding the best materials for the game.

Science Process Skills

Focused observing

Organizing and
   communicating observations

Science Vocabulary

bowling

easy

hard

heavy

heavier

light

lighter

Materials

balls of various sizes, blocks, and other objects to use for knocking the bottles over

funnel

markers

poster board

sand

several 1-liter and 2-liter bottles

Science Content Standards

The children will experiment with tools that work to knock things over. The children will learn how to use the tools and describe which tool works best. (Physical Science—Force and Motion; Science and Technology)

Before the Activity

Fill the bottles with different amounts of sand. (Use the funnel.)

What to Do

1. Show the children how the bottles contain different amounts of sand. Also, show the children a sampling of objects they might use for knocking the bottles over. Then place the bottles upright in a triangle, as they would appear in a bowling alley.

2. Show the children how to roll or slide something at the bottles to knock them down. Be sure to emphasize that the children roll or slide the objects, rather than throw them.

3. Let the children use the various objects to try to knock over the bottles. Afterward, talk about what happens: "Did some things work better than others? Were some bottles easier to knock over than others? Were any too hard to knock over?"

Children's Books

In Cathy East Dubowski and Mark Dubowski's *Cave Boy*, Harry, the cave boy, is an inventor who creates a drum, a wheel, and many other things. With his inventions, he can even make a grumpy chief smile.

Keep It Simple

● For some children, you may want to begin with three empty bottles clustered together. Once they understand how to knock down the bottles and experience success, challenge them with the heavier bottles.

Add a Challenge

● Some children may enjoy keeping score by counting how many bottles they can knock down in two tries, just like real bowlers.

Theme Connections
Our Environment

This activity is perfect for investigations about games and Reusing and Recycling.

Observing and Assessing the Child's Science Learning

● Can the child tell you or show you which of the bowling objects worked best to knock down the bottles?

● Can the child show you which of the bottles were hardest or easiest to knock down?

Connecting Science to the Curriculum

• **Mathematics**—In this activity, the children collect and analyze data by making a large chart to show the number of bottles they knock over.

• **Music**—Recycled plastic bottles completely or partially filled with sand make interesting and varied sounds when they are hit with sticks. When the children tire of bowling, invite them to make drumbeat music with their recycled bottles and experiment with the sounds the bottles make. Can the children hear the difference between the sound of a partially filled bottle and a completely filled bottle?

Tool Shuffle

Exploring Tools

Science Process Skills

Focused observing

Observing to classify

Organizing and
communicating observations

Science Vocabulary

various tool names

various tool uses

Materials

small plastic toolbox (or a
plastic bucket labeled
"toolbox"; this provides a
safe container for
transporting the tools)

variety of tools, some of a
traditional nature, such as an
ice scraper, spoon, shovel,
screwdriver, hammer, pliers,
broom, sponge, bucket, or
funnel; and some contrived
tools, such as a round piece
of wood, paper towel tube,
or a block of wood

This game can be played indoors but might be better suited for
outside. The children should get some good exercise while
illustrating that they understand a lot about tools and their uses.
This activity works best in small groups, ensuring that everyone can
participate and no one has to wait too long for a turn.

Science Content Standard

After having been given the chance to work with many tools, the
children will be asked to play the game described in this activity and
explain or demonstrate the functions of various common tools by
indicating that:

- Tools are made for specific purposes.

- We can manufacture tools to accomplish certain tasks.
(Science and Technology)

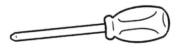

What to Do

1. Line up the collection of tools and the objects that the children can use as tools. Show the objects to the children and talk with them about how all the objects can serve different purposes and help us do work.

2. Ask the children to walk away from the tools. Explain to the children you have some specific jobs for them to do. After naming a job, the children should all think about the job and what might be a good tool to complete it. Tell one child it is his turn, and have that child run to the tools, pick up the tool he thinks is best one for the job, put it in the toolbox, and walk back using careful "on-the-job" steps. (This is a safety strategy. Just like real workers, the children have to be very careful when they are working and making things with tools.)

3. Describe another job. It could be completely imaginary or an actual classroom job that needs to be completed; this will make the assignment even more realistic (and the game more fun). For example, spill some sawdust and ask a child go get the right tools to clean it up. If there are no actual tasks, the children can simply pretend to have a job to do.

4. Continue until everyone has had at least one turn.

Observing and Assessing the Child's Science Learning

- Watch to see if the child picks the best tools for the jobs you describe. If the child has trouble picking the best tools, talk with the child about the tools he selected. For instance, if a child chooses a hammer to drive a screw, it may be something he has seen done at home, or perhaps he thought it would be faster than using a screwdriver. If the child is unsure what the differences are between a nail and a screw, describe the differences to the child.

Chapter 6

Working with Water

Working with Water

Science Concepts

This chapter explores the following science concepts:

- Water can change shape.

- There are many different liquids.

- When water is frozen, it becomes a solid.

- Some objects float in water and some sink.

Introduction

Water is a safe, inexpensive material and is ideal for exploring what liquids do. The activities in this chapter challenge children to discover the properties of water in a fun and thought-provoking atmosphere. Be part of the excitement and receptive to the children's ideas and theories. Children need to fully experience a liquid if they are to later understand the concept that matter exists as solid, liquid, and gas. Let's see what your children discover about water and other liquids as they engage in the activities in this chapter.

Getting Ready

Place the following materials, along with any other interesting objects that can effectively show the properties of water, in the Discovery Center or other appropriate places in your classroom for the children to explore during Free Discovery:

- supply of water

- buckets and dishpans

- bulb basters

- paper towels, towels, sponges, and newspaper

- containers of all sizes and shapes, including soft-drink bottles and similar plastic containers

- funnels

- measuring spoons and cups

- medicine cups (the 30-ml or 1-oz cups used to dispense medicine)
- medicine droppers or pipettes
- spoons
- syringes
- waxed paper

Free Discovery

Begin Free Discovery by talking with the children about all the things they already know about water. Before starting the first activity, create a class Discovery Chart of what the children already know about water. You might ask such questions as, "What do we use water for? Where can we find water? Are there things water can do that other things can't do?" Have the children brainstorm all the ways they have used water since they woke up: brushing their teeth, giving water to the dog, rinsing dishes, washing hands, and so on. Challenge the children to think of as many words as they can to describe water, and write these words on the Discovery Chart. Keep the chart posted in the room throughout your study of water, and from time to time ask the children if they would like to add to the chart or change any of the information it contains.

Introduce the children to the materials they will use in the water activities. If any materials require special care, talk about it with the children. Newspapers spread under a bucket or dishpan will absorb the inevitable drips and spills. Keep towels available so the children can clean up easily. This will allow the children to manage and clean the Discovery Center on their own.

Now is the time to begin the class Discovery Books for this chapter. You may want to make several books, each focusing on a specific activity, or you may want to make a general book with drawings and captions showing what the children are learning about water. Either method works, as does making both types of Discovery Books. The children can also draw and write or dictate about what they do and observe in their own Discovery Journals.

Working with Water

Science Process Skill

Focused observing

Science Vocabulary

create
mural
partner
rain
wet
dry
painting

Materials

colored chalk
colored pencils
crayons
glue sticks
large sheets of mural paper (or easel paper taped together to cover a table)
tissue paper (in a variety of colors and white)
watercolor paints and markers

Children's Books

Wong Herbert Yee's *Who Likes Rain?* follows a young girl on a walk in a gentle April rain.

Art Partners: Creating with Rain

Mural painting is always fun for children. Involve the entire class in a creative indoor/outdoor partnering art adventure. This activity requires a cooperative light rain, so be sure to check the forecast the day you want to do this activity.

Science Content Standard

The children will observe how water, in the form of rain or a sprinkler, will change shape and cause some of the paint they have used to float away. (Physical Science—Properties of Matter)

Before the Activity

Place a long strip of mural paper on the floor or on a long, wheelchair-accessible table. Set up a table with a collection of different art media.

What to Do

1. Talk with the children about how they use water with art materials. Do they remember using watercolor paints? Show the children how lines made with watercolor markers change when you brush them with a wet paintbrush. Show the children how crayon lines do not change much at all when you brush them with a wet paintbrush.

2. Talk with the children, saying, for example, "We're all going to work as partners helping each other to create this mural. Who else do you think could help us as an art partner? Do you think rain could be an art partner? Let's try it! We get to go first. Then we will see what happens when rain has a turn." Encourage each child to choose one or two art-making materials to make his own unique contribution to the mural. Let the children play and create with the materials in any way they like.

3. After all of the children have an opportunity to participate, let the mural dry and take a digital photograph of the children's work. Now it is time for the rain!

Working with Water

Keep It Simple

● Sprinkle powdered tempera paint on paper. What happens to it when it rains? If no rain is in the forecast, try spraying it with water.

Add a Challenge

● Can the sidewalk be an art partner? Have the children paint the sidewalk with tempera or another washable, nontoxic paint, and press paper on the art to make prints of the children's work. The prints will be textured because of the concrete.

Theme Connections

Colors

This is a great activity to use when the children are exploring colors, weather, and artists.

Seasons

Rain is a part of spring weather in many parts of the country. What other signs are there that spring has arrived?

4. Take the mural outdoors and place it on a paved or grassy area (avoid muddy or deep puddle locations). Secure the mural by placing rocks around its edge so it will not blow away. Talk with the children about how they predict the rain will change the mural. Write the children's predictions on chart paper.

5. After the mural has a short exposure to light rain, return it to the classroom to dry.

6. Ask the children to describe what they see. Say, "See what you and your rain partner have created. Has our mural changed?" Show the children the photograph of the mural before it was exposed to the rain. Help the children notice the different ways the various media changed because of the rain. Have the children examine the mural from time to time as it dries to see if it continues to change.

Observing and Assessing Child's Science Learning

● Can the child describe how rain changed the artwork on the mural?

Working with Water

Ice Colors

Many of the children have had colored lips from eating frozen ice treats. They will quickly recognize how ice can be used as a watercolor tool. It is also interesting to observe how the colors change as the paper dries.

Science Process Skill

Focused observing

Science Vocabulary

change
color
dry
feel
ice
melt
mix
see (observe)
touch
wet

Materials

food coloring

ice-cube trays

mittens, gloves, or washcloths to use to hold the ice (optional)

sponges or towels (for cleanup)

white construction paper or other absorbent paper

Science Content Standard

The children will use ice cubes in watercolor painting and observe how water can change shape when melting. (Physical Science—Properties of Matter)

Before the Activity

Try this activity once before doing it with the children so you have a sense of how strong the colors need to be to remain visible when dry. Using water colored with food coloring, fill and freeze ice-cube trays. Use a variety of colors. If possible, have the children help mix the food coloring into the water. Then pour the water into the ice-cube trays.

What to Do

1. Pop the ice cubes out onto a tray or large cake pan. Say to the children, "Let's pretend that instead of ice cubes, these are frozen crayons. What do you think will happen if we draw with them? What do you think our fingers will feel like? I wonder what kind of marks they will make."

2. Give each child two or three colored ice cubes. Let the children enjoy sliding the cubes around on the paper. Encourage the children to talk about what they see. Talk about how the hard ice is melting into water. Wonder aloud what is making that happen: "Is the water the same color as the ice cube? Do you notice the new colors that are appearing?" Consider giving the children paper towels or old mittens to use to hold the ice cubes if their fingers get too cold.

3. Talk with the children about how the ice feels and how it changes the way the paper feels. After the cubes melt or the children's hands get too cold, set the papers aside to dry.

Children's Books

The Snowy Day by Ezra Jack Keats is a classic story of a playful day in the snow and a snowball that becomes a wet spot in Peter's pocket.

Jan Brett's *The Three Bears* is the tale of Goldilocks moved to the Inuit land of snow and ice.

Keep It Simple

● Repeat this activity outside on a white bedsheet.

Add a Challenge

● Challenge the children to draw Ice Color equations: a blue ice cube plus a red ice cube equals a purple puddle.

Theme Connections
Colors
This activity provides a great way for children to explore and combine colors.

Seasons
Incorporate this activity into a theme on the Seasons. In winter, snow and ice are common. In summer, ice helps us cool down

Snack and Cooking
Use fruit juices to make edible ice cubes as a snack.

Dual Language Learners

Say the name of the color of each piece of ice the child handles, as well as the names of the colors the children create when they mix the initial colors together.

4. Talk with the children about how they think their papers will change as they dry. Ask, "What do you think will happen to the colors?"

5. When the papers are dry, talk with the children about what they see.

Observing and Assessing the Child's Science Learning

● Can the child describe what happens to ice when it gets warm?

● Can the child describe some of the differences between the wet and dry papers?

● Does the child notice that the colors are blending?

Connecting Science to the Curriculum

● **Taking It Outside**—Freeze colored water in cake pans, plastic tubs, and other containers. Unmold them when they are frozen solid and let the children build sculptures with them. Provide a spray bottle of water to help the children "glue" the shapes together. This is fun to do in winter if you live where the water will freeze outside. It is also fun to play with the frozen shapes to cool off when it is hot!

How Much Did It Rain?

Rain is a common and easy form of water for children to observe. Measuring the amount of rainfall during a storm provides children with an opportunity to observe rain even more closely.

Science Content Standards

As the children observe the rain they will discover that water can change shape based on the container holding it. (Physical Science—Properties of Matter)

The children will measure the rain. (Measuring—Nonstandard: Linear)

What to Do

1. On a day with a rainy forecast, take the children outside to place containers in open areas around the building.

2. After the rainfall ends, bring the children outside to look at the containers. Help the children measure the amount of rain in each container by placing the tongue depressor in the container and marking the depth with a marker or crayon.

3. As the children compare the containers, see whether they notice that the depth is about the same in all of the containers. You may also help them notice that the rainwater forms the same shape as the container it is in.

Science Process Skills

Focused observing

Organizing and communicating observations

Science Vocabulary

deep

deeper

depth

measure

rain

rainfall

shallow

shallower

weather

Materials

crayon or permanent marker

margarine tubs, coffee cans, or assorted containers

tongue depressors or craft sticks

Children's Books

Bringing the Rain to Kapiti Plain by Verna Aardema, *Listen to the Rain* by Bill Martin, and *Come on Rain* by Karen Hesser all celebrate the importance of rain through appealing stories and illustrations.

Keep It Simple

● After a rain, go outside and look for water. Big puddles are easy to find. Can the children find tiny ones, too?

Add a Challenge

● During a period of frequent rain, measure daily rainfall and make a graph to record the results. This activity gives the children the opportunity to talk about rain and storms—frightening experiences for some children. Encourage the children to share their experiences and feelings.

Theme Connections
Me and My World

This activity is a natural fit when the children are learning about and exploring their world.

Observing and Assessing the Child's Science Learning

● Can the child describe what she observed?

● Does the child notice that the water was the same depth in each container, regardless of its shape?

Connecting Science to the Curriculum

• **Mathematics**—In this activity, the children compare the depths of the water in various containers.

• This is one of many activities in this book (for example, see "How Far Can You Jump?" on page 92, and "Shade Tree Shadows," on page 216) that can be a part of a measurement investigation. What else is outside for the children to measure?

• **Taking It Outside**—In the winter after a snowstorm, take the children outside with rulers to stick in the snow to measure its depth. Bring some snow inside in containers of various shapes and sizes and invite the children to observe the snow as it melts.

Family Involvement

Encourage families to make their own rain gauges with recycled containers from home to reinforce this activity.

Using Museums and Other Community Assets

Listen to radio and television weather reports to learn if their rain measurements are similar to those the children found. Bring this information in to the class and talk with the children about the factors that might result in different findings.

Working with Water

Bobbers and Bottomers

This activity provides a new way to investigate the concepts of *sink* and *float*. This time, instead of placing all objects on the water surface and observing whether they sink or float, children hold objects down on the bottom of the water container and release them. The "bobbers" will float to the surface and the "bottomers" will stay on the bottom.

Science Process Skill

Observing to classify

Science Vocabulary

bobber
bob
bottom
float
heavy
light
sink

Materials

paper and markers to make signs

sponges (for cleanup)

variety of things that will sink or float—plastic counters, shells, a potato, an orange, a block, acorns, twigs, and so on

water table or large, flat container filled with water

Science Content Standards

The children will classify objects that float and sink in water and describe the pressure of the floaters on their hands. (Physical Science—Properties of Matter; Physical Science—Force and Motion)

Before the Activity

Make two signs, one saying *Bobbers* and the other saying *Bottomers*. Consider adding simple illustrations of an object on the surface of water and an object on the bottom to help clarify the two groups for the children.

What to Do

1. Show the children the collection of items you have gathered. Say, "We are going to be scientists and do a special test to sort all these things into groups."

2. Select a bobber and a bottomer, put them in the water, and hold one down with each hand. While the children are watching, release both objects. Ask, "What happened? This one bobbed to the top. We'll put it by the sign that says 'bobber.' We'll put the one that stays on the bottom by the 'bottomer' sign."

3. Ask one of the children to pick something to hold on the bottom of the tub. Ask, "Do you feel it pushing up against your hand or is it just sitting on the bottom? Do you think it will bob to the top or stay on the bottom? What is your hand telling you? Okay, move your hand away. What happens? Is it a bobber or bottomer?" Have the child place the object by the correct sign.

4. Depending on the size of your water container, two to four children can work at a time to create piles of bobbers and bottomers.

Children's Books

The Amazing Story of Lucky the Lobster Buoy by Karel Hayes tells of the adventures of one special bobber.

Keep It Simple

● Make a chart with one side for *Bobbers* and the other side for *Bottomers*. Have each child test a new object and place it or draw it on the correct side of the chart.

Add a Challenge

● Make a two-column graph of *Bobbers* and *Bottomers*. Ask the children which group has the largest number of objects.

5. Leave a collection of objects and the tub of water in the messy materials area. Encourage the children to continue to investigate which objects are bobbers and which are bottomers and to place them in their appropriate group.

Observing and Assessing the Child's Science Learning

● Does the child accurately place the objects in groups?

● While she is holding an object down, ask the child to predict whether the object is going to stay on the bottom or bob to the top. The child should come to associate the upward push from an object as a predictor of floating.

Connecting Science to the Curriculum

• **Mathematics**—In this activity, the children create two groups of objects; those that bob to the surface and those that stay underwater.

• **Taking It Outside**—This is a great activity to do outside, where splashes are of little concern. How many outdoor bobbers and bottomers can the children find? Can the children find more bobbers inside or outside?

• Place several magnets in the bottom of a small wading pool or tub. Tie a magnet to the end of a string on a fishing pole. Attach a small bobber to the string at a point that will allow it to be pulled under if the magnet on the string is attracted to the magnets on the bottom of the pool. Go fish!

Family Involvement

Invite children's family members who use bobbers for fishing to come for a visit and show their bobbers to the class and talk about how they use them to catch fish.

Science Process Skills

Focused observing

Observing to classify

Measuring—nonstandard:
 mass

Science Vocabulary

aboard

float

heavy

large

light

sink

small

Materials

materials of different weights
 that the children can place in
 the jars or containers, such
 as plastic or wooden spoons,
 rocks, fishing weights, corks,
 and metal washers

plastic containers with lids

small plastic jars with lids

water table or large, flat
 container filled with water

Children's Books

The Boat Alphabet Book by Jerry
Pallotta tells just about
everything about boats using
entertaining text and clear,
precise illustrations.

In a spin on the classic tale of
one too many, *Who Sank the
Boat?* by Pamela Allen gives us a
humorous take on sink and float.

Bring It Onboard

What happens when objects are added to a floating jar "boat"?
Children can compare the objects that sink their boats to objects
that can be floated by their boats.

Science Content Standard

The children will observe the effect of heavy objects on their play
boats as they classify objects that float or sink in water. (Physical
Science—Properties of Matter)

What to Do

1. Float a closed plastic jar on the water in front of children. Talk
 about floating. Ask, "Do you have toys that float in the bathtub?
 What happens when you push your frog down to the bottom? It
 pops right back up. Anna, try pushing the jar to the bottom. What
 happens when you let go of it? Up it pops! Let's pretend this is a
 boat. We're going to see what it can carry without sinking."

2. Remove the lid and place a large, heavy object in the jar. Say, "Let's
 see what happens when we bring this onboard our boat." The
 object should not be heavy enough to sink the jar, though it
 should make it noticeably lower in the water. Ask the children to
 talk about what they see.

3. Select a heavier object, one that will sink the jar. Repeat the
 process of placing the jar in the water. Talk about what happens:
 It was too heavy and sank the boat.

4. Allow the children to explore with several more objects and
 containers. Ask, "Which objects let the jar boat float and which
 sink the boat?" Have the children group the objects in these two
 categories. Discuss the size, weight, and other characteristics of
 the objects in the groups. Ask, "Which things make our jar
 boats sink?"

Keep It Simple

● Can the children find objects that will sink if placed in water by themselves but will float when placed in the jar?

Add a Challenge

● Do the activity using only sand or water as a weight. Add varying amounts to identical jars. How much does it take to sink the jar? Challenge the children to keep track of how many scoops of sand they put in the jars.

Children with Special Needs

Children with pervasive developmental disorders and autism spectrum disorders may feel comfortable standing near the water table for a minute or two, watching the teacher and the other children in action before participating.

Observing and Assessing the Child's Science Learning

● Does the child recognize that the heavier an object is, the more likely it is to sink the "boat"?

Connecting Science to the Curriculum

• **Water Table**—Make a collection of boats for the children to explore and provide materials for them to make their own boats. Teach the children "Rub-a-dub-dub, Three Men in a Tub" and "Row, Row, Row Your Boat."

Family Involvement

Ask the children's families to send clear plastic jars and plastic containers with lids so the children can engage in more experimentation.

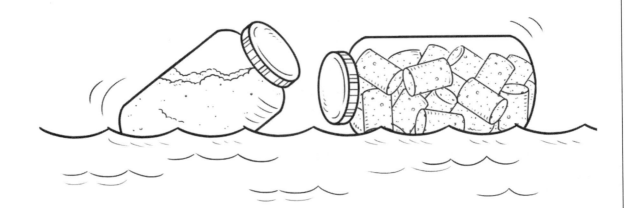

Freeze It

How many ways can you squish a balloon and how can you make it stay that way? This activity is a "cool" exploration of liquids turning into solids and then turning back into liquids again.

Science Content Standard

The children will freeze many balloons filled with water to observe that water can change shape when it is frozen to become a solid. (Physical Science—Properties of Matter)

What to Do

Safety Note: Ensure that no children have latex allergies before proceeding with this activity.

1. Help the children use funnels to fill balloons with water. (Be careful of the water pressure from the faucet, and don't make the balloons too full!) Tie the balloons closed. Let the children use yarn, string, rubber bands, pipe cleaners, and anything else they can think of to change the shapes of the balloons. Consider having the children do this portion of the activity over dishpans or trays to help contain any spills or leaks.

2. When each child finishes "sculpting" a balloon, label them with the child's names and place all the balloons in a freezer. Ask, "What do you think will happen to your balloon sculptures?" Write the children's ideas on a Discovery Chart.

3. When the water in the balloons freezes, take the balloons out of the freezer and return them to the children. Help the children remove the balloons and other materials to expose the piece of ice. Talk with the children about the fact that water, a liquid, is now ice, a solid. It now has a definite shape. Ask, "Will this water fit in a bottle now?"

4. Ask the children to draw their ice shapes in their Discovery Journals and label them. Provide help as needed. Ask, "What will happen to the ice when it warms in the air? Will it keep its shape?"

5. Place the children's sculptures in the dishpans so the children can watch and see what happens to the ice over time.

Science Process Skill

Focused observing

Organizing and communicating observations

Science Vocabulary

H_2O
liquid
shape
shape names
solid
volume
water

Materials

balloons (small)
freezer
funnels
pipe cleaners (wrap the sharp ends with tape)
pitchers
rubber bands
string
towels
trays or dishpans
water
yarn

Children's Books

Read *Angelina Ice Skates* by Katherine Holabird and Helen Craig, then clear some space for an indoor skating rink. Let the children skate in their socks. Can they spin like Angelina?

Keep It Simple

- Freeze juice into shapes to make juice pops. Does juice behave just like water?

Add a Challenge

- Mold pieces of wet fabric over various shaped objects, leaving the bottom portion of the fabric open. Freeze them and remove the object. Talk with the children about what makes the fabric stay in one shape. Can the children see the very thin ice that makes the fabric hold its shape? Observe how long the pieces of fabric keep their shapes before the ice melts. Ask, "Does it take more or less time for these fabric shapes to melt than it took for the balloon shapes to melt?"

Theme Connections
The Seasons

This activity works very well in a winter-based theme. If possible, freeze the shapes outdoors.

Shapes

Circles, triangles, and squares are regular shapes. The shapes the children make in "Freeze It" are irregular. Challenge the children to help you find a way to make regular ice shapes. Ask, "What could we use as molds?"

Children with Special Needs

Children with motor impairments may need assistance pouring water into funnels and tying the variety of materials around the balloons to form shapes.

Observing and Assessing the Child's Science Learning

- Does the child's journal entry reflect an understanding of the way liquids change shape?

- Can the child describe how water holds a definite shape when it is frozen, but does not when it is a liquid?

Connecting Science to the Curriculum

- **Taking It Outside**—If you live in an area where it gets cold enough to freeze water, it is fun to let Mother Nature do the freezing for you. You will have much more room and can make larger shapes. Consider attaching a collection of frozen shapes to string or yarn to construct an outdoor ice mobile.

Marble Catchers

How can you capture underwater marbles without capturing the water, too? This activity gives children a chance to experiment with how to make holes in cups so that the cups can catch the marbles and leave the water behind.

Science Content Standard

The children will observe that water can change shape as it pours through small holes; the children will observe that some objects float in water and some sink. (Physical Science—Properties of Matter)

Before the Activity

Safety Note: If you are concerned about the children using nails to make their own marble catchers, make a variety of them in advance and skip Step 2.

What to Do

1. Show the children a sieve and colander and ask them if they have ever seen someone use these objects. Children may mention seeing someone use them for draining macaroni for macaroni and cheese or some similar purpose. Talk about how the macaroni stays in and the water goes out. Ask the children what they think will happen if you pour water into the sieve or colander. The children may say things like, "They'll leak" or "Water will go out." Pour water through the sieve or colander to show the children what happens; the water changes shape and pours out through the holes, just like the children predicted.

2. Tell the children they are going to make marble catchers—the marbles will stay in and the water will go out, just like macaroni stays in a sieve. Set out several cups. Show the children how to turn the cups upside down and poke holes in the bottoms and sides of the cups with the nails to make their marble catchers. Have the children put on their safety goggles and carefully push a nail into the cup. Encourage the children to try different cups and different sizes of nails. Provide help as needed. **Safety Note:** Observe the children very closely as they use nails or any other sharp objects to poke holes in the cups. Be sure to collect all the nails immediately after the children finish using them.

Science Process Skill

Focused observing

Science Vocabulary

colander

drain

hole

poke

sieve

Materials

colander or pasta strainer

marbles (or bear counters, plastic cubes, or other small items)

nails in a variety of sizes

paper cups in a variety of sizes

safety goggles

sieve or strainer

sponges (for cleanup)

water table or large, flat container filled with water

Children's Books

Old MacDonald Had a Woodshop by Lisa Shulman shows the children another way to use nails, complete with sound effects.

Caldecott winner *Flotsam* by David Wiesner is a wordless book that illustrates the amazing surprises that can be hidden in water.

Keep It Simple

● Provide a collection of sieves, colanders, slotted spoons, as well as cups, spoons, and small plastic containers and jars. Have the children sort them into things they predict will hold water and things that won't. Have them test their predictions. Were they right?

Add a Challenge

● Have the children count the number of marbles they catch in each scoop. Make a chart for the children to record how many marbles they captured in their first, second, and third scoops.

Theme Connections
Colors

Put a variety of colored items in the water and challenge the children to sort them using their "color catchers."

Tools

Help the children make another tool—a skimmer—with pantyhose and a coat hanger. Twist the hanger into a diamond shape. Bend the hook closed to form a handle. Cover the hanger with pantyhose. Pull the hose toward the hook and wrap the hook, hose and all, in duct tape to form a handle. The children can use the new tool to skim things that float from the surface of the water.

Children with Special Needs

For children with autism spectrum disorder, this activity encourages active participation and interaction with other children in the class in a predictable way.

3. Place several marbles on the bottom of the water table. Show the children how to use the marble catchers to pick up the marbles from below the surface of the water. Hold up the cups to allow the water to drain through the holes, leaving only marbles in the cups. Talk with the children about the ways that the different cups drain water, and the effect the size and number of holes have on the process. Are there some cups the children think work better than others? Can the children make their own catchers work more effectively?

4. Give the children time to refine their marble catchers by adding more holes or using different nails. The children may want to make new catchers. (If you are in charge of making the catcher, follow the children's directions for making new ones or refining the ones they have.) Give the children ample time to explore. Do the marbles catchers need more holes on the bottom? Maybe they need a few on the sides. Can the children think of other things to capture with their catchers? Maybe some plastic toy bears could have a bath, or perhaps the frog counters can go for a swim.

Observing and Assessing the Child's Science Learning

● Does the child understand that making more holes or larger holes in her marble catcher causes the water to drain more quickly?

Connecting Science to the Curriculum

● **Mathematics**—In this activity, the children can count the number of marbles they catch in their cups.

Water to Ice to Water

Working with Water

Science Process Skills

Focused observing

Organizing and
communicating observations

Science Vocabulary

freeze

liquid

solid

thaw

Materials

collection of fun objects
("freezables") that will sink in
the cups of water and not
dissolve, such as crystals,
bright coins, colorful rocks,
and hard plastic spiders that
almost sink

small, clear plastic cups

Simple though it might be, this activity gives us a great way to see how well the children understand that ice and water really are the same substance. To make this scientific fact clear, the water freezes then thaws in the same container.

Science Content Standard

The children will be able to observe the same water melting and freezing. They will describe how water will change shape as it goes through the phases from liquid to solid. (Physical Science—Properties of Matter)

What to Do

1. Pour your collection of "freezables" out and give the children a chance to explore the assortment. Encourage the children to share what they know about ice and freezing things. Wonder aloud about what might happen if the children were to freeze these treasures in ice. Then let each child choose something to freeze.

2. Partially fill several plastic cups with water, making one per child.

3. Have the children drop their prizes into the bottoms of their cups. Collect all of the cups and put them in the freezer overnight.

4. The next morning, bring the cups out for the children to see. Talk with the children about their observations. Ask, "What has happened to the water? What has happened to their prizes? They're all frozen in ice!"

5. Show the children their treasures trapped in the ice. Ask the children how they are going to get their special treasure back. Do they have any ideas? They might talk about pouring hot water on

the ice. Some children might have seen a parent or family member put salt on an icy sidewalk to melt the ice. The children might suggest smashing the ice with a hammer. Tell the children, "This time, we are just going to wait and see how long it takes for our ice to melt by itself."

Close Observation

- **Show It**—Give the child her cup of ice and have her put the cup somewhere in the room: by the window, on a shelf, or in the water table. Ask the child to show you when she notices the ice changing.

- **Tell It**—Talk with the child about what will happen to the ice if she leaves the cup out. The child should mention that the ice will eventually turn back to water, releasing the treasures frozen in the ice. Encourage the child to give frequent reports about what is happening in her cup.

- **Draw It**—Encourage the child to draw pictures of what she thinks happens when her treasure is frozen in ice. Also consider drawing several cups on a sheet of paper for the child and having her draw in the cups what she sees happening when she periodically checks her cup as the ice melts.

- **Write It**—Have the child take her cup and put it in different places in the room, such as in the sunlight, under the desk, or on top of the heater. Encourage all the children to do the same. Have each child go around the room on a regular basis and see what is happening to everyone's cups of ice. Have each child draw and write about her observations in her Discovery Journal. Or, she can come back to you and report what is happening for you to record on a Discovery Chart.

Observing and Assessing the Child's Science Learning

- Choose from the above strategies to see how observant the child is, and to determine how well she can describe the process by which water turns to ice and ice turns to water.

Pass the Water

Expect a wet and messy time as the children explore all the shapes water can make. Whether the children work individually or in small groups, have towels and newspapers ready to clean up the inevitable spills and drips.

Science Process Skill

Focused observing

Organizing and
   communicating observations

Science Vocabulary

H_2O

liquid

shape

shape names

solid

volume

water

Materials

clear containers of various
   shapes and sizes, including
   cups, bottles, cartons, old
   vases, perfume bottles, and
   plastic bags

cups (1 per child)

food coloring

pitchers

towels

trays or dishpans

water (lightly tint the water
   with food coloring)

Children's Books

A Drop of Water by Walter Wick
is a collection of beautiful
photographs that show the many
shapes of water.

Science Content Standard

The children will observe and describe in journals how water can change shape by pouring it into various containers of different sizes and shapes. (Physical Science—Properties of Matter)

Before the Activity

Prepare pitchers of lightly colored water. The coloring will help the children see the water levels more clearly.

What to Do

1. Gather a small group of children around a table and show them your collection of containers. Say, "Just look at all this stuff. Gracie, your daddy brought us these yogurt cups. Lourdes, your family gave the baby food tubs. Instead of throwing them away we can use them to play 'Pass the Water.' Are you ready? Find a container you like. Look, the water is round like my jar. I'm going to pour the water into Max's tub. It's square! It's just like Max's tub. Now it's Max's turn. You pour the water into Lourdes' bottle. The water is round again. The water got tall and skinny when Mya poured it into the bottle that used to have sprinkles in it. I think there's enough left in your bottle to fill Jess' cup. Pass the water around the table until everyone has a turn."

2. Continue to make enthusiastic comments about the children's explorations, and encourage the children to make their own comments as well. Pass the water quickly enough to keep this activity challenging and fun, while respecting the children's differing abilities. Also, consider using a funnel to help children who may have trouble passing the water to another child's cup.

Working with Water

Keep It Simple

- Place the various containers in the water table for the children to continue to explore independently.

Add a Challenge

- Provide bulb basters, syringes, plastic tubing, and similar tools. Challenge the children to figure out a "really tricky way" to get water from one container to another.

Theme Connections
Opposites and Shapes

Use opposite and shape words as you talk with the children about their actions. Their containers are *empty* then *full*; some containers are *short*, while others are *tall*. The water goes *up* and *down*, *in* and *out*. Water can take the *shape* of a *cube* or a *cylinder*; and the water's *surface* can make a *circle* or a *square*.

3. Get out the Discovery Journals so the children can draw some of the shapes they make with their water. Encourage the children to write captions for their drawings as they choose, helping those children who are not yet able to write. Introduce the children to the chemical symbol for water, H_2O. The children might enjoy the novelty of being able to write a scientific symbol.

4. Keep the water and containers out in the messy materials area so the children can continue to explore the many shapes water can make.

Observing and Assessing the Child's Science Learning

- Does the child's journal entry reflect an understanding of the way liquids change shape?

- Can the child explain that water in liquid form takes the shape of whatever container it is in?

Connecting Science to the Curriculum

- **Mathematics**—In this activity, the children begin to explore conservation of volume as they pour the same quantity of water into a variety of containers.

- **Taking It Outside**—Repeat this exploration outside with larger containers, such as gallon jugs, 2-liter bottles, buckets, and tubs.

Through Thick and Thin

Objects move through liquids in different ways. This activity gives children the opportunity to explore the properties of a variety of liquids by observing how objects move in them.

Science Content Standards

The children will observe how other liquids compare to water. (Physical Science—Properties of Matter)

The children will observe how objects placed in the liquids move. (Physical Science—Force and Motion)

Before the Activity

Send home a note asking the children's families to send in clear bottles and jars with lids. Prepare two or three bottles with a liquid and a few objects each, and label them with the name of the liquid. To prepare the sugar syrup, mix equal amounts of water and sugar and boil the mixture until it thickens. This mixture will be very hot, so let it cool before pouring it into the container.

What to Do

1. Show the children the bottles you have prepared. As you invert the bottles, ask the children to describe the way the liquids move. Do some things move faster or slower than others?

2. Let each child choose a liquid, fill a container under adult supervision (using funnels if needed), and choose two or three items to place in the container. Have them drop the items into the liquids.

Children's Books

At Grandpa's Sugar Bush by Margaret Carney and Janet Wilson tells the story of a boy and his grandfather making maple syrup. It also captures the adventure of being in the woods with all its shy creatures in early spring.

From Maple Tree to Syrup by Melanie Mitchell uses clear, sharp photographs to share the syrup-making process.

Science Process Skill

Focused observing

Science Vocabulary

dense

density

descriptive words, such as *thicker, slowly, runny, watery,* and *quickly*

float

liquid

liquid names

sink

Materials

clear bottles and jars with tight lids, such as spice jars, beverage bottles, salad dressing bottles, and peanut butter jars

funnels

liquids, such as vinegar, carbonated water, honey, mineral oil, salad oil, motor oil, liquid detergent, corn syrup, and sugar syrup

small objects, such as beads, stones, sequins, marbles, paper clips, and metal and rubber washers

towels

water

Working with Water

Keep It Simple

● Fill clear plastic bottles of various sizes with half colored water and half cooking oil. Let the children enjoy rolling and shaking them to see how the liquids interact.

Add a Challenge

● Make a Discovery Chart with the children. Ask the children to come up with a rule about how objects move in different liquids. The children may say something like "It moves slow in thick things and fast in water." Encourage the children to think of as many ways as possible to describe differences in the liquids and in the objects as they move. Write down all of the children's observations.

Theme Connections
Snack and Cooking

Take the opportunity to expose the children to all the different kinds of liquids we eat and use in cooking. Compare smoothies and juice and water. What happens to milk when you make pudding? What happens to milk when you make ice cream? What happens to milk when you make muffins? Help the children make a simple oil-and-vinegar salad dressing to taste.

Children with Special Needs

For children with sensory integration issues, do this activity in a quiet place, where the children may interact with materials alone or with an adult.

3. Help the children put the lids on very tightly. Now, turn the bottles over and see what happens. Encourage the children to look at each other's bottles. Can they find one in which the objects move faster than their own and another in which the objects move slower? They may not be able to find both. Talk with the children about their observations and support them in talking with each other to make comparisons.

4. Repeat the activity, having the children select a different kind of liquid, but putting the same items in the liquid so the children can see how the same objects move through different liquids. Ask the children to describe the differences. For children having difficulty observing differences, put the container holding the first liquid beside the container holding the second liquid, turn them, and compare directly.

Observing and Assessing the Child's Science Learning

● Is the child able to describe the ways the objects move in different liquids?

Connecting Science to the Curriculum

• **Mathematics**—In this activity, the children compare the ways similar objects move through different liquids.

Working with Water

Water Movers

We can use all kinds of things to move water, but certain tools work best for specific tasks. An eyedropper moves water precisely. A cup moves a greater volume than an eyedropper. This activity allows the children to learn for themselves how to move water in a way that is best for the job.

Science Content Standards

The children will observe and describe the ways that various tools can be used to move water from one container to another. (Science as Inquiry; Science and Technology; Physical Science—Properties of Matter)

What to Do

1. Let the children experiment with the collection of water movers. Talk about all the different ways they work. Some scoop water while others suck it up. Some, like a funnel, make water into a narrow shape so it will pour into a bottle. Talk about the containers. Which containers hold a little water? Which containers hold a lot of water?

2. Talk with the children about the various water movers. Say, for example, "Ethan, which one would you use if you wanted to move a lot of water really fast? Megan, what do you think would be the best water mover to get water into this little, bitty bottle? Tyler, which would you pick to water our plant? Which one could we use to pour a glass of juice? Which one would work best to squirt a friend?"

3. Ask the children to predict which water mover is the best tool to move water from one container to another with the fewest spills. Have them try it to see if their prediction was correct. Challenge the children to count the number of scoops it requires to transfer all the water from one place to another.

Science Process Skill

Focused observing

Science Vocabulary

best
better
little
tool names
worst

Materials

basters
containers to hold water, such as plastic cups, tubs, and buckets
eyedroppers
other water-moving materials, such as buckets, jars, basters, hoses, funnels, and sponges
pieces of aquarium tubing
sponges and towels
spoons
straws
water table or a large, flat container filled with water

Children's Books

Frank Asch uses watercolors to create beautiful images of water in all its forms in his book *Water*.

The photographs in Barbara Kerley's *A Cool Drink of Water* show people enjoying water all around the world.

Working with Water

Keep It Simple

- With some children, consider beginning with just two or three water movers. Add more water movers as the children become more interested and proficient.

Add a Challenge

- Continue your explorations as the children clean up. Do the children like using towels or sponges better for cleaning up spilled water? Does everyone agree? Try using different kinds of mops for floor spills. Ask, "Why don't we usually use mops on table tops? How should we empty the water table?"

Theme Connections
Community Helpers

For a Community Helpers theme, build a structure outside, pretend it catches on fire, and put out the fire with a bucket brigade!

Children with Special Needs

Children with motor impairments may need assistance with some of the water-moving tools.

Observing and Assessing the Child's Science Learning

- Can the child describe how each tool moved the water?

- Does the child understand that water is a liquid and as a liquid will take the shape of its container?

Connecting Science to the Curriculum

- **Mathematics**—In this activity, the children count the number of times it takes a tool to transfer water from one container to another. The children also compare how much water the various containers can hold.

- **Taking It Outside**—Bring the collection of water movers outside. Add buckets, large tubs, and wagons to the collection. Challenge the children to move water to various outdoor locations. How many ways can the children find to fill the birdbath or water the flowers without using a hose?

Water Pressure Pushers

When one plunger goes down, the other goes up. Observing this sort of cause-and-effect relationship fascinates children. In exploring water pressure plungers, the children are exploring the principles of pressure in a closed system. Children observe how the exertion of pressure on one part of a system causes changes in another part of the system. Although the children may not fully realize why the phenomenon takes place, they will enjoy controlling and observing pneumatic pressure in action.

Science Content Standards

The children will observe and describe how water can change shape as it moves through the syringe and tubing system. (Science as Inquiry; Science and Technology; Physical Science—Properties of Matter)

What to Do

1. With the children, pour food coloring into the water in the water table. Draw colored water into a large syringe. Show the children how to make the syringe go up and down, and then give the children several syringes to explore. Can the children make their bodies go up and down slowly, just like the plungers in the syringe? If the children have not used syringes before, give them plenty of time to play with the syringes and become comfortable with how they work. Also, consider providing a target the children can use for squirting water to get that urge out of their systems.

2. Connect the dispensing ends of two syringes with a piece of plastic tubing. Show the children how, by pushing down on the plunger of the full syringe, the plunger of the empty syringe pushes up. Even more interesting is that when the plunger of the empty syringe is pulled up, it pulls the full syringe's plunger down.

Science Process Skill

Focused observing

Science Vocabulary

down
in
out
plunger
pressure
pull
push
syringe
up

Materials

clear plastic aquarium tubing that fits the ends of the syringes
food coloring
large plastic syringes (available as medicine dispensers at drugstores, livestock stores, or through science supply companies)
sponge or towels
water table or large, flat container filled with water

Children's Books

In *Curious George Cleans Up*, edited by the Houghton Mifflin Company, George spills some juice, which leads to cleanup with water, which leads to too much water. Before long, George needs a big pump to clean up his mess!

Keep It Simple

● Make targets for the children to squirt with the plungers. This provides an entertaining way to strengthen small hands.

Add a Challenge

● Can the children find other things to use to squirt at targets? Maybe a salad-dressing bottle from the recycle bin will work. What about a dish soap bottle? What can they do with a hand soap pump bottle?

Theme Connections
Opposites

This activity gives the children a great chance to observe and create a lot of up-and-down and in-and-out movement!

Summer Fun

On a warm summer day, take the syringes and other things that squirt outside for wet and messy play.

Dual Language Learners

For children for whom English is not their home language, model and supplement spoken directions with eye contact and gestures.

3. Place the materials in the water table for the children to explore. The children may need your guidance and some practice to learn how to move the syringes' plungers without pulling them out of the syringes. Expect some unexpected squirts!

Observing and Assessing the Child's Science Learning

● Can the child describe what will happen when one of the plungers is moved?

What Holds Water?

Cups, juice boxes, water bottles, and other such containers are a part of children's everyday world. Do the children know what makes a good container for liquids? Let's give it some thought!

Science Content Standards

The children will observe what happens to water when it is stored in various containers and will classify the containers as being able to hold water and not being able to hold water. (Physical Science— Properties of Matter; Science as Inquiry)

Before the Activity

Place several containers around the room.

What to Do

1. Talk with the children about what they know about water containers. For example, say, "What about water bottles? If we put water in an empty water bottle, would the water stay in or would it leak out? What about a paper bag? Let's try it. Look, it's holding the water. Wait . . . it's starting to leak. Wow! There is water everywhere! I guess a paper bag doesn't hold water for long!"

2. Ask the children to look around the room for various containers. The children can select those you set out earlier, as well as other containers they see. Have the children divide the containers into those they think will hold water and those they think will not.

Science Process Skills

Focused observing
Observing to classify

Science Vocabulary

container
hold
leak
liquid

Materials

containers of a variety of shapes, some that will hold liquids and some that will not, such as oatmeal and cereal boxes, plastic bags, paper bags, cans, bottles, cardboard boxes, sieves, nets, and jars

small pitchers or cups for pouring water

water

water table, tub, or dishpan

Children's Books

Kathleen Garry McCord provides illustrations for the humorous American folk song of the same name in *There's a Hole in My Bucket*. It will make a great sing-along as the inevitable leaks occur.

The photographs in Barbara Kerley's *A Cool Drink of Water* show us many ways people carry water.

Keep It Simple

- Provide a collection of containers that clearly will and will not hold water, such as various sizes of cups and sieves. After ample exploration time, ask the children to sort them into the two groups.

Add a Challenge

- Set out a timer for the children to see how long it takes for the containers to leak. Are there some containers that leak right away and others that never leak?

- Challenge the children to make a collection of things people use to carry water. The collection can include photographs as well as actual items. Invite families to email or send photographs of special water containers, such as a family baby cup or a favorite vase.

Theme Connections
Camping

Campers and hikers have all kinds of ingenious containers. Let the children try out canteens, collapsible cups and buckets, water bottles, thermos jugs, and nesting cooking sets.

Dual Language Learners

Model and demonstrate the use of single words or short phrases, gesturing in order to clarify the meaning of terms such as *hold* and *leak*.

3. Separate the children into pairs and ask each pair to test a pair of containers. The children can take turns holding the containers and pouring the water. Have them work in the water table to contain spills or leaks.

4. After testing each container, ask the children to separate them into two groups, those that were good at holding water, and those that were bad at holding water. Observe how the children separate the containers. Did they put any of the containers in the wrong categories? Why might the children have done so? Are there some containers that hold water at first and then leak? Talk with the children about their choices.

5. With the children, make a list of characteristics of a container that can hold a liquid. Ask the children to describe how a container that is good at holding liquids differs from one that is bad at holding liquids.

Observing and Assessing the Child's Science Learning

- Can the child show you some containers that hold water and some that do not?

- Can the child explain why certain containers do not hold water well? For example, the child might say that water soaks through paper bags.

Working with Water

Sink or Float: That Is the Question

Science Process Skills

Focused observing

Observing to classify

Organizing and communicating observations

Science Vocabulary

sink

float

predict

volume

Materials

assortment of fun and unusual sinking and floating objects—small toys, a cork fishing bobber, plastic worms or frogs, fruit (apples, grapes, bananas, coconuts), a bobblehead athlete figure, a pork chop squeak toy, and anything else you find that might be fun

assortment of interestingly shaped clear bottles (olive oil, mustard, ketchup, or any other differently shaped bottles)

several sheets of paper divided lengthwise with a wavy blue line representing water surface waves

Your children are coming to the end of a fascinating study that has allowed them to explore the properties of one of the most important substances in their young lives. With the information they now possess, the children will be able to better understand the unusual but predictable behaviors of water and be able to work with and manage this important resource.

Science Content Standards

The children will be using their knowledge of water to describe how:

- Water can change shape.

- When water is frozen it becomes a solid.

- Some objects float in water and some sink. (Physical Science—Properties of Matter; Science as Inquiry)

What to Do

Part 1

1. Gather a small group of children around you and talk about all the fun and excitement they have had exploring water and ice.

2. Say something like: "Let's think about all we have learned. Look at this big pitcher of water and all these funny-shaped bottles and glasses. Will water fit into all of these different shapes?" Hold up a familiar cup, perhaps one they use for snack. Say, "I know water will make this shape. We pour water into cups like this all the time, but I wonder about these other shapes."

3. Hold up the first bottle, turn it sideways, upside down. Looking thoughtful, ask, "Will water fit itself into this strange bottle?" If the children say yes, ask, "What makes you think so? It's a pretty

odd container." Continue to probe with questions until it is clear the children are aware that all containers, even oddly shaped containers, will hold water.

4. Invite the children to try putting water into all the different containers to be sure they are right. Can they find any containers to which the water cannot conform?

Part 2

1. Show the children the collection of unusual sinkers and floaters. Tell the children that you are wondering whether these interesting objects will float or sink. Ask, "Will you predict which ones will float and which ones will sink?" Write the children's predictions on a piece of chart paper. The children's predictions may or may not be accurate. What is more important is that when you ask the children how they can find out if they sink or float, the children want to go test them in water. This indicates that the children know a way to find an answer to your question.

2. Help the children bring the objects to the water table so they can test their predictions. Compare the results of each test to the children's predictions. Were the children correct? Provide two tubs into which the children can separate the objects based on whether they sink or float.

3. After the children complete their investigation, give each child a sheet of paper with a wavy line across the middle to indicate the water surface. Then ask the children to draw or place the floaters on the water line and the sinkers under the water. Do the children place the objects in the correct places on the paper?

Observing and Assessing the Child's Science Learning

- Does the child indicate that she understands that water will fill any shaped container?

- Does the child understand that some objects float on water and some do not?

- On the picture charts, does the child place the objects in the correct locations?

Light and Shadows

Chapter 7

Light and Shadows

Science Concepts

This chapter explores the following science concepts:

- Light comes from many things.
- You cannot touch light.
- Light travels through some materials and not others.

Introduction

The study of light is fascinating. While children will not completely understand the nature of light, especially what generates light, children will have an exciting time investigating many of its readily observable properties. What will the children discover about light as they engage in the activities in this chapter?

Getting Ready

Place the following materials, along with any other interesting objects, in the Discovery Center or other appropriate places in your classroom for the children to explore during Free Discovery:

- light sources that can be handled safely, such as flashlights of several types and sizes; battery-powered lanterns; lamps; a filmstrip projector; a pen light; a lava lamp; a halogen light; a fluorescent light; a wind-up, crank-operated flashlight; a high-intensity flashlight; an overhead projector; a strobe light; a camera flash; a neon light; a miner's helmet light; and chemical stick lights

    Note: Do not allow the children to have access to light sources that get hot. Also ensure that children do not shine lights into one another's eyes.

- colored transparent sheets of material, such as colored transparencies, term-paper covers, cellophane, and plastic wrap

- one or more clocks or timers

- an assortment of transparent materials, such as plastic (hard and soft), magnifiers, and glass; enough light passes through these materials that objects can be clearly seen

- an assortment of translucent materials, such as colored plastic, plastic milk jugs, cloth, thin plastic chips, paper, waxed paper, and plastic grocery bags; the light they permit to pass through is insufficient to allow objects to be clearly seen

- an assortment of opaque materials, such as wood blocks, ceramic or plastic tile, rubber, heavy paper and cardboard, metal, foil, and rocks; these materials allow no light to penetrate

Free Discovery

Before starting the first activity, create a class Discovery Chart of what the children already know about light and shadows. Talk with the children about where light comes from and what it is. Ask the children to name some sources of light that are familiar to them. Guide the discussion with questions such as: "What is the biggest light you can think of? What is the smallest? What do you know about shadows? Where have you seen them?" Probe to see whether the children have any questions about light and shadows that you can incorporate into the activities that will follow. Challenge the children to think of as many words as they can to describe light and shadows. Keep the chart posted in the room while doing the activities in this chapter, and from time to time ask the children what they would like to add to it.

Introduce the children to the materials that will be used in the light activities. If any materials require special care, talk about them with the children.

During Free Discovery, talk informally with the children about their explorations. Ask questions to assess what the children are doing and thinking about as they explore. While the children may need some guidance or suggestions when they first begin to explore these materials, it is important to let the children explore freely, not to overdirect their exploration.

Light and Shadows

Science Process Skill

Focused observing

Science Vocabulary

alike
different
predict
transparent

Materials

crayons or colored markers

flashlights (optional)

small cardboard box or boxes

small objects of different colors

tape

transparent plastic in 4 colors (from colored transparencies, term-paper covers, plastic wrap, or cellophane)

Children's Books

Little Blue and Little Yellow and *A Color of His Own*, both by Leo Leonni, are rich stories about how color may or may not reflect who we are. The books give the children something to think about.

Color Boxes

This activity provides an opportunity for children to observe the spectrum of colors that compose light. It does not require having a rainbow to see these colors; children can create their own box of colors with cardboard and a few colored transparencies.

Science Content Standard

The children will observe colors that occur when objects are placed under transparent color sheets. (Physical Science—Properties of Matter and Light)

Before the Activity

Make color boxes by cutting windows in each of the four sides of the box and covering the windows with four different colors of transparent plastic.

What to Do

1. Put the color boxes out for the children to play with and explore. The children can put their hands into the boxes to see what colors their hands appear to be as they observe them through the different windows. The children can place different-colored objects into the color boxes. Ask the children what colors the objects appear to be through each of the windows. Consider providing the children with flashlights so they can direct more light into the color boxes.

Keep It Simple

● Create a class Discovery Chart that lists a few of the objects the children observed. Create five columns, one for the actual color of the objects and one for each of the colors the objects appeared to be when observed through each of the colored windows.

Add a Challenge

● Give the children a new set of objects. This time, ask the children to draw or write in their Discovery Journals about the actual colors of individual objects before they go into the color boxes. Challenge the children to predict and record the colors that they expect the objects to be when viewed through the various windows. Following the activity, have the children record their actual results.

Theme Connections
Colors and Rainbows

This activity makes an interesting addition to an exploration of colors and how to make new ones.

Summer Fun

Help the children make their own sunglasses using colorful strips of transparent plastic.

Dual Language Learners

Name and label the colors of each transparent plastic sheet. Clearly state the color and name of each object that is placed in the box. Ask the children to say the names of the colors and objects in their home languages as they put the objects into the boxes. After the children name the colors and objects in their home languages, say the names of them in English.

Children with Special Needs

A child in a wheelchair will need accomodation. Be sure to place the box at a level that is wheelchair accessible.

2. Ask the children to record in their Discovery Journals the most unusual or favorite observation they made. Using drawings or words, the children can show the colors of their objects and what colors they appeared to be when they were in the boxes.

Observing and Assessing the Child's Science Learning

● Can the child describe the changes in appearance that occur after placing objects in a color box?

Light and Shadows

Sun Pictures

Direct sun will bleach most construction paper in a very short time, usually after a day or two depending on how long it is in bright sunlight. All you have to do is lay the pieces on a shelf near the window. Add a few opaque items and the children can observe how the power of sunlight makes sun pictures.

Science Process Skill

Focused observing

Science Vocabulary

bleach

change

color names

comparative words, such as *lighter* and *darker*

fade

rays

sunlight

Materials

several opaque items, such as blocks, child-safe scissors, paper clips, and puzzle pieces (flat objects work best)

squares of colored construction paper in various colors (be sure it is not fade resistant)

tape

Science Content Standard

The children will observe how light shining on an object can change the object's colors. (Physical Science—Properties of Matter and Light)

What to Do

1. Engage the children by saying something such as: "We know the sun gives us light and makes us warm. Did you know the sun can make pictures, too?"

2. Let each child select a color square and a few of the opaque items.

3. Take a sun tour of the classroom or of the building, giving the children several opportunities to find sunny spots where the sun can do its work.

4. Let the children tape their squares in the spots they choose and set the items on top of the paper.

5. After a few days, have the children collect their squares. Ask, "What happened? Did the sun make a picture? Did some colors change more than others? Look at all the different pictures the sun made!"

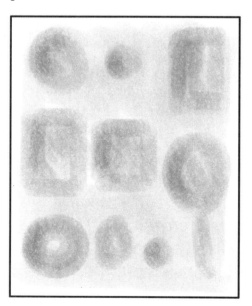

Children's Books

Black and White and *Who Are They?* by Tana Hoban may have babies as the target audience, but these books can inspire preschoolers to use their sun pictures to make their own simple image books.

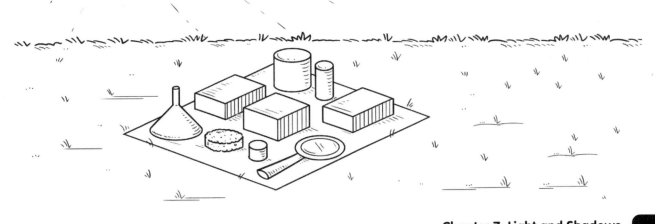

Keep It Simple

● The children can use developmental writing to label their pictures with the items they used. Assemble the pictures into a Sun Pictures class book.

Add a Challenge

● Challenge the children to find examples of the sun fading colors inside and out. Perhaps they can find some examples at home. You can list their finds on a chart or use a digital camera to take pictures that show the power of the sun to fade colors.

Theme Connections
Puzzles

Use the sun art pictures as simple puzzles. Can the children figure out what their friends used to make sun art?

Dual Language Learners

Repeatedly describe the changes that occur to the paper to reinforce the children's understanding of how the sun affects and ages objects.

Observing and Assessing the Child's Science Learning

● Can the child describe what happened to the piece of paper when left in the sun?

Connecting Science to the Curriculum

● **Taking It Outside**—Locate a piece of outdoor furniture or playground equipment that needs a new coat of paint. Bring the children outside and show the children the object, talking with them about how the object's color is fading. Apply a swipe of new paint of the same color and talk with the children about the differences they see. Explain that the paint fades because it is constantly exposed to the weather and the sun.

Family Involvement

Give each child a resealable bag of colored construction paper squares. Ask the children to explain what they did at school and to ask their parents and families to make sun pictures with them by placing the squares and objects in different windows around the home.

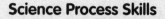

Light Collages

Light comes from many different sources. Just how many different kinds of light sources are there? Send the children on a hunt through the pages of old magazines and catalogs to see how many they can find.

Science Process Skills

Focused observing
Observing to classify

Science Vocabulary

bright
dim
electricity
light
names of light sources
power
source
switch

Materials

child-safe scissors
collection of pictures of light sources taken from magazines
glue sticks
posterboard

Science Content Standard

The children will use a set of posters and magazine pictures to classify light sources; the children will describe the many sources they find that emanate light. (Physical Science—Light and Energy)

Before the Activity

Draw shapes of a light bulb, a fire, and the sun on separate sheets of poster board.

What to Do

1. Explain to the children that they will be going on a light hunt. Challenge the children to locate pictures of light sources in the magazines and then use the scissors to cut them out. You might say, "Look for things such as fire, sun, flashlights, candles, headlights, lamps, and anything else you can find."

2. Once the children cut out some pictures, have them glue the images to the posters that most closely represent the light sources they have found.

3. As they work, talk with them about how the light sources work. For example, someone has to light a candle or a fire. Other lights use electricity and have a switch that turns them on.

Children's Books

Day Light, Night Light: Where Light Comes From by Franklyn M. Branley discusses many different sources of light, including flashlights, campfires, stars, and lanterns.

Keep It Simple

● Use a digital camera to take photos of all the light sources in and around your building. Give the children the images and help them assemble the images into an "Our Lights" book.

Add a Challenge

● Challenge the children to find a specific type of light source, such as natural light, electric light, light sources with a flame, and so on.

Theme Connections
Community Helpers

Talk with the children about how police, firefighters, and emergency medical personnel have flashing lights on their vehicles to let people know that help is on the way.

Homes

People around the world have a variety of light sources in their homes. How many different kinds of night lights do the children know about? Do any of the children have interesting lamps in their homes?

Toys

Many children's toys and games incorporate lights. Invite the children to bring in some lighted toys and games from home to share with each other.

Dual Language Learners

Say the names of each of the light sources as you describe them and show them to the children.

Observing and Assessing the Child's Science Learning

● Can the child accurately identify pictures of light sources?

● Can the child identify the source of the energy for each light?

Family Involvement

Ask the children's families to donate magazines that contain images of light sources.

A Lot, a Little, Not at All

Science Process Skills

Focused observing
Observing to classify

Science Vocabulary

opaque
translucent
transparent

Materials

cards with the words
transparent, translucent,
and *opaque* written on
them (optional)

common objects and
materials that are
transparent, translucent,
and opaque

flashlights and/or a sunny
window

Children's Books

All About Light by Lisa
Trumbauer uses clear color
photographs and a simple
text to explain some big ideas
about light.

The difference between *transparent* and *translucent* is a fairly subtle
distinction for young children to make; *transparent* and *opaque* are
much easier to grasp. Give the children plenty of opportunities to
test objects and ask questions to help them clarify their developing
understanding of these distinctions. After their explorations, help
the children develop group definitions of *transparent, translucent,*
and *opaque*—the kind of big words children this age love.

Science Content Standard

The children will observe light coming through a variety of objects
and classify the objects into three groups using a Discovery Chart.
(Physical Science—Properties of Matter and Light)

What to Do

1. Put the collection of materials out for the children to explore. Say,
   "We have been spending time investigating with light. All these
   things I collected will help us find out some more about light. Can
   you find something you can see through? Rosita found a clear
   plastic bottle. I can see your hand right through it. See if the light
   shines through it. It does! If you can see right through something,
   we call it *transparent*. Do you see anything else that's transparent?
   We're going to put all the *transparent* things we find right here."

2. Ask the children if any of them can find something they cannot
   see through at all. For instance, say, "Look, Suneel found a block
   and Josh found some
   cardboard. What
   happens when you
   test them with the
   light? Does it shine
   through? We call things light
   can't go through *opaque*. Let's
   put the *opaque* things here."

Keep It Simple

● Let the children hold a flashlight against their open hands to determine whether their hands are *transparent*, *translucent*, or *opaque*.

Add a Challenge

● The children can create a chart in their Discovery Journals to record their findings by placing each object tested under the headings *transparent*, *translucent*, or *opaque*.

Dual Language Learners

Involve the children's families and community members as classroom volunteers to work with dual language children using both English and their home languages. This may require some guidance and/or training.

3. Test all the objects and sort them into piles. Eventually a child will pick up a translucent item, such as a thin plastic grocery bag or a piece of plastic cut from a milk jug, and not be sure where to place it. Wonder aloud: "Here is a tricky one. Why don't you hold it up to the light? You can kind of see through it so it isn't opaque. You can't see through it completely like you did with the clear bottle. We call this *translucent*. It means you can see through it a little."

4. Encourage the children to continue to investigate the materials and search the room for more. Have them use the light to help them sort the objects into groups based on whether they are *transparent*, *translucent*, or *opaque*.

5. Create a three-column Discovery Chart listing all of the things the children investigated and sorted into the categories *transparent*, *translucent*, or *opaque*.

Observing and Assessing the Child's Science Learning

● Can the child group items as *transparent*, *translucent*, or *opaque* with or without using the correct terms?

Connecting Science to the Curriculum

● **Taking it Outside**—Bring the children outside with the flashlights. Can the children find things for light to go over, under, around, and through?

Shadow Dancing

Using a shadow on a sheet to observe a person's motion makes this activity fun and playful. This is the children's chance to play—and an opportunity for them to use some descriptive words about light and motion.

Science Content Standards

The child will observe how light not passing through objects casts shadows that can be studied. (Science as Inquiry; Physical Science—Properties of Matter and Light)

Before the Activity

Tie a length of rope across the room, and hang a white sheet over it so that the sheet reaches the floor. Set a lamp on one side of the sheet.

What to Do

1. Put on some music and tell the children: "It's time to shadow dance!" Let the children take turns going behind the sheet and moving while other children watch. Some children will be comfortable dancing individually while others may prefer to dance in pairs.

2. As the children move behind the sheet, bring to their attention the location of the light. Say to them, "For you to make (cast) a shadow, you must be between the light and where the shadow will be. Remember that and you will know where to look for your shadow anywhere."

3. Can the children in the audience describe the movements they see? For example, Kayli might hop up and down. Mason might do a wiggle dance. Can the audience move just like the shadows?

4. Now really look at the shadow. Can the children see the dancer's nose or eyes? Why? What if the dancer faces another way? A shadow is a place where no light from the light source reaches, so it is darker. It is a two dimensional copy of a three dimensional object, the child. It only shows the outline of our bodies.

Science Process Skill

Focused observing
Organizing and
    communicating observations

Science Vocabulary

between
cast
directional terms, such as *up, down, right,* and *left*
light source
move
movement
shadow

Materials

lamp
length of rope
music source
white sheet

Children's Books

Rabbit loves dancing with his shadow in Ann Tompert's *Nothing Sticks Like a Shadow.* When Woodchuck bets Rabbit that he cannot get away from his shadow, the adventures begin.

Keep It Simple

● Show the children how to make some simple hand-shadow animals. See if the children can identify the animals.

Add a Challenge

● Show the children how to make simple shadow puppets with cardboard cutouts. Challenge the children to create puppets and act out a favorite book, nursery rhyme, or story.

Theme Connections
Dancing

Explore the many ways people dance. Bring in all kinds of music for the children to listen to and create their own dances. Teach the children some simple dances as a way to develop motor memory. Many children's recordings have related dances the children can learn.

Children with Special Needs

Have children with visual impairments sit close to the sheet to help them distinguish the various shadow movements.

Observing and Assessing the Child's Science Learning

● Can the child observe the movement of another child's silhouette behind the screen and describe or imitate the way that child's silhouette is moving?

● Can the child make a simple drawing of the positions of the light, child, and shadow?

Discovery Center

Light and Shadows

Standing in the Way of Light

When we stand in a beam of light, we stop the light from passing through us. If light is absent, so are shadows—the two go together. In this activity, children explore the relationship between an object and the shadow it produces as it blocks light from passing through.

Science Content Standards

The children can observe how light from a very bright source does not pass through some objects, creating shadows; the child will observe how light not passing through objects casts shadows that can be studied. (Science as Inquiry; Physical Science—Properties of Matter and Light)

What to Do

1. Darken the room and shine a bright light on a wall at about the children's height. Ask a child to stand in front of the light so that a shadow is cast on the wall.

2. What do the children think will happen to the shadow if the light were turned off or if the child moved out of the light? Try it. Were they right?

3. Now have the child stand still while you move the light. What happens to the shadow when the light is moved? Show the children the pattern: light, object, shadow. It can work no other way.

4. Allow the children to experiment with holding a variety of objects—including their hands—between the light source and the wall. Talk with the children about what they see.

5. Hold a piece of cardboard between the children and the objects casting the shadows so the children cannot see the objects. Hold up an object so that it casts a shadow but is not visible to the children. Ask the children, "Can you guess what this is from its shadow?"

Science Process Skill

Focused observing

Organizing and communicating observations

Science Vocabulary

between

bright

dark

far

light

near

shadow

Materials

bright light source, such as a lantern, flashlight, or a projector

piece of cardboard

variety of objects for casting shadows

Children's Books

Bright Lights, Shadowy Shapes by Jennifer Waters and *What Makes a Shadow?* by Clyde Robert Bulla provide lots of fun and useful information about shadows and making shadow pictures.

Keep It Simple

● Provide cardboard cutouts shaped like animals or people to encourage shadow puppet play.

Add a Challenge

● In their Discovery Journals, have the children draw the relative positions of the light source, object, and shadow. Have them draw or write something about the shadows they made.

Theme Connections
Reduce, Reuse, Recycle

Provide reusable materials for the children to use when they make shadows.

6. Create a class Discovery Chart with two columns. In the first column, list what the children think each object is; in the second, write the actual object.

7. Keep the equipment available so the children can play "guess the shadow" with each other.

Observing and Assessing the Child's Science Learning

● Can the child draw pictures or describe the elements necessary to produce a shadow?

● Can the child identify shadows produced from simple shapes?

To See or Not to See

Light and Shadows

Science Process Skills

Focused observing
Observing to classify

Science Vocabulary

dark
light
opaque
shadow
shine
translucent
transparent

Materials

flashlights
large lantern flashlight or
  overhead projector
large selection of objects,
  some transparent (clear
  plastic cups, beads, counters,
  or water bottles) and some
  opaque (washers, blocks, or
  silverware)

By exploring enough transparent and opaque objects, children can learn to predict which objects light will pass through clearly and which objects will make shadows.

Science Content Standard

This assessment activity looks at the children's ability to describe, through example, how light travels through some materials and not others. (Physical Science—Properties of Matter and Light)

What to Do

1. Darken the room and tell the children they are going to find out if light from the flashlight (or overhead projector) travels through any of the materials you have collected.

2. Show the children how to hold an object in front of the light and see what happens. Ask, "Does it make a shape on the wall because it blocks the light or does the light shine right through it?" Show the children how to hold the materials so the opaque objects make a clearly defined shadow on the wall. The transparent object will make little or no shadow when held the same way.

3. Give a small group of children a collection of objects. Have each group use the light source to test whether objects create shadows or light passes through them. Ask the children to separate the objects into two piles based on their findings.

Close Observation

• **Show It**—Give the child a flashlight and a new set of materials. Ask the child to show you which objects the light does and does not pass through.

• **Tell It**—Ask the child to describe what he sees happening when the light from the flashlight shines on the objects. Ask the child to describe what would happen if he held the object in the sun. Ask, "Would the light go through that object?" Try it.

• **Draw It**—Ask the child to draw what he observed. The child might make one page for objects that make clear shadows and another for objects that do not make clear shadows. The child may be able to draw beams of light, the object blocking it, and the shadow that appears on the wall.

• **Write It**—Have the child write or dictate to you a list of the objects that make shadows and objects that do not. The child might also make drawings of the objects and provide his own labels.

Observing and Assessing the Child's Science Learning

● Choose from the above strategies to determine if the child can classify objects into groups based on whether or not the objects allow light to pass through them.

Star Chamber

The Star Chamber, your own classroom planetarium, provides children with a new and exciting way to explore light and darkness. To see how a small light changes darkness is a revelation for children. The glow-in-the-dark stars provide another element of light to explore.

Science Content Standards

Using this specially constructed Star Chamber, the children will discover that light comes from many things. (Science and Technology)

The children will observe how this chamber tries to represent the night sky. (Earth and Space Science—Objects in the Sky)

Before the Activity

Cut a door in the box so the children can comfortably enter it. (**Safety Note:** Adult-only step.)

What to Do

1. Prepare the Star Chamber with assistance from the children. Since some young children have a fear of darkness, it is a good idea to involve the children in every step of the process. The children can paint the outside of the box and decorate it with creations that depict the night sky. Cover the interior of the box with black construction paper (optional), and then decorate the interior with the luminescent stick-on stars. The children can place the stars randomly or try to form constellations. Leave the box's door open for a while or place a light inside the box to "charge" the stars.

Science Process Skill

Focused observing

Science Vocabulary

glow
light
night planetarium
sky
star

Materials

black construction paper (optional)

crayons (for a Discovery Book)

flashlight

large box, such as a refrigerator packing box, for the children to play in

box cutter (adult-use only)

luminescent (glow-in-the-dark) stick-on stars

masking or duct tape to cover box seams

paper (optionally cut into large stars)

Children's Books

Night in the Country by Cynthia Rylant and *Forest Bright, Forest Night* by Jennifer Ward invite children into a quiet, peaceful world at night.

In Monica Wellington's *Night City*, children learn about the bustling city life that goes on while they sleep.

Keep It Simple

- Talk about real stars and other things that children see at night.

Add a Challenge

- Have the children individually or with a partner make a book about things that happen at night. They may also want to learn about nocturnal animals.

Theme Connections
Space, Sun, Moon, and Stars

The Star Chamber provides a way for the children to think about stars during the day. Sing "Twinkle, Twinkle, Little Star" and "Star Light, Star Bright," just two of the many songs, poems, and books about stars. Are there other places in the room where the children might enjoy luminescent stars?

Children with Special Needs

For children with autism spectrum disorder, go into the chamber with them to ease the children into this activity, as it might be scary for them initially. This strategy is appropriate for any other children that may have a fear of darkness.

2. Select a few children at a time go into the Star Chamber with the flashlight. Ask the children to observe the stars and tell you what they see. Tell them not to use the flashlight until they find out how well they can see without any light. Let the children decide whether or not to leave the door open.

3. Now have the children turn on the flashlight. They will discover that they can see better. Say, "We can see better with more light." They will see the stick-on stars as well. Ask, "What happens to the stars when you turn off the flashlight?" Talk with the children about what they see inside the Star Chamber.

Observing and Assessing the Child's Science Learning

- Does the child understand that he sees better when there is more light?

Light and Shadows

Pajama Party

Bringing nighttime activities into the daylight hours is a novel way to explore how light affects what people do. Children love wearing pajamas at school, and it can be pretty comfy for teachers, too.

Science Process Skills

Focused observing
Observing to classify

Science Vocabulary

dark
day
light
night
pajamas
sky

Materials

blankets
large sheet of newsprint and markers (for Discovery Chart)
pajamas
paper and crayons (for Discovery Book)
sleeping materials
teddy bears and dolls

Children's Books

Good Night, Gorilla by Peggy Rathmann chronicles the nighttime tasks of a zookeeper and the mischievous gorilla that follows him on his rounds *and* to bed. *Goodnight Moon* by Margaret Wise Brown is a classic story of a bunny's soothing bedtime routine.

Where the Wild Things Are by Maurice Sendak is a goodnight story for the more adventurous.

Science Content Standards

The children will use play time to explore the difference between day and night; the children will explore objects in the night sky. (Earth and Space Science—Objects in the Sky)

The children will explore how light changes day to night. (Physical Science—Light)

Before the Activity

Several days before this activity, inform the children's families that the children will be having a pajama party to share what they do at night. Ask the families to have their children wear pajamas and bring in sleeping materials, such as blankets and teddy bears. Encourage families to set the stage for the pajama party by drawing their child's attention to the appearance of the sky at various times of the day and night. Before their children's bedtime, parents can take them outside for a few nights to look at the night sky. Suggest that they watch the setting sun and point out the moon and stars. Early risers can enjoy the rising sun. You might have some family members who can show children a planet—Saturn, Mars, Jupiter, and Venus are the ones easy to see. Point out to the families that stars twinkle and planets do not.

What to Do

1. Designate a special day at school as "Pajama Party Day." On this day, the children and the teachers wear their pajamas and bring their blankets and favorite sleeping pals (teddy bears, dolls, blankets) to school.

2. Throughout the day, have several discussions about special things the children do at night, such as hear a story, go to bed, and sleep. Have the children compare the ways they get ready for bed and what they wear to bed.

Keep It Simple

● Make a Discovery Book using the children's drawings of different things they do during the day and the night. Help the children make captions beside their drawings.

Add a Challenge

● Have children either individually or as a group dictate a story of an imaginary nighttime adventure. Make the story into a book the children can illustrate. They might even want to act it out.

3. Try to do all the favorite night things the children suggest. Discuss special characteristics of the night—such as the appearance of the sky, stars, moon, and darkness. Compare them to what we see during the day.

4. End the day by making a Discovery Chart with the children. Draw a line down the center of the board. On one side, write "At nighttime we usually...," and on the other side, write "At daytime we usually...," and copy down all the ways the children complete these statements.

Observing and Assessing the Child's Science Learning

● Can the child name or describe at least one characteristic of the night sky?

● Can the child describe some things people do during the day and at night?

Connecting Science to the Curriculum

• **Mathematics**—Explore clocks. Talk with the children about what time they go to bed. Ask, "Is everyone's bedtime the same? What time do we get up?"

Light and Shadows

Science Process Skill

Focused observing

Science Vocabulary

dark

light

light sources names

Materials

candle

chemical light stick

crayons

empty paper towel tubes

flashlight

glue sticks

lamp

large sheet of newsprint and markers (for a Discovery Chart)

scrap pieces of paper

Children's Books

In *The Very Lonely Firefly* by Eric Carle, a lonely firefly searching for a friend finds many other lights, including a candle, a flashlight, headlights, and fireworks before he finally finds some firefly friends.

Light Finders

It's a light extravaganza! Children will have a great time exploring some light sources that are very different from one another.

Science Content Standards

The children will observe light from many sources that are brought into the classroom. (Science as Inquiry)

The children will observe that the light coming from the source must hit an object in order for them to see it, and that putting something in front of the light source blocks the light. (Physical Science—Light)

Before the Activity

Set up a table or other area with the light sources you have collected.

What to Do

1. Create Light Finders with the children using cardboard tubes. The children can decorate the tubes using paper, scrap material, and crayons. (**Note:** Do not use water-based markers because the ink will come off on their faces and hands when they use the Light Finders.) Tell the children not to cover the ends of the tubes. They need to be able to see through them to find light.

2. As they work, ask the children, "How do you think light helps you?" The children might say that light helps them see things in the dark. Ask if any of the children have a nightlight. What about a flashlight? Talk about the things that make light outside. "During the day, the sun makes light. What makes light at night?" Talk with the children about the moon and stars. Ask, "Has anyone seen fireflies?" Being afraid of the dark is a big issue with some children. Exploring with an adventurous spirit may encourage some children to view darkness in a friendlier way.

3. Darken the room. Cover doors, pull shades or drapes over windows, and turn off the lights. Ask, "Where does our light come from? Use your Light Finders to look around the room to see if you can find some places where there is light." (For example, the children may see light coming in around the door.) "When

Keep It Simple

● Discuss the various light sources that the children see on the way to and from school, such as traffic lights, headlights, signs, and streetlights. Make a Discovery Chart as the children share their knowledge of the many light sources they know. What light sources do the children's families use at home? Add these light sources to the Discovery Chart.

Add a Challenge

● Give the children a flashlight. Challenge them to find different ways to hide it and the light it makes so their friends cannot find it with their Light Finders.

Theme Connections
Camping

Talk with the children about how campers use many sources of light at night: lanterns, flashlights, and campfires. They also see fireflies often.

Space

Investigate the sun, moon, and stars as sources of light in space that are visible to children.

you see something that is giving light, tell me so I can look at it, too." Some of the children may spot light coming in at the edge of a window shade. Ask, "Where do you think that light is coming from?"

4. Turn on the flashlight and move the beam around the room. Say, "The light from this flashlight helps us see better in the room. Can you find where I point it? What happens when I cover it with my hand?" Repeat this process as you light the lamp, the candle, the light stick, and the room lights. Help the children focus on the light source each time. If you like, count the number of different light sources with the children. Encourage the children to talk about how each light changes the way the room looks.

Observing and Assessing the Child's Science Learning

● Can the child describe how light changes the room?

● Can the child indicate the sources of light in the room?

Connecting Science to the Curriculum

• **Mathematics**—In this activity, the children count the various light sources.

Family Involvement

Invite the children's families to lend the children flashlights and other light sources for this activity.

Encourage families to explore the phases of the moon with their children by having them look at the moon twice a week. Then suggest that the families make drawings of the moon for their children to share with the class.

Light and Shadows

Science Process Skills

Focused observing

Observing to classify

Organizing and
communicating observations

Science Vocabulary

shadows

sundial

sunlight

Materials

blocks

class Discovery Book

handful of stones

pencils or markers

Children's Books

The Sun Is My Favorite Star by
Frank Asch follows a young child
through a day with the sun,
combining playfulness with
factual information.

Sun Up, Sun Down by Gail
Gibbons uses simple text and
clear illustrations to tell young
children all about the sun.

Rocks Around the Clock

People have been using sundials to tell time for centuries. This
activity gives children the opportunity to build a simple sundial and
use rocks to mark the passing of time.

Science Content Standard

The children will use rocks to construct a simple sundial that they
can use to observe time passing as the shadows move. (Science and
Technology)

What to Do

1. On a clear, sunny morning, when the children all arrive in the
   classroom, ask them to gather several large wooden blocks and a
   handful of rocks and then follow you outside.

2. Talk with the children about outdoor light. Ask the children
   where light comes from outside.

3. Ask the children to find a sunny area away from anything that
   might shade it later in the day, such as trees, buildings, or
   playground equipment.

4. With the children, stack the blocks one on top of the other,
   building a tower that is tall enough to cast an observable shadow.
   Explain to the children how this tower can function as a sundial
   that will indicate the passage of time. Point out to the children the
   current time of day, the location of the sun in the sky, and the
   position of the tower's shadow on the ground.

5. Have one of the children place a stone at the very top of the
   shadow the sundial is making. Ask the children to make drawings
   of the sundial, and then bring everyone inside. Once inside,
   gather the children around a clock with a dial face. Show the
   children the hour hand on the clock as an introduction to a
   discussion of time. Write the time in the Discovery Book. Tell
   the children this identifies the time when we made our first
   sundial drawings.

Keep It Simple

● Trace the shadow of a plant or other item of manageable size. Trace it again later in the day. Ask the children what they notice about how it has changed.

Add a Challenge

● If the space is available, challenge your children to design and build a more permanent sundial.

Theme Connections
Time and the Seasons

This activity works well in lessons that relate to time and the seasons.

Dual Language Learners

Each time the children observe the time of day, repeat that time to children whose home languages are not English. Ask the children to name the numbers in their home languages and then again in English.

6. At regular intervals throughout the day, bring the children back out to the sundial, each time asking a different child to add a new stone at the top of the shadow. Give all the children enough time to make new drawings of the tower, its shadow, and the stones. Talk with the children about their observations. What do they see the shadow doing? What do they notice about where the stones are relative to the shadow? Record the clock time as well.

7. The following morning, at the same time the children made their first visit to the sundial, bring all the children back out to the sundial and talk with the children about what they see. Ask, "Is the dial's shadow back where it was yesterday?" Repeat these trips outside to verify that the sun is following the same schedule as it did yesterday.

Observing and Assessing the Child's Science Learning

● Does the child understand that the shadow is moving over the course of the day?

● Can the child draw a picture showing how to create a sundial?

Science Process Skills

Focused observing
Observing to classify

Science Vocabulary

branches
graph
leaves
line
measure
shade
shadow
size
tree names
width

Materials

glue sticks
posterboard
tree leaves

Children's Books

Animals make shadows, too, as the children will discover in *Whose Shadow Is This: A Look at Animal Shapes* by Claire Berge.

Footprints and Shadows by Anne Wescott Dodd explores the beauty of nature and the seasons through extraordinary watercolors.

Shade Tree Shadows

All trees cast shadows that create shade on a sunny day. However, some trees make larger shadows and provide greater shade than others. Children can have outdoor fun as they try to locate the trees that are the best shade makers. If there are no trees nearby, look for other shade makers.

Science Content Standards

The children will use their knowledge of shadows to classify structures, such as trees or porches, as useful shade producers. (Science as Inquiry; Earth Sciences—Changes in the Earth and Sky)

What to Do

1. Locate a tree that casts a large shadow, and ask the children to form a line across the widest part of the shadow.

2. Record the number of children who can stand in a line across the width of the shadow.

3. Ask, "What makes this tree a good shade tree?" Observations might include size, direction of branch growth, and number of leaves.

4. Let the children measure a few other tree shadows in the same way.

5. Ask the children to collect one leaf each from the trees they think provide the best shade.

6. Bring the children back inside, write the names of each tree type on a sheet of poster board, and help the children use glue sticks to attach their leaves to the poster board, creating a graph that shows which trees are the most popular shade makers.

Keep It Simple

● Measure the tree shadows at another time of day. What do you discover? Substitute playground structures for trees.

Add a Challenge

● Challenge the children to use a meterstick or a yardstick to measure different kinds of shadows. The climber shadow might be five metersticks, and the trash can shadow might be half a meterstick.

Theme Connections
Seasons

Incorporate this activity into a discussion of the seasons. Children will appreciate how helpful a tree's shade can be on a hot summer day.

Dual Language Learners

Label and name each tree in both English and in the child's home language.

Observing and Assessing the Child's Science Learning

● Can the child identify which tree (or structure) provides the most shade or the best shadow?

Connecting Science to the Curriculum

• **Mathematics**—In this activity, the children count the number of children it takes to measure the shadow, as well as graph the shadow measurements.

Our Light and Shadows Book

Light and Shadows

Science Process Skills

Focused observing

Observing to classify

Organizing and
   communicating observations

Science Vocabulary

bright

dark

light

opaque

shadow

translucent

transparent

Materials

crayons, markers, and pencils

materials to write and
   illustrate a book

paper

All the activities in this chapter give children the opportunity to explore various aspects of light and shadow. Now it is time to put it all together—literally! In this activity, the children work together to create their own class book about light and shadows.

Science Content Standard

The children will be assessed on their understanding of the following concepts:

● Light comes from many things.

● You cannot touch light.

● Light travels through some materials and not others. (Physical Science—Properties of Matter and Light)

What to Do

1. With the children, discuss the ways people use and make light and shadows. Look at the charts, Discovery Books, and Discovery Journals the children made during all of the previous activities, as well as any other books or materials they might have used. Encourage the children to recall all the different things they have done with light and shadows.

2. Set out crayons, markers, pencils, and paper. Ask the children to write or make a drawing of some particular memory they have from learning about light and shadows. Help the children add captions or descriptions to each illustration.

3. When all of the children complete their pages, as a group decide on a title for the book. Write the title on a cover. Use staples or other fasteners to make the pages into a book and place it in the classroom book area.

Observing and Assessing the Child's Science Learning

- Use the book of the children's light and shadow memories as a discussion guide. Each child should be able to relate one or more of the activity's concepts to the captions and illustrations in the class book.

- Can each child describe the light and shadow activities that prompted his contributions to the book?

Chapter 8

Getting to Know Our World

Getting to Know
Our World

Introduction

The environment is possibly the single most important science topic we introduce to children. All of our scientific knowledge is of little value if we cannot protect and maintain the environment in which we all live. This chapter explores children's immediate environment, helping children see how interesting their world is, no matter where they live. There are clouds, birds, living things growing and changing, and exciting weather changes everywhere.

Everything around us is part of our environment. This includes the natural world and everything that people manufacture and build. Creating in children a desire to nurture and care for the Earth begins with helping children develop an appreciation for their immediate environments. Young children need to experience pleasure and excitement in outdoor play and discovery, in simple explorations with plants and animals, and in learning about the sun and wind. Young children do not yet need to learn about legitimate environmental concerns, such as pollution, the damaged rainforest, and endangered wildlife. Give children joyful experiences with nature now, and they will care enough to learn to be good stewards when they are older.

Getting Ready

Place the following materials, along with any other interesting objects, in the Discovery Center or other appropriate places in your classroom for the children to explore during Free Discovery:

- collection of natural objects, such as soil samples, clean sand, sticks, twigs, rocks, and other materials native to your environment

- collection of manufactured objects, such as small plastic bags, pencils, plastic straws, plastic insects, pieces of concrete, bricks, and artificial flowers

- tools to enhance the children's observations, such as magnifiers, magnets, picture identification books, containers for sorting objects, funnels, rulers, thermometers, microscopes, forceps, and eyedroppers

Free Discovery

Before starting the first activity, create a class Discovery Chart of what the children already know about their environment. Ask, "What living things are nearby? Have you ever seen ants in the pavement cracks? Are there any plants around? What is the biggest plant you know about? A tree? Do you have plants where you live? Are there squirrels or lizards or bees anywhere? What do you know about our weather?" Encourage the children to think of as many things as they can that are found in their environment. As the children share their ideas, consider ways to incorporate their questions about the environment into the activities that will follow.

Post the Discovery Chart in the room, and leave it up while doing the activities in this chapter. From time to time, ask the children if they would like to add to the Discovery Chart or if they would like to change any of the information it contains.

Allow the children ample opportunity to investigate the new materials in the classroom. While the children may need some guidance or suggestions when they first begin to explore these materials, it is important to let the children explore freely, not to overdirect their exploration.

As the children do the activities in this chapter, add their discoveries to the Getting to Know Our World Discovery Chart.

Getting to Know
Our World

Draw It: A Matter of Scale

This activity introduces two terms that define differences: *large* and *small*. Drawing *large* and *small objects* helps reinforce for the children the meanings of these terms. The drawings may not be realistic, but even very young children can indicate size differences in their work. This sort of differentiation is a beginning form of *measurement*.

Science Content Standards

The children will note similarities and differences of objects to separate them into groups. (Science as Inquiry; Measurement—Nonstandard: Linear)

What to Do

1. Show the children two objects. Talk with the children about which object is *large* and which is *small*. Consider using the words *big* and *little*. Ask the children to tell you about how the objects are alike and different. Focus the children's observations on size more than the other ideas they may have.

2. Invite the children to handle the objects and talk about how they feel in their hands. Say, "Look, the little rock fits on your thumb. The big rock fills up your whole hand!"

3. Encourage the children to place the objects on the table and trace around them with their pointer fingers or use their fingers to create a circle around each object. Can the children make circles that just fit each object? Encourage the children to use comparative language as they observe the two objects.

4. Provide paper, markers, pencils, and so on, and ask the children to think of two objects or shapes and then draw them. Ask the children to compare the sizes of the two images they created. Then ask the children which shapes are larger and which are smaller.

5. Challenge the children to make new drawings of the same images or shapes, but to exaggerate the sizes of the shapes so that the small image is much smaller than the large object. Or let the children change the sizes of the objects so that the smaller object is now the larger object. Help the children label the images as *large* and *small*.

Science Process Skills

Focused observing
Observing to classify

Science Vocabulary

alike	little
big	same
different	size
large	small

Materials

2 similar objects, one large and one small, such as 2 rocks, 2 balls, or 2 plants

crayons

large sheet of newsprint and markers (for a Discovery Chart)

paper

Children's Books

Tana Hoban's beautiful photographs in *Is It Larger? Is It Smaller?* will give children many ideas about large and small things in their world.

In *Ladybug Girl* by Jackie Davis and David Soman, Lulu, Ladybug Girl, is "too little" to play with her older brother, but is big enough to come to the aid of tiny ants. From her perch on the branch of a tree, her big brother becomes the little one. You'll enjoy adventures, big and small, with Lulu, Ladybug Girl!

Keep It Simple

● Encourage the children to work with other materials, such as clay, paint, or crumpled paper.

Add a Challenge

● As children become skilled with large and small, add more objects and challenge them to compare all the objects' sizes. Some children will be able to represent the size differences and order three or more objects from largest to smallest.

Theme Connections
Opposites

This experience with large and small is a perfect addition to a study of opposites.

Shoes

Ask families to donate several old shoes to the class, and then open a pretend shoe store. The children will be able to explore the concepts of *large* and *small* as they work with baby shoes, kid shoes, adult shoes, work shoes, play shoes, night shoes, and day shoes. With the children, observe, measure, classify, and study all the different kinds of shoes people wear.

Observing and Assessing the Child's Science Learning

● Looking at the pairs of objects and shapes that the child drew, can she indicate which the smaller and larger images are?

Connecting Science to the Curriculum

● **Language and Literacy**—Make a Discovery Chart that has two lists of words—one that describes big things and one that describes small things. The children might use *teeny, tiny,* or *itsy bitsy* to describe small objects and *gigantic, humongous,* and *really, really, really big* to describe large objects.

● **Mathematics**—In this activity, the children measure objects by visually comparing their sizes.

● **Taking It Outside**—Take clipboards and drawing materials outside. Talk with the children about the large and small plants they see. Can the children make themselves large like a tree and small like an acorn? Ask the children to draw something large and something small. The children might choose a large plant, such as a shrub, and a smaller one, such as a dandelion. Can the children make these two plants look different? What other large and small things can they find outside?

Family Involvement

Send home a booklet of each child's drawings of large and small objects. Ask family members to repeat this activity with their children, using large and small objects available in the home. Also, encourage families to look at their children's drawings and then do a household hunt for objects that they identify as *large* or *small*, or *big* or *little*.

Incorporating Technology

Use various hand lenses to make things look larger or smaller. The children can look through both ends of binoculars.

Getting to Know
Our World

Hot Spots

The sun not only gives us light, it gives us heat as well. This simple experience with thermometers introduces children to the idea of measuring temperature. Choose a sunny day and let the children hunt for hot spots.

Science Process Skill

Focused observing

Science Vocabulary

cool
hot
measure
temperature
thermometer
warm

Materials

cake pans or other flat, stable containers, one of cool water and one of warm water

several inexpensive but easy-to-read thermometers

Children's Books

A Hot Day and *A Cold Day*, both by Lola M. Schaefer, show children how daily temperatures affect what we do.

One Hot Summer Day by Nina Crews follows a city child through her hot summer day, complete with panting dogs and purple popsicles.

Science Content Standards

The children will observe changes in the thermometers when they are placed in locations with different temperatures. (Science as Inquiry; Measurement—Temperature)

What to Do

1. Show the children the thermometers and say, "These are special thermometers that scientists use. Today, you are going to be scientists and find out what the thermometers do. Has anyone ever seen other kinds of thermometers?" Some children may share experiences with having their temperature taken. Some may have weather thermometers at home. Say, "Let's see if our hands can tell what temperature something is. Feel the sides of this pan of water. Now put your hands on the sides of the cake pan. How does it feel? You are right. One is warm and one is cool."

2. Encourage the children to examine the thermometers, asking the children what they notice about the thermometers: "Can you find the little red line on them? We are going to find out what it does. Are you ready to investigate, scientists? Do you see the little round ball on the end of your thermometer?" Then have the children put that part of the thermometer in the pan of warm water. Say, for example: "I wonder what our thermometers will do. You are right, Demetri. The line is getting big. It's going up the thermometer. Let's try the cool water and see what happens. It is going down, Julie. I see it, too."

Keep It Simple

● Have the children draw thermometers on paper or in their Discovery Journals showing the thermometers measuring something hot and cool. Encourage the children to write at their own level about their observations.

Add a Challenge

● Have the children record the actual temperature of the various spots and items using the actual numbers.

Theme Connections
Games

Play "Thermometer." Call out locations and have the children move their bodies like the thermometer's red line: stretched up tall with their hands reaching up for hot, arms by their sides for medium, and squatting down for cold. For example, say, "You are in the sun on the hot blacktop playground," or "I just put you on an ice cube." Keep the pace quick for an active game that will reinforce how thermometers work.

Tools

Thermometers are tools people use to give us information about the weather, our bodies, and cooking. What other tools can the people use to get information? For example, bring in a scale for the children to use. Give them practice weighing different objects.

Weather

Thermometers are a great way to explore changes in the weather and the seasons.

3. Challenge the children to use their hands to find warm and cool spots inside or outside to test with the thermometers. As they try various spots, ask the children whether the lines on their thermometers are going up, down, or not moving much at all.

4. Call the little scientists together to discuss their observations. What have they observed about the red line in the thermometer? Share their excitement: "You discovered how the thermometer tells us about temperature. The red line gets long and tall when it is measuring something warm. Can you make yourselves long and tall? When the thermometer is measuring something cold, the red line squeezes down toward the ball. Can you make yourselves shivery little balls?"

Observing and Assessing the Child's Science Learning

● Can the child describe how the line on her thermometer changes when the thermometer moves to a location with a different temperature?

Connecting Science to the Curriculum

● **Mathematics**—In this activity, the children read numbers on thermometers and use thermometers to measure temperature. The children also compare temperature readings at different locations and times.

Recycling

This activity relates directly to the recycling activities going on in many communities. The children will learn and practice good environmental habits while cleaning up litter. Children in the older grades at your school may already have a recycling program. If so, ask some of the children from those grades to come to your room to help start your program. If your school does not have a recycling program, it may be time to start one.

Science Content Standard

The children will note similarities and differences among objects in order to separate them into groups; the children will begin to use simple descriptive language about objects. (Science as Inquiry)

Before the Activity

Find out about recycling guidelines in your community. Some communities sort materials into paper, plastic, and metal; some require more specific sorting; some do not require any sorting. Do the materials all go in the same bin? Think about how to remove the recycled materials from your site. Do you have community pick-up? Are there volunteers among the families or staff who would be willing to take turns taking materials to the recycle center? If so, set up a schedule and post it. You may need to send out reminders until the program gets established and it becomes a habit for everyone.

What to Do

1. Engage the children in a discussion about recycling. Ask the children if they have heard the word before and what they think it means. Explain recycling to the children, and talk about how it helps the environment and reduces waste.

2. Put out the collection of recyclable materials for the children to examine. Include newspapers, mail, extra copies of school calendars, cans, bottles, and so forth. Say, "These are all things we do not need anymore, so we are going to recycle them." Ask the children if their families recycle at home. Some children may volunteer that they do. Ask them what they recycle. "Where do you put things that are to be recycled? Do you have recycling bins at home?"

Science Process Skills

Focused observing
Observing to classify

Science Vocabulary

less
least
litter
names of categories
more
most
recycle
sort

Materials

boxes to be used as recycling bins
markers, pens, crayons
things to recycle

Children's Books

The illustrations and titles of *I'm Dirty* and *I Stink* by Kate McMullan and Jim McMullan will make children laugh as they learn about garbage and recycling.

I Drive a Garbage Truck by Sarah Bridges, Derrick Alderman, and Denise Shea and *Trashy Town* by Andrea Zimmerman, David Clemesha, and Dan Yaccarino can spark conversations about how people can reuse and recycle useful items instead of throwing them away.

Keep It Simple

● Some children may be overwhelmed by large amounts of materials. Give them a box with a small collection of items to sort.

Add a Challenge

● Weigh each bin and compare the amounts. Compare the volume in the boxes. Which material fills its box the most? Is it the heaviest?

Theme Connections
Dramatic Play

Have the children use the reusable materials to make props for dramatic play. They can make their own vehicles or flying machines, their own pretend food, or instruments for the doctor's office.

Our Neighborhood

Reusing and recycling should become a familiar part of community life, along with environmental stewardship for all our children.

3. Show the children the boxes you have brought to school to use as recycling bins. Set out several markers, pens, and crayons. With the children, make recycling labels. Be sure the signs align with your community guidelines. Consider making separate signs for metal, paper, and plastic even if there is mixed recycling in your community. This will give the children experience with sorting.

4. Ask for the children's help in sorting the recyclables you have brought in. Some children may be able to count the items as they sort them.

5. Wonder aloud whether there are other things around the classroom that the children could recycle. Suggest that the children check the wastebasket for paper. At snack time, ask what the children think they should do with their empty milk jugs and the boxes the children's snacks came in. If there is litter outside, talk with the children about whether it is something that they can recycle. Let the children place the materials in the proper bins. Proper placement of some items may initially be difficult to determine, but will allow for lively discussions. Have the children compare the amount of material in each bin. Ask, "Which bin has the most material in it? Which bin has least amount of material in it?"

Observing and Assessing the Child's Science Learning

● Given a collection of recyclables, can the child sort most of the materials into the proper bins?

Connecting Science to the Curriculum

● **Mathematics**—In this activity, the children compare the quantities of the recycling bins, using terms such as *more*, *most*, and *less*. The children also count the items they put in the recycling bin.

Animal Watchers

An animal walk is an excellent way to gather information about the many animals living in your environment. Enjoy the children's excitement as they locate, identify, and count the animals they see on their journey.

Science Content Standards

The children will observe an area of the outdoor environment for animal life. (Science as Inquiry; Life Sciences—Characteristics of Organisms)

What to Do

1. Share with the children your curiosity about what animals live around your world. Tell them that you are going to go on a walk to look for animals. Before doing so, however, they are going to make an important tool—binoculars. Then show the children how to make pretend binoculars. Help those children who are having difficulty assembling two cardboard tubes with a strip of masking tape. Provide crayons so the children can decorate their binoculars if they like. **Note:** Do not use washable markers, as the color will wash off onto the children's hands and faces as they use their binoculars.

2. As the children work, ask them what kinds of animals they saw on the way to school this morning. They might say they saw a squirrel, a lizard, a dog, or a cat.

3. Say, "Today we are going to take a walk. We will use our binoculars to see how many different kinds of animals we can spot."

4. Take the children on a walk outside. Remind the children that it is important to walk quietly so they do not disturb or scare the animals away. Say, "When you spot something, tell me what you think it is." Depending on the area, the children might see birds, dogs, cats, insects, squirrels, or even cattle or horses.

5. Keep a tally of animals the children see on the walk. Help the children expand their use of descriptive language by providing new vocabulary as you talk together. On subsequent walks, make comparisons about what they see this time that is different from their last experience.

Science Process Skills

Focused observing
Organizing and
   communicating observations

Science Vocabulary

animal names, such as *insect, worm, bird, dog, sparrow,* and so on
binoculars
tool
wildlife

Materials

clipboard and tally sheet
crayons
empty cardboard tubes
large sheet of newsprint and markers (for a Discovery Chart)
masking tape

Children's Books

Caterpillars, Bugs and Butterflies; Birds, Nests and Eggs; and *Rabbits, Squirrels and Chipmunks* by Mel Boring are helpful books in the Take Along Guide series. Although the reading level is for older children, four- and five-year-olds love them, too. They are delighted to find out more about the animals they see nearby.

Getting to Know
Our World

Keep It Simple

- Have the children draw the animals they see in their Discovery Journals and then add descriptive text if they are able. Alternatively, consider transcribing the children's comments for them.

Add a Challenge

- Encourage the children to browse through books about birds, insects, and other animals. Can the children find images of the animals they saw outside? Look for animals during different seasons. Do the children notice different animals at different times of the year?

Theme Connections

Community Helpers

Encourage the children to look for community helpers when they are outside; write down which community helpers the children see.

Transportation

The children can find various examples of transportation. Challenge the children to sort the modes of transportation in different ways.

6. After returning to the classroom, talk about the animals the children spotted, using the list as a reference. Make a Discovery Chart listing the animals they saw. In another color, add to the list as the children tell you about other animals they see during subsequent walks. Consider making another chart that lists the children's pets.

Children with Special Needs

Make sure that visually impaired children are familiar with the places you are going to on your animal walk. Keep those children near the front of the line so that you can describe the animals as the other children observe them.

Observing and Assessing the Child's Science Learning

- Can the child identify by name the common animals she observed?

Connecting Science to the Curriculum

- **Mathematics**—In this activity, the children count and compare the numbers of different kinds of animals.

Birds: They're Everywhere

Showing children birds that live in their environment may be their introduction to an interesting hobby: bird watching. The behavior of birds is different in every season. Birds migrate and mate in the spring, raise their young in the summer, migrate in the fall, and find ways to survive in the winter.

Science Content Standards

The children will observe birds in the outdoor environment; the children will begin to use simple descriptive language about birds. (Science as Inquiry; Life Sciences—Characteristics of Organisms)

Before the Activity

Place the bird feeder in the schoolyard before doing this activity. The Audubon Society, one of the nation's most active environmental groups, is made up of people who like to watch birds. You may want to contact a member of this organization to help you take the children on the bird walk.

What to Do

1. Take the children on a bird-watching walk around the playground or neighborhood park. When the children spot a bird, ask them to watch it closely. Ask, "How is the bird moving? What colors do you see on the bird?"

2. Using the clipboard and paper, write the children's observations on several Discovery Book pages for them to illustrate later. Try to identify and name the birds and note differences among them. For example, pigeons move much differently than do sparrows or robins.

3. If you do not know the names of the birds you see, ask the children to describe them. Then check the field guide to identify what kinds of birds they are. The children can develop their own ways of identifying birds by color, markings, or behavior, such as "the one that hangs on the side of the tree" for woodpeckers. They may also learn bird names if you use the ones you know.

Science Process Skill

Focused observing

Science Vocabulary

animal
beak
bird
bird species names
feather
flying
nest
wing

Materials

bird feeder
clipboard
field guide
paper and crayons (for a
   Discovery Book)

Children's Books

Birds by Kevin Henkes and Laura Dronzek is a delightful blend of a concept book and wonderful imaginings about birds that begins with the simple experience of hearing a bird sing.

About Birds: A Guide for Children by Cathryn Sill and John Sill provides solid information through clear text and appealing illustrations.

Fancy Nancy: Explorer Extraordinaire! by Jane O'Connor shows how to make a pinecone bird feeder.

Keep It Simple

● Take pictures of birds common in your area and make a field guide with the children. Laminate the photographs, punch a hole in one corner of each one, and put them on a ring to make an easy take-along guide.

Add a Challenge

● Encourage the children to continue their observations and make additional drawings of familiar birds. The more they observe and draw the birds, the more accurate their observations and drawings will become.

Theme Connections
Animals
Use this activity to observe and learn about other kinds of animals in your environment.

4. Talk with the children about the birds, asking things such as: "Where do we see birds? Are they in water, on the ground, on a branch, on tree bark, in a shrub, or high up in a tree? What are the birds doing? Are they running, flying, hopping, sleeping, sitting, eating?"

5. Repeat this activity while watching the bird feeder. Do the children notice that some birds are much more common than others?

6. Bring the children back inside. Hand out the pages from the Discovery Book on which you wrote the children's descriptions of the birds they saw. Provide markers, crayons, and colored pencils and invite the children to draw the birds they saw.

7. As the children illustrate the Discovery Book pages with drawings of the birds they saw, review the observations they made earlier to help them recall details, such as how many legs birds have, the colors of their feathers, and their sizes.

Observing and Assessing the Child's Science Learning

● Can the child use words or actions to describe the birds' behavior?

Connecting Science to the Curriculum

● **Mathematics**—In this activity, the children compare the sizes and relative numbers of birds. The children can also count the number of birds they see.

Family Involvement

People from all walks of life enjoy watching and feeding birds. Ask your families if they or someone they know would like to share their knowledge of birds with the children.

Sharing with Friends

Getting to Know
Our World

Science Process Skills

Focused observing

Observing to classify

Organizing and
communicating observations

Science Vocabulary

environment

nature

plant and animal names and
other vocabulary unique to
your setting

Materials

crayons, paint, markers, and
so on

paper

By showing, telling, drawing, and writing, the children share with their friends the understanding that has grown out of the previous activities. This information provides the teacher with a quick reference point about when to share more challenging discoveries about the wonders of their world.

Science Content Standards

The children will begin to use simple descriptive language about their environment; the children will note and describe similarities and differences among living and nonliving things in their environment; the children will communicate their observations. (Science as Inquiry; Earth Sciences; Life Sciences)

What to Do

1. Invite another class, a director or principal, or another adult friend to the classroom. Talk with the children about how they need to let their friend or friends know about what they have been observing and learning about their world.

Close Observation

• **Show It**—The child shows her friends some of the things she has been making or collecting to share what she has been learning about her world.

• **Tell It**—Each child takes a turn telling her invited friends about her discoveries and the interesting things she is learning about her world.

• **Draw It**—Let the child create a piece of original art that depicts some aspect of the environment that she has learned about or observed. Display the child's work in the room for her friends to observe.

• **Write It**—Let the child use developmental writing to write captions for drawings in her Discovery Journal describing all that she is learning about their environment. The child can share her journal with her invited friends.

Observing and Assessing the Child's Science Learning

• Does the child's individual contribution indicate a growing understanding and appreciation of her immediate surroundings?

Getting to Know Our World

Science Process Skills

Focused observing
Observing to classify

Science Vocabulary

cirrus clouds
clouds
cumulonimbus clouds
cumulus clouds
sky
stratus clouds

Materials

cotton
crayons, chalk, or white and gray paint
glue
paper, various shades of blue and gray, if available

Children's Books

The Cloud Book by Tomie dePaola is a simple field guide to clouds and also provides some interesting folklore.

Charles G. Shaw's *It Looked Like Spilt Milk* is a well-loved classic with an easy, repetitive refrain that looks at all the shapes clouds can make.

Eric Carle's *The Little Cloud* is a similar story.

Thunder Cake by Patricia Polacco provides a tasty way to help deal with children's fear of thunderstorms.

Cloud Pictures

Clouds come in all kinds of shapes and sizes. This is part of what makes them fun to draw and paint. Help children notice light and wispy cirrus clouds. They are very different from big thunderhead clouds, the cumulonimbus.

Science Content Standard

The children will note similarities and differences among clouds in order to separate them into groups; the children will and begin to use simple descriptive language about clouds. (Earth Sciences)

What to Do

1. Take the children outdoors on a day with good cloud formations. Invite the children to lie on the ground to watch the clouds. Talk with the children about what they see. Are the clouds puffy or long and skinny? Stratus clouds have layers. Can the children see the lines? Can they make the shapes of the clouds with their hands or bodies?

2. Show the children the collection of art materials. Say, for example: "We've looked carefully at the clouds. Now we're going make pictures of them. Sometimes we make things any way we want. This time we're going to be scientists. We're going to make pictures that will help us remember just how the clouds looked today. Look at all the materials we have to use. What do you think will work best for you to make a picture of the clouds you see?" Let the children choose what they want to use to make their own representations of the clouds. As they work, remind the children to think about making a picture of real clouds.

3. Repeat this activity on various days so the children can see a variety of clouds and weather conditions. Talk with the children about how the different clouds are alike and different.

Keep It Simple

● When you are observing the clouds, note the direction that they are moving. Make a list of associated weather events, such as wind, rain, snow, thunder, and lightning.

Add a Challenge

● Create a bulletin board with the three common cloud types: *cirrus*, *cumulus*, and *stratus*. Talk with the children about these three types of clouds, and challenge the children to put their drawings under the correct names. Some of the children may use the names of the clouds when you supply the words. Ask the children, "How are the clouds you see alike?"

Theme Connections
Art

Examine photographs of clouds, the children's cloud pictures, and clouds painted by artists such as Vincent van Gogh, Claude Monet, or Winslow Homer. They all look different! Talk about the differences between scientific observational drawings and creative art and have the children do some of both.

Observing and Assessing the Child's Science Learning

● Does the child's picture show an awareness of the cloud's unique shape in the sky?

Connecting Science to the Curriculum

• **Language and Literacy**—In this activity, the children use their own words to describe the clouds they see.

• **Mathematics**—In this activity, the children compare the sizes and shapes of the various clouds.

Science Process Skills

Focused observing
Observing to classify

Science Vocabulary

bud
dandelion
flower
leaf
root
seeds
taproot
tool
weed

Materials

garden trowel

Children's Books

Share one or more of the many versions of the Russian folktale *The Enormous Turnip* to show the children that dandelions aren't the only roots that are hard to pull up.

Tops and Bottoms, a Caldecott winner by Janet Stevens, is a humorous tale in which a trickster shows how people use the tops and bottoms of plants.

Digging Dandelions

The dandelion is a wonderful tool for exploring the parts and states of a plant. Dandelions have many leaves and a distinctive flower and seed arrangement. The dandelion is a composite flower that belongs to the same group as the sunflower and daisy. And they grow nearly everywhere.

Science Content Standards

The children will begin to use simple descriptive language about plants; the children will communicate their observations. (Science as Inquiry; Life Sciences—Characteristics of Living Organisms)

What to Do

1. Explore a nearby grassy area for dandelions. Show the children a dandelion with flowers, flower buds, and flowers that have gone to seed. Talk with the children about how flowers grow old, just like people. They are young, grow old and change, and finally die.

2. Show the children how to use the trowel to uproot several plants at various stages of growth. Ask the children, "What makes these plants so hard to dig up?" Examine the taproot with the children. Ask, "Is it like the roots of the surrounding grass? How is it different?"

3. Have the children look at the plants very carefully. Point out the different stages of the flowers' development, from very young buds to those that have shed their seeds. See if the children can arrange the plants according to their stages of development.

Keep It Simple

● Have the children draw images of dandelion plants in their Discovery Journals. Encourage the children to label their drawings.

Add a Challenge

● Boiled dandelion roots make a brown- or yellow-colored. Dye strips of white cotton cloth or yarn, set these strips out, and challenge the children to use them for weaving or other purposes.

Theme Connections
Art

Show the children art images that contain flowers. Ask, "How does van Gogh paint sunflowers? How does Renoir paint roses? How does Georgia O'Keeffe paint wildflowers? How do the illustrators of our picture books create flowers?" How do the children create dandelions?

Children with Special Needs

Children with sensory integration issues may feel uncomfortable touching the soil and the dandelions. Let these children work with a classroom buddy who will do the digging and handling of the plant.

Observing and Assessing the Child's Science Learning

● Can the child arrange the dandelions according to the stages of their development?

Connecting Science to the Curriculum

● **Mathematics**—In this activity, the children arrange the plants according to the stages of their development.

● **Science and Nature**—This activity provides an easy way to introduce and explore the root structures of plants.

Family Involvement

After the children have an understanding of plant parts and are familiar with the trowel's function, encourage the children to share this activity at home with their families.

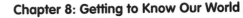

Getting to Know Our World

Feather Wind Gauge

Wind direction and velocity are important weather information given to us each day in the weather report. The children, too, can determine the direction wind moves by using a simple weather vane as a tool.

Science Content Standards

The children will begin to use simple descriptive language about wind; the children will communicate their observations. (Science as Inquiry; Earth Sciences)

What to Do

1. Help the children tie a piece of string to the quill of the feather, one feather per string.

2. Encourage the children to pretend to be wind and to take turns blowing on one another's feathers. Ask, "What happens to the feathers when we stop blowing?"

3. Go outside with the feather wind gauges. Ask the children whether it is a still or a windy day. Challenge them to find places where there is a lot of wind and less wind. Ask the children what happens when they run with their wind gauges.

4. Bring the children back inside. Set out paper, markers, crayons, and colored pencils and ask the children to draw the feather wind gauge in no wind, on a very windy day, and on a breezy day.

Science Process Skill

Focused observing

Science Vocabulary

blow

calm

fast

gauge

gentle

hard

still

slow

storm words such as *wind, thunder,* and *blow*

tool

Materials

feathers (available at craft stores)

markers, crayons, and colored pencils

string

Children's Books

The Wind Blew by Pat Hutchins and *Gilberto and the Wind* by Marie Hall Ets provide two very different looks at all that can happen on a windy day.

Keep It Simple

● Let the children use their wind gauges as draft detectors for air that may be coming into the school around windows and doors.

Add a Challenge

● Consider marking the number of windy and still days over a given period on the daily calendar. Challenge the children to make a graph and compare the number of windy days to still days.

Theme Connections
Weather

A Feather Wind Gauge is one of many tools children can use when investigating the weather. Use it to test the wind to see if it is a good day for kites or sailboats.

Observing and Assessing the Child's Science Learning

● Can the child use the wind gauge as a tool to tell whether the wind is blowing? The child may be able to look out on a windy day and predict that the feather wind gauge will move today.

Connecting Science to the Curriculum

● **Mathematics**—In the Add a Challenge portion of this activity, the children create a graph to compare the number of windy days to the number of still days.

Family Involvement

Have the children bring their feather wind gauges home to show their families how the gauges work.

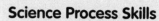

Science Process Skills

Focused observing

Observing to classify

Organizing and
   communicating observations

Science Vocabulary

bark	tree
branches	tree names
leaf	trunk
roots	veins

Materials

collecting bags

leaves from each of three
   species of trees

school area or nearby park
   with at least three varieties
   of trees

Children's Books

Caldecott Medal Winner
A Tree is Nice by J. M. Udry is a
beautifully illustrated classic
about trees.

A Busy Year by Leo Leonni and
Our Tree Named Steve by Alan
Zweibel and David Catrow are
thoughtful stories about loving
and caring for trees.

Some books, such as *Tell Me
Tree: All About Trees for Kids* by
Gail Gibbons and *Trees, Leaves
and Bark* by Diane Burns, are
more advanced but provide good
references for both you and the
children.

The Great Tree Match

Knowing the names of the trees in many schoolyards and
neighborhoods is fairly easy because there are usually only a few
varieties. Knowing the names and the leaves of each of these trees
can give children a sense of knowledge and confidence about the
outdoors, and may lead to more exploration. When fall arrives and
leaves are everywhere, go collecting.

Science Content Standards

The children will note similarities and differences among leaves in
order to separate them into groups; the children will begin to use
simple descriptive language when discussing the leaves. (Science as
Inquiry; Life Sciences)

Before the Activity

Collect leaves from three nearby trees. Place one leaf from each type
of tree in each child's bag.

What to Do

1. Take the children on a leaf-collecting walk. Talk with the children
   about the shapes of the leaves as well as their colors and textures.
   Say, "Some leaves feel very rough, while others are smooth. Some,
   like holly, are prickly and can hurt."

2. Hold up a leaf and identify it. For example, if it is a maple leaf, say,
   "This is a leaf from a maple tree. One way we can identify a tree is
   by looking at its leaves. All leaves from a certain type of tree look
   the same."

3. Give a collecting bag to each child, and ask the children to look in
   their bags. Say, "Three leaves are in your bag. I want you to take
   out a leaf that looks like the leaf I am holding."

Keep It Simple

● Use the collected leaves to make a leaf identification book. Find a local tree expert to come to the area to help the children name the trees and find new ones.

Add a Challenge

● If several tree types are available nearby, let the children make up their own leaf bags, adding three leaves that they have not already identified. Have the children trade bags with another child and challenge everyone to identify the trees from which the leaves came.

Theme Connections
Nature

Use other elements from nature to create matching activities. What other natural elements in your area could children match? Possibilities include rocks, pinecones, and clover flowers.

Children with Special Needs

Pair children in wheelchairs with a peer buddy to assist in leaf collecting.

4. When all the children have found the leaf, say, "Let's try to find a leaf like that on a tree." Walk to the various trees and match the leaves until they find the proper match. The children will discover that each tree has its own special type of leaf, and that all leaves on a tree are usually alike.

Observing and Assessing the Child's Science Learning

● Given the leaves of three trees, can the child find leaves in the area that are like those in her bag?

● Can the child describe the differences among the leaves?

Connecting Science to the Curriculum

● **Language and Literacy**—In this activity, the children use descriptive terms to talk about the shapes, textures, and colors of the leaves.

● **Mathematics**—In this activity, the children find leaves and match them to the sample leaves already in their bags. The children also group and classify the leaves.

Science Process Skills

Focused observing

Observing to classify

Organizing and communicating observations

Science Vocabulary

map

relationship terms, such as *up, below, under, next to,* and so on

Materials

glue

large sheet of newsprint or butcher paper

markers

scissors

small pieces of paper

tape

Children's Books

Fancy Nancy: Explorer Extraordinaire! by Jane O'Connor shows the children a map of a "fancy" journey among birds, wildflowers, and butterflies.

Read *Ladybug Girl* by Jackie Davis and David Soman or *Little Fur Family* by Margaret Wise Brown and make a map of where the main character's adventures take them.

Mapping Our World

Make a map of your outdoor space with the children and use it to help keep track of all of your special finds. It is yet another way to get to know our world.

Science Content Standards

The children will begin to use simple descriptive language about their environment; the children will note and describe similarities and differences among objects in their environment; the children will communicate their observations by creating a map. (Science as Inquiry; Earth Sciences; Life Sciences)

What to Do

1. As the children watch, make a map of the schoolyard. Be sure to draw it with the same orientation as the buildings. Draw in the building and sidewalks, and outline major areas, describing what you are doing as you draw: "I am drawing a map. A map is a special kind of picture of our outdoor space." Introduce the idea of scale by talking about how the little map is a drawing of the big schoolyard.

2. Ask, "What else do we need to show on our map? Look around. What do you see? That is right. We need to show where our jungle gym is. Draw it on this little piece of paper for me, and then we will glue it on our map." Then cut a piece of paper the correct size to keep the drawing roughly in scale for the map. Ask the children, "What else do we need to draw?" Include the fixed play equipment, trees, shrubs, and other large objects. Use relationship and position terms, such as *up, below, under,* and *next to,* as you create the map. Say things such as: "What goes next to the slide?" Talk about how the map is a drawing or model of your schoolyard.

3. Walk around the area with the children to be sure the basic map is complete.

4. Add details to the map as things change with the seasons or the children make new discoveries. Have a child add the praying mantis she found under the slide. Ask someone to add the daffodils that are coming up.

Keep It Simple

● Help the children begin to understand that maps represent places and pathways by making maps of the roadways they have made with blocks in their play.

Add a Challenge

● Take the children on a mapping expedition to locate objects around the schoolyard. While on the adventure, follow the map you and the children already made. Allow each child to collect one small, easily movable object from the walk. Remind the children to remember where they found their objects. Cover the entire area. Return to the classroom and ask each child to describe what she found and to point out on the map where she found it. Have the children tape or glue the objects on the map.

Theme Connections
Our Neighborhood and Community

Make a three-dimensional map of your immediate surroundings, using shoe boxes or other small boxes to represent each building. Take the children out to make observational drawings of the buildings. If they are capable, the children can then paint the boxes and label them with appropriate signs.

Observing and Assessing the Child's Science Learning

● Can the child point out common objects on the map?

● Does the child recognize the map as a model of the schoolyard?

Connecting Science to the Curriculum

• **Mathematics**—When the children look at the map outside, they are matching drawings to real places and things, in one-to-one correspondence. This activity also introduces the children to the notion of scale as the children compare the map to the actual schoolyard.

Family Involvement

The children can show the schoolyard map to their families when they arrive to pick up their children at the end of the day. Encourage the children's families to work with their children to make similar maps of the areas around their homes.

Getting to Know Our World

Science Process Skills

Focused observing

Observing to classify

Organizing and communicating observations

Science Vocabulary

camera

outdoors

outside world

photos

picture

Materials

battery charger

digital cameras

rechargeable batteries

Children's Books

The illustrations in *The Usborne Complete First Book of Nature* by Rosamund Kidman-Cox will inspire children to look for living things to photograph in their own environment.

Picture Our World

A digital camera can give children the opportunity to discover and record lasting memories of what the world looks like from their perspective. In the process, the children develop a deeper appreciation for all that is around them.

Science Content Standards

The children will begin to use simple descriptive language about their environment; the children will note and describe similarities and differences among living and nonliving things in their environment; the children will communicate their observations through photographs and words. (Science as Inquiry; Earth Sciences; Life Sciences)

Before the Activity

Ask the children's families and your friends and colleagues if they have unused digital cameras. Many people have cameras going unused because they have moved on to a newer model. Purchase or acquire by donation a battery charger and rechargeable batteries. Show the children how to use the camera and practice inside taking pictures of classroom activities and anything else they find interesting. You may be surprised to find that some of the children already have a lot of experience with digital cameras.

This is a small-group activity. Groups of three to five children can share a camera.

What to Do

1. Talk with the children about taking the cameras outdoors, including the need for extra care. Say, for example: "We have used our cameras to take pictures of the many things that we do in our classroom. Now we are going to go outdoors so you can take pictures of our outside world." Encourage the children to think about what would be interesting to photograph. What do they think is important to photograph and why?

2. Consider suggesting a few images the children might look for outside, such as a mud puddle when it rains, cracks in the dirt when it gets really dry, dandelions, spiderwebs, rain, snow, or the

Keep It Simple

● Let the children place some of the photographs in their Discovery Journals and add captions themselves, or write captions for the children based on their dictations.

Add a Challenge

● Select an outdoor landmark such as a tree or shrub. Each month, photograph all of the children next to this landmark. With the children, examine the photographs for differences from month to month. Ask the children how their clothes change in the different images. Ask, "Does the sky change? What about the plants?"

Theme Connections
All About Me

Group the children in pairs and have them take photos of one another's hands, ears, and so on. Challenge the children to identify themselves and their friends based on these images.

wind blowing their friend's hair on a windy day. Do not overdirect the children. Silly photos are just fine, too. Expect some nose shots as children take pictures of themselves. Expect some funny faces when they take pictures of their friends.

3. Bring the children inside and look at the photos that the children took. Review the photos with the children, and tell them to look for those they like most and would want to include in a class book. Talk with the children about why they think certain photographs illustrate something about the world. Say, "A picture of Molly making her monster face is fun, but it may not be right for this book."

4. When the children finish making their selections, print them for a class book, "About Our World." Add captions of the children's observations.

Observing and Assessing the Child's Science Learning

● Can the child select photographs that convey something about the immediate environment?

Family Involvement

Plan a family meeting where the children can share their "Our World" photographs and class book with their parents and other family members.

Incorporating Technology

Use the children's photographs to make a PowerPoint presentation to use during family meeting times.

If cameras have video features, encourage the children to explore taking short videos of what they see.

Sounds Around Us

Children enjoy exploring the world of outdoor sound. There are all kinds of interesting sounds out there—from nature and from people. Looking in the outdoors is important, but so is listening.

Science Content Standards

The children will begin to use simple descriptive language about sounds in their environment; the children will note and describe similarities and differences among the sounds in their environment; the children will communicate their observations. (Science as Inquiry; Life Sciences)

What to Do

1. Take the children outside and find a place to sit. Talk with them about listening. Say, "When I read a book to you, everyone listens to what I'm reading and looks at the pictures. Outside, we are going to listen to the sounds of our world. Instead of looking at pictures, we can look around and see if we can figure out what is making the sounds. If we are really quiet, I wonder what we will hear. Hmm—I hear a humming sound. I think it is the cars driving by, don't you? I hear a rattling, rustling sound. I wonder what it is. Does anyone else hear it? What do you think might be making that sound? I think you are right. It is the leaves blowing. What do you hear? Let's sit quietly for a minute or so. If you hear something, just think about it in your head until I say it is time to tell." (This activity may take some practice for some of the children.) Consider capturing the sounds on a tape recorder to play back and discuss at a later time.

2. After a minute or so, pause to let the children tell you what they have heard. Do they know what made the sound? Did anyone else hear it? Encourage the children to describe the sounds. Talk about loud sounds, pretty sounds, annoying sounds, distant sounds, sounds from animals, and sounds from machines. If you are using a recorder, listen to the sounds again as you play back the tape. Ask, "Can you tell me what you hear now? Are there any sounds you don't recognize?"

3. Return to the classroom. List the sounds the children can remember on the Discovery Chart. Also, if the children can identify it, list the source of the sound.

Science Process Skills

Focused observing
Observing to classify
Organizing and communicating observations

Science Vocabulary

ear
hear
listen
record
sound
source names

Materials

large sheet of newsprint and markers (for a Discovery Chart)
tape recorder (optional)

Children's Books

Too Much Noise by Ann McGovern is a well-written version of the folktale about a man who complains about too much noise. He is made to fill his house with all kinds of noisy animals. Once they all leave, the man decides his home is not too noisy after all. The "noisy" words such as *creak, squeak,* and *swish* will inspire children to think of their own noisy words.

Getting to Know
Our World

Keep It Simple

● Have the children draw something that makes sounds outdoors in their Discovery Journals and label their drawings. Also consider having the children draw separate pages for indoor sounds and outdoor sounds. Are there some sounds the children can hear both inside and out?

Add a Challenge

● Make a tape recording of some of the various sounds that are made at different areas of the school, such as in the playground, in the kitchen, and in the restroom. Possible sounds include running water, toilet flushing, door closing, and telephone ringing. Play the tape for the children and see if they can identify and name the source.

Theme Connections
Me and My Body

Help the children think about sound. Ask, "What is the softest sound you can hear? When is it noisiest outside? What is the noisiest nearby location? How many animal ears can you see when you are outside?"

Sounds

As they explore sounds, help the children pay special attention to the sounds nature makes. Do the children hear different sounds where they live? Compare sounds that come from living things to those that come from manufactured things.

Children with Special Needs

Hearing the various sounds may be difficult or impossible for a child with a hearing impairment. When possible, let these children place their hands on the sound producer, such as a telephone, refrigerator, car, or any item that vibrates as it produces sound.

4. Repeat the experience from time to time. Walk around the school or neighborhood. Ask the children, "What new sounds do you hear? Do you hear different sounds in different seasons or at different times of day?" Add any new sounds to the Discovery Chart.

Observing and Assessing the Child's Science Learning

● Can the child name the sources of some of the sounds she hears outside?

● Can the child identify the sources of the sounds she hears on a recording?

Family Involvement

Ask families to make lists or recordings of the sounds around their homes. They can send the lists or recordings to school so the children can discuss the sounds and what they mean.

Welcome to Our World

Getting to Know
Our World

Science Process Skills

Focused observing

Organizing and
communicating observations

Science Vocabulary

words used throughout the
activity, such as *environment,
nature, animal and plant
names,* and *investigate*

Materials

all of the items children
collected and created while
getting to know their world,
such as leaves, rocks,
photographs, Discovery
Books, and Discovery
Journals

art materials, such as paper,
markers, crayons, paint,
tape, and glue

digital camera (optional)

large sheet of paper

marker

After everything the children have experienced and learned about
their immediate environment, it seems only natural for the children
to share their discoveries with fellow citizens of this wonderful place
in which they live.

Science Content Standards

The children will begin to use simple descriptive language about
their environment; the children will note and describe similarities
and differences among living and nonliving things in their
environment; the children will communicate their observations.
(Science as Inquiry; Earth Sciences; Life Sciences)

Before the Activity

Meet with teachers from another class to arrange to have the
children come together to discuss their local environment.

What to Do

1. Engage the children in a conversation about all the recent
   activities they have been doing and all they have discovered about
   their environment. Talk about how interesting and valuable they
   have found the world to be.

2. Tell the children that children in other classes want to come and
   see what they have been doing, as do the children's families. Say,
   "They want to come and learn about all the interesting things we
   have been discovering about our world."

3. Look at the Discovery Chart you created at the beginning of this
   activity. Are there things the children want to add? Now make an
   "Ideas for Sharing" list on a large sheet of paper. Ask the children
   to describe all the pictures they have taken and all the drawings

they have made that they can share with their classroom visitors. Add each suggestion to the list.

4. Working in groups or as individuals, let the children decide what they would like to display for the open house. There might be a need for a few more art projects or a class song focusing on some aspect of the children's immediate environment. Consider having the children clean the playground or some other area around the school in anticipation of the visitors' arrival. Record the experience with a digital camera and display the photographs in the classroom.

5. When visitors arrive, let the children do most of the sharing. Simply observe the children, occasionally commenting on all the children have done and have come to understand about their immediate surroundings.

6. Send the visitors off with something to remember this visit by, such as a litter bag or a take-action flyer. Litter bags can be donated by a local car wash. "Do not litter" flyers can be made with a simple printout available from various environmental organizations. Find one on a website or make your own and print out copies for all the visitors.

Observing and Assessing the Child's Science Learning

- Can the child discuss her immediate environment with the classroom visitors?

- What kind of information is the child sharing? How accurate are her statements?

Index of Children's Books

Index